CW00733605

The Off-Comers of

Windermere

The Off-Comers of

Windermere

Birth of a
Vibrant Victorian Township

1800 - 1900

Ian Jones

Copyright © 2022 Ian Jones

The moral right of the author has been asserted.

The author has asserted his moral rights. The right of Ian Jones to be identified
as the author of this work has been asserted by him in accordance with the
Copyright, Designs and Patents Act 1988.

All rights reserved. No part of this book may be reproduced, stored or introduced
into a retrieval system, or transmitted in any form or by any means
(electronic, mechanical, photocopying, recording or otherwise) without
the prior permission in writing of Ian Jones.

The author has made all efforts to trace copyright and apologises if
any have been inadvertently breached.

© Copyright of photographs and graphics printed in this book is
the property of the author, except where otherwise stated.

Maps are based on Ordnance Survey County Series (Westmorland 1859, 25 inch,
Sheets 32/7 and 32/8; and their equivalents from Series 3, 1912).

Matador
Unit E2 Airfield Business Park,
Harrison Road, Market Harborough,
Leicestershire. LE16 7UL
Tel: 0116 2792299
Email: books@troubador.co.uk
Web: www.troubador.co.uk/matador
Twitter: @matadorbooks

ISBN 978 1803133 157

British Library Cataloguing in Publication Data.
A catalogue record for this book is available from the British Library.

Printed and bound in the UK by TJ Books LTD, Padstow, Cornwall

Typeset in 11pt Times by Troubador Publishing Ltd, Leicester, UK
Front cover: St Mary's Abbey ca.1865 © Ian Jones

Matador is an imprint of Troubador Publishing Ltd

Foreword

This book is intended to fill a gap in the literature of the Lake District. It presents a social history of the many in-comers who built their villas and mansions in a sylvan virgin landscape, and created the village we know today as Windermere. Who were these folk, wealthy and not, artisan and not, mostly strangers who came from *'off '*, to shape a Northern Arcadia amongst the lakes and fells of Westmorland? All too often the memory of them and their contribution to the genesis, institutions and heritage of the place has faded, or been lost completely in the mists of time. This volume attempts to revive their memory, and assemble a definitive record before the facts are lost forever.

It is written in a cross-over style, aiming to appeal to widely differing readerships. The casual reader will find a fascinating story and interest in the many previously unpublished photographs and illustrations from Victorian times. The serious historian will also find a wealth of material to stimulate deeper research.

If I have succeeded in reaching such diverse groups, then the project has been worthwhile.

Enjoy, whatever your interest.

I wish to thank the very many people who have helped with this research, especially the staff of Cumbria Archive Centre, Kendal; the Local Studies Department of Kendal Library; Sandra Bowness for Roger's superb collection of photographs; Kenneth Clarke for his expert knowledge of early photography; and David Lewis of Adelaide for an off-comer's critique of the initial manuscript.

Thank you to you all.

Ian Jones
January 2022

I dedicate this book to

Edna

whose endless love and support have given me space to write.

Contents

Villas, Grand Houses and Quality

Illustrations

Illustrations in Chapter 1

1. Thomas West's map
2. Peter Crosthwaite's map
3. St Catherine's Rise
4. Ogilby's strip map
5. Jeffreys' map

Illustrations in Chapter 2

6. Keyplan of Birthwaite roads in the early 1800s
7. Map of Orrest Head House and Farm
8. Orrest Head House
9. Map of Elleray Estate
10. Old Elleray Cottage (Christopher North's Cottage)
11. John Wilson's Elleray mansion
12. Girt, yalla haired Wilson of Elleray
13. Rt Hon. George Canning and Sir Walter Scott
14. Statue of Professor John Wilson
15. The Wood
16. Cook's House estate
17. Footprint of Cook's Farmhouse
18. View south from High Field, by Joseph Farington
19. Rayrigg and Calgarth, Clarke's map
20. Map of Millerground
21. Millerground House
22. Ferryman's Cottage at Low Millerground
23. Winlass Beck at Millerground
24. Footprint of Rayrigg Hall
25. Philipson armorial
26. Asymmetric south aspect of Rayrigg Hall
27. William Wilberforce
28. Rayrigg Hall east elevation and driveway
29. Cottage at Mill Beck Stock
30. Myln Beck, Applethwaite and Undermillbeck boundary
31. Low Birthwaite
32. Map of Birthwaite farm estate
33. Round House on Long Holme, with Birthwaite and Orrest beyond
34. Daniel Gardner and Pennington brothers
35. Graphical reconstruction of Birthwaite Hall
36. Monumental inscription to George Gardner at St Martin's Church
37. Drawings of ladies, Jane Gardner's sketchbook

Illustrations in Chapter 4

Abbreviations

CAC	Cumbria Archive Centre
CAC(C)	Cumbria Archive Centre (Carlisle)
CAC(K)	Cumbria Archive Centre (Kendal)
CAC(W)	Cumbria Archive Centre (Whitehaven)
CWAAS	Cumberland & Westmorland Antiquarian & Architectural Society *(now known as Cumbria Past)*
JP	Justice of the Peace
K&WR	Kendal & Windermere Railway
KM	*Kendal Mercury*
LRO	Lancashire Record Office
OS1	Ordnance Survey map Issue 1 (surveyed 1857)
OS2	Ordnance Survey map revised (surveyed 1897)
OS3	Ordnance Survey map Issue 3 (surveyed 1911)
solr	solicitor
TNA	The National Archives
UK	United Kingdom
WG	*Westmorland Gazette*

View of Windermere Lake from Orrest Head, looking south over wooded land
beyond the station where part of the village was built.
J.B. Pyne ca.1850

Chapter 1 – Preamble

*'Few things are more interesting than the place we live in, and yet it is
sometimes true that there are few places we know so little about.'*

So said C.T. Phillips writing on Troutbeck in 1933,[1] and surely his words resonate today. How many of us could name the founding fathers of the village of Windermere, where they came from, what the source of their power and influence was, their knowledge and skill, and how they acquired their wealth – if any? Was there an architectural or civic plan for the village, and if so, by what authority did it shape the embryonic community? This book seeks to redress the balance by tracing a social history of the many people, mostly in-comers,[2] a few native-born, some half remembered, but mostly long forgotten, who shaped the physical, social and cultural fabric of the place. What determined its architecture, construction, institutions and traditions that bestowed a rich and enduring heritage on the Victorian township we know today as Windermere? In the words of William Wordsworth,

'–– make men that have been reappear'.

This book deals not only with wealthy off-comers – merchant princes, bankers, brokers, cotton-tots, ship owners, retirees and gentlefolk – but also with the ordinary working folk, the labourers, artisans and masons, shopkeepers, tradesmen, hand-maidens and servants whose labour brought vitality and growth to the community. In their various ways they implanted on the virgin soil of Applethwaite[3] in Westmorland the seeds and seedlings, fabric and framework, of a vibrant and elegant township, which rose from a tranquil sylvan landscape below the southern slope of Orrest Head.

In the spectrum of British townships Windermere is young, and of no great size. It owes its genesis to the advent of steam power and eight miles of iron-way that linked Kendal to Birthwaite.[4] The Kendal & Windermere Railway opened to travellers on 20 April 1847, immediately attracting a surge of visitors of every social class.

Nearby, the ancient fishing hamlet of Bowness had nestled on the eastern shore of Windermere Lake at least since Norman times. It is home to St Martin's Church, confusingly also known as Bowness Church, and the Parish Church of Windermere. Around 1800 in Applethwaite there existed nothing remotely resembling a village, only four widely separated and isolated rural cottages and vernacular farmhouses, *'–– old world abodes of sturdy statesmen'.*[5]

Although in 1800, Ambleside and Bowness were being gently stirred by tourism, in the 1900s the independence of Bowness fell victim to the irrepressible expansion of its near-neighbour, the fledgling township of Windermere. Today the two places appear seamlessly as one, but the heritage of Bowness is sufficiently distinct, both topographically and socially, to deserve a separate volume.[6]

1. *Part of Thomas West's 1778 map of Westmorland. The small estate called Birthwaite, which became the site of much of Windermere village, was too insignificant to be marked on the original map. It would have appeared between Rayrig and Calgarth, as shown here in red, 1½ miles from the lake shore.*

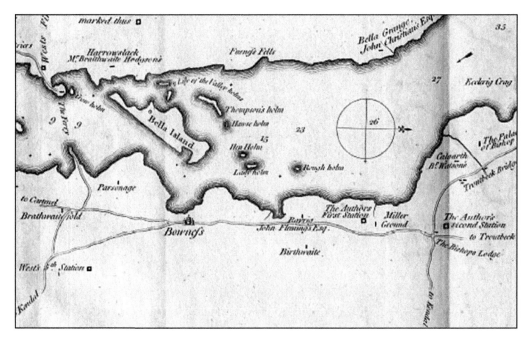

2. *Part of Peter Crosthwaite's map, surveyed in 1783. For the first time Birthwaite appears on a contemporary map (lower-middle).*

Courtesy of Cumbria County History Trust

In the 1700s the farm named Birthwaite comprised a solitary farmstead, probably built a century earlier in the vernacular style of Lakeland,[7] using undressed stone and rubble. It nestled below the western slope of Orrest Head, 1½ miles to the north and east of Bowness.[8] The nearest contemporary dwellings were scattered a mile apart along the turnpike road, nestling inconspicuously amongst the trees, betrayed only by curling smoke from their chimney pots – Orrest Head Farm, old Elleray Cottage, and Cook's House Farm. Not a hotel in sight, nor shop, nor bank, nor school, nor church, nor any other man-made thing intruded upon the scene. Only a mix of mature and majestic trees, rock-strewn awkward pasture, and *watter* rushing down the rocky becks. Lancelot Steele estimated that around Birthwaite in 1800 there were not more than 20 souls.[9] By 1900 the permanent population had increased one hundred-fold.

In the 1600s the only direct route linking Kendal to Ambleside, Keswick, and the far west coast, was little more than a narrow and treacherous track,

> '–– *very dangerous and incommodious to travellers by reason of the steepness and narrowness thereof*',

often deeply rutted and mired, suited only for lines of plodding packhorses. It meandered through Staveley and Ings, climbed past Broadgate, to cross Applethwaite Common to the north of Bannerigg and Orrest Head, following a Roman route past Causey[10] Farm, and Crosses. From there it dove steeply downhill past the little medieval Chapel of St Catherine, to Troutbeck Bridge. The track was barely six feet wide in places, too narrow for horse-drawn vehicles; and too steep for lumbering wagons or the carriages of gentlemen; even packhorses had difficulty passing when laden. In 1730 Benjamin Browne of Troutbeck, High Constable and Bridgemaster of Kendal, described it as:

> '–– *ffrom ye foot of St Catherine's Brow to the top, very narrow and bad road, and so on to Misled Moor, bad road and very narrow in some places.*'

After the passing of the Turnpike Acts in 1761/62, the roads from Kirkbie Kendale to Ambleside, and from Plumgarths to the Windermere Ferry at Bowness, were partly improved or diverted,[11] and turnpikes, toll-bars, and tollhouses were erected. Side lanes were sometimes gated to prevent livestock from straying. On a line from Crook via Ings to Troutbeck, names like Broadgate and Fusethwaite Yeat survive today, relics of such gates. And Stybarrow Cottage[12] at Cook's Corner may have served as a gatehouse for two intersecting roads.[13] Unofficial barriers were sometimes manned by children or older folk, seeking pence for the service of opening the gate for travellers to pass.

To cope with the difficult roads of the county, a primitive design of narrow cart evolved in Westmorland. Its 22-inch wheels – solid discs fashioned from balks of solid timber, joined by dowels – were locked rigidly to a solid axle shafts for strength and stability. But wagons of any kind were uncommon and liable to sink to their bellies in mud, or fracture their wheels on unyielding rocks, such was the state of the roads. Plodding packhorses were the carrier's transport of choice, capable of negotiating the narrow un-engineered tracks, with loads of two hundredweight per beast[14] – wool, slate, timber, charcoal – even iron, lead and gunpowder. Occasionally, primitive sleds were employed for heavier loads, hauled by teams of up to 30 horses.

3. A steep and narrow stretch of the ancient packhorse track, known variously as St Catherine's Rise or St Kathern's Brow, where it rises steeply from Troutbeck Bridge to The Crosses and Causey Farm. It once formed part of the main and only route from Kendal to Ambleside, and was probably part of a Roman road between the forts of Watercrook and Galava.

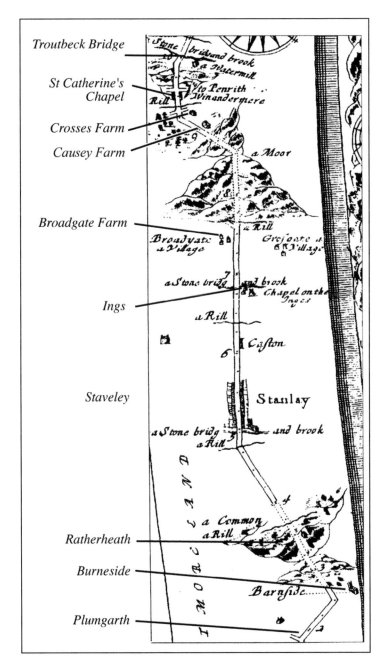

Troutbeck Bridge

St Catherine's Chapel

Crosses Farm

Causey Farm

Broadgate Farm

Ings

Staveley

Ratherheath

Burneside

Plumgarth

4. In his report of 1675 on the 'Principal Roads in England and Wales', cosmographer Ogilby described the route from Kendal to Ambleside – 'It is as bad a road as any in England, being very hilly, stony and Moorish'.

Courtesy of Cumbria Archive Centre, Carlisle [15]

The packhorse track over Applethwaite Common was *turnpiked* around 1763 with tollgates at Plumgarth, Staveley and Waterhead near Ambleside.[16] But by the 1800s the direct line past Causey and Crosses was all-but abandoned in favour of a longer route south and west of Orrest Head, with easier gradients from Ings to Elleray and Cook's House, before descending more gradually to Troutbeck Bridge.[17] In spite of easement in the 1800s, bends and declivities remained, notorious scenes of accidents to gigs and mail coaches travelling at speed on the section from Allis How to Cook's Corner. Increasing numbers of travellers, and all manner of produce, lumbered along its hard-rolled gravel, conveyed by packhorse, cart and increasingly by wagon. Today, this road is the main artery from Kendal to Windermere, Ambleside and Keswick.

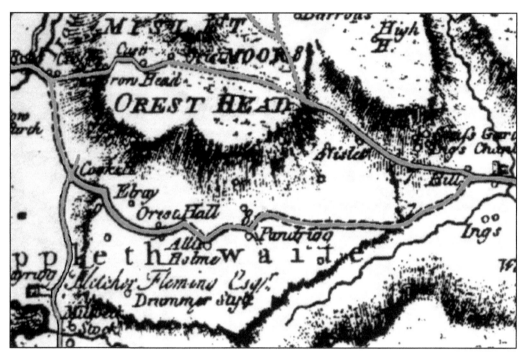

5. *Jeffreys' map of 1770 showing northern and southern routes past Orrest Head, much of their length ill-defined and difficult.[18] The northern route was turnpiked first, by the Cockermouth to Kendal Turnpike Act of 1763. Gradually the longer southern route gained favour since it bypassed the steep and rocky gradient of St Catherine's Brow, from 'Cusie' to Troutbeck Bridge. Birthwaite is marked on this map – but not named (below 'Elray').*

With kind permission of CWAAS

Prior to the 1800s the isolated inhabitants of central Lakeland were self-sufficient in most essentials of a simple rural life. Some gained meagre earnings at the flesh markets in Kendal and Ambleside, selling wool, meat, foul and dairy produce. Their income was sometimes augmented by cottage industries, weaving cloth, manufacturing swills, clogs, hoops, charcoal for the iron furnaces of industrial Lancashire – and gunpowder for quarrying slate. Small water-driven corn and fulling mills were found along the many fast flowing becks of the region. Birch and ash saplings were coppiced on otherwise unproductive hillsides. Staple foodstuffs consisted of oats for *poddish* and clap-bread, supplemented by smoked meat, rabbit or poached fish. Ale brewed from barley was safer to drink than spring water, consumed by all ages at any time of day or night, and brewed in every village and hamlet. Malting floors were worked in cottages and farms of every Lakeland valley. Gambling, wrestling, cock-fighting, nag-racing, and hunting with dogs provided primitive sport and entertainment.

Late in the 1700s a growing awareness of the unexplored pastoral beauty of this remote, and largely inaccessible corner of England permeated a section of the nation's intellectual élite – poets, writers and painters. Deprived of their grand tours through Europe by Napoleonic conflict, the more curious and wealthy classes came to gaze in wonderment at the grandeur of lake and mountain scenery. A few of these worthies settled in the district – de Quincy, Coleridge, Southey, Harden, Wilson and Wordsworth (returning to his roots)[19] – where they formed the nucleus of an intellectual aristocracy.

The opening in 1847 of the Kendal & Windermere branch from the Lancaster to Carlisle Railway, marked a watershed in accessibility for tourists – like the opening of a flood gate. The line was strenuously opposed by Wordsworth, who feared invasion of his homeland by the uneducated masses, incapable of comprehending the splendour of the scenery.

Prior to the railway, travellers on the turnpike road from Kendal passed the pretty little Chapel of Ings, built by Mr Bateman on the profits of his Italian trade in wool and marble. For the next mile they climbed past Bannerigg,[20] where briefly could be glimpsed the wall of western fells, before dipping to cross the soggy mire of Mislet Common. They crested the final rock-strewn rise at Alice Howe – with the shoulder of Orrest Head rising on the right – to gaze amazed at a wondrous panorama. In his diary of a tour to the Lake District in 1798 John Harden wrote

> '–– the first view of Windermeer water –– the impression was sublime –– we were on an immense summit, stretched out before us the almost unbounded range –– of Westmorland mountains –– the sun hid his head behind the distant hills and threw his golden beams resplendent across the whole atmosphere, 'twas an inspiring sight –––'.

There, as the near-horizon dropped away at the feet of the traveller, suddenly was revealed the first expanse of '*the Queen of Lakes*', a panoramic ribbon of shimmering silvery water, stretching as far to the north and south as the arms of a man could reach. The western fells stood prominently above the slopes of Claife. Descending gently towards Elleray, in 1847 the imposing facade of Windermere Hotel rose from the hillside, to offer hospitality to travellers arriving both by road and rail. Above the lone hotel on the southern slope of Orrest, the view of Windermere was one of the finest in the land. Here, the full length of the Lake meandered like a river, from the double knob of Langdale

Pikes at the north and west; Crinkle Crags, Weatherlam and Coniston Old Man sweeping left; and the heights of Graythwaite and Gummer's Howe far off to the south.

Suddenly the pace and style of pastoral life around the little Birthwaite farm, with its ancient cottage and gentleman's villa of only 20 years,[21] was to change dramatically forever. The newfound ease and convenience of rail travel attracted the *nouveaux riches* – merchants, industrialists, ship-owners and gentlefolk from Lancashire and beyond. They were accompanied by middle-income managers and traders, travelling 2nd class. But as predicted by Wordsworth, the working masses also arrived increasingly on cheap day excursions. Tickets were snapped up by mill-workers, shop assistants, miners, labourers, and their families, conveyed on open *toast-rack* carriages exposed to billowing clouds of steam and soot, belching from primitive locomotives. Gradually, a tiny population near the terminus expanded to serve the demands of hungry and inquisitive travellers, and the needs of a slowly expanding resident population. Visitors arrived in ever increasing numbers, and a vibrant and stylish township rose in the space of 50 years, transforming forever the rough and empty sylvan landscape below the station. Initially, the village took its name from Birthwaite Farm, on whose land the station and much of the village were built. But by 1860 it was re-named *Windermere* at the insistence of traders and wealthy in-comers, despite the distance of the fledgling township from the Lake.[22] They desired a more prestigious and familiar name than Birthwaite

It is to the eternal credit of the early builders (Harrison, Medcalf, Atkinson and several Pattinson generations) that increasingly high standards of construction, building material and architecture evolved into a comfortable and recognisable Lakeland style. The local greystone,[23] augmented by imported Lancashire sandstone and limestone for quoins, door and window reveals,[24] became the standard building materials, beneath steeply pitched roofs of blue-grey Lakeland slate. The solidity and style of these early buildings – shops, villas and humble terraced cottages alike – bestowed on Windermere an enduring charm and elegance, a feeling of solid quality which survives to this day.

Many coffee-table books have appeared in the intervening years, comprised of lithographic prints, paintings, and photographs, but usually short on text; books which serve as sweeteners, ephemeral introductions to Lakeland life and scenery. There have been other more learned and academic analyses of particular aspects of Lakeland life and industry, such as those of J.D. Marshall; authoritative and academic works for academic people, documenting the onset of tourism and industry, and their effect on the underlying economy of Victorian Lakeland.

Harriet Martineau, who took up residence in Ambleside from 1845, was the first to pen a contemporaneous account of the surging tide of events and people she witnessed. Her *'Guide to Windermere'* was published in 1854 as a walking tour of central Lakeland. Disappointingly, only four pages touch all-too-briefly on the infant village of Birthwaite. She included a gazetteer of property owners and yeomanry of the day, drawn mainly from Mannex's directory of 1849, *'A History, Topography and Directory of Westmorland'*.

The first extensive account of the village and its residents was penned by G.G. Cunningham.[25] Published privately in 1900, it recorded the first 50 years of St Mary's Church. He presented a lawyer's meticulous account of the social and parochial history of the village, events which embraced his central ecclesiastical theme. He came to Windermere from Edinburgh in 1856, at the age of eleven years, when his parents[26] built the villa named Elleray Bank, high on the western slope of Orrest Head.[27] The young Scot became a barrister in Edinburgh and married a Fleming lady, of Rydal Hall near Ambleside.[28] Throughout his career he continued to visit Elleray Bank in summer months, until his death in 1904. Although G.G. Cunningham[29] was absent for long periods in Scotland, and the house was permanently let in the 1880s, he was well placed to observe the changing pace of life, and growth of the village over time. His account represents the first substantial and contemporaneous narrative of life in Windermere, and its residents, during the fifty years to 1900.

Remarkably, there has only been one other account which sought to record the *'Growth and History of Windermere'*. This booklet was dictated from the recollections of Lancelot Steele aged 83, in 1928, the year before his death. He recalled events witnessed first-hand during most of his long life, and earlier events learned second-hand from acquaintances who preceded him in Windermere. His account is a nostalgic journey, one which he clearly enjoyed. As Cunningham observed before him,

'--— nothing is so new as what has been long forgotten'.

Perhaps understandably, *'Lanty'* Steele's recollection after 70 years should be viewed with a little caution. Nevertheless, his remembrances are of great value, alongside those of Harriet Martineau and G.G. Cunningham, as the only first-hand accounts of the birth and early growth of the village.

Young Lanty Steele was barely six years old when he first visited Birthwaite in 1853; but it was a further six years before his widowed mother came to live. As a teenager he was fascinated by the hustle-and-bustle and rapid expansion of the place. He found employment as a stable lad at the Windermere hotel, eventually rising to the position of foreman ostler,[30] and finally to agent for Rigg's Coaches. He was well placed to observe village life, the many visitors passing through, and those returning for longer acquaintance. In later years, as a worthy member of Windermere Urban District Council and Windermere Schools Board, Lancelot Steele was immensely proud to have served on equal terms with more wealthy neighbours, to have known them personally and had their respect.

As well as various trade directories, the columns of local newspapers have been invaluable sources of information, for their contemporaneous and sometimes patronising reporting of events.[31] Later writings on Windermere are less authoritative, second-hand accounts at best, written many years after the events they describe.

The book which follows here takes a middle-line between informality and academic rigour, to present a comprehensive social history of the people who created the village of Windermere, its architecture, civic amenities and culture. As far as possible the narrative is rooted in records, seeking to build on first hand accounts of events, wherever they survive. It draws heavily on archival documents[32] from which to weave a broad and colourful tapestry of the village from 1800, through its inception in the 1840s, to completion around 1900. Inevitably there are gaps in the records, and they have only been interpolated, where essential, with the greatest of circumspection.

Arrangement of the Book

To observe the evolving historical scene this book employs the popular device of many early Lakeland guides – the walking tour. We will circle several times around the southern half of the ancient rural landscape of Applethwaite where the village of Windermere rose, to observe its birth over the course of a century from 1800 to 1900. For the first and widest circuit, starting at Orrest Head House in 1800 we will travel anti-clockwise, stopping at landmarks of interest to reveal the pastoral quietude of those early years. For succeeding tours we will step forward in time, spiralling inwards to finish around 1900 at Ellerthwaite, close to the centre of the vibrant village we know today. As we shall see, the owners of Orrest Head House, Birthwaite Hall, St Mary's Abbey, and Ellerthwaite are particularly significant to its genesis.

Inevitably, during each tour our path will meander in time as well as in space, to observe the comings and goings of people, the evolving social scene, and building developments of every kind. We will see a dramatic transformation of the civic and built environment within the landscape of Applethwaite, in three significant time periods

- **1800-1840** – a wide sweep of the pastoral landscape, south and west of Orrest Head, to paint a portrait of the sylvan quietude that preceded the railway;
- **1840-1860** – a second tour, retracing our earlier footsteps, to witness the sudden and penetrating thrust of a railway built primarily for tourists; the arrival of the first of the off-comers, and their dominant influence on the development of the place;
- **1860-1900** – a third and more disorganised stroll through increasing urbanisation, to observe the dynamic growth at the centre of an elegant Victorian township, and how the landscape and populace were transformed forever.

During each tour we will examine the dominant role of off-comers, some from near and others from 'far, some with wealth and others with none, seeking retirement and leisure – or employment of their labour, artisan skills and entrepreneurship – all of them swamping the tiny indigenous population. Together, they fashioned a stylish and thriving Victorian township which has served the needs of tourists and residents alike for 170 years – and continues to do so today.

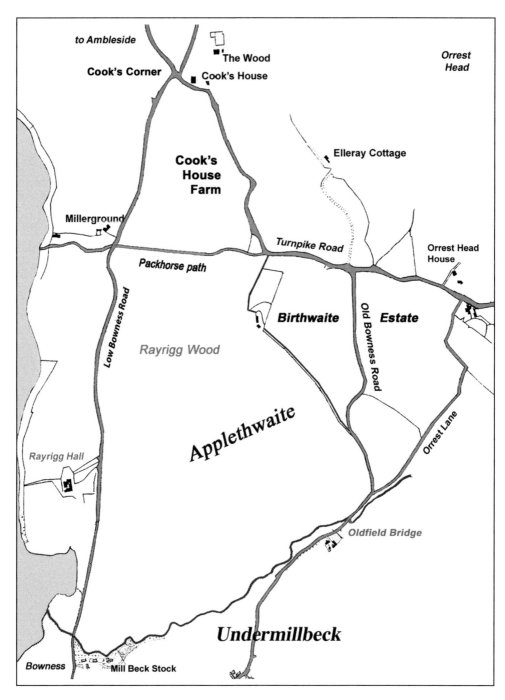

6. Roads and tracks passing Birthwaite, Elleray and Cook's House in 1800

24

Chapter 2 – Portrait of a Sylvan Quietude

For our first walk we will take a winding route around a sylvan landscape to the south and west of Orrest Head, to observe the tranquil rural scene that preceded the arrival of the railway. Starting from Orrest Head House, we will travel west and north along the turnpike road to Cook's Corner; turn left and south towards Bowness, stopping at Rayrigg Hall, and Myln Beck Stock; then east to Oldfield Bridge; and return north by the long climb up Orrest Lane, to finish at Orrest Head Farm again. Inevitably, our path will meander to and fro, both in time as well as in space, to witness the slow pace of life and a gradual awakening in the early 1800s. In the words of a local paper

> '--- the general character of Westmorland landscape is a pastoral quietude, almost loneliness, dotted here and there with a village or solitary farmhouse, the green and rounded hillside occasionally giving place to bolder and more barren elevations.'[33]

The geology of Applethwaite, like all of Lakeland, has been sculpted and scarred many times by ice. The underlying rock is technically Silurian[34], comprised of slate-like material, anciently folded strata forming the Windermere basin of hills. They are usually of lower scale than those of the Borrowdale volcanics to the north and west. Glaciers which receded 10,000 years ago dumped vast quantities of loose and shattered rock, coarse detritus carried down from the higher reaches of the fells, laying bare the rugged tops of hillocks and knolls around Orrest Head. Soil which weathered in the intervening millennia has nowhere accumulated to any great depth, except in pockets and mires. It is generally laden with stone and debris, strewn with larger rocks and outcrops,

> '--- barren, producing little or nothing but wood'.[35]

The steep southerly face of Orrest Head, spilling down to Birthwaite farmhouse, has for long been clothed in native broadleaf trees, fine specimens of oak, sycamore, birch and ash. In more recent times they were in-planted with timber for saw mills and bobbin mills at Troutbeck Bridge, Thickholme and Myln Beck. For centuries it was surrounded by more sparsely wooded pasture, suited only for grazing by hardy Lakeland sheep.

The villages of Windermere and Bowness occupy today a gently sloping terrain which descends steeply at first from Orrest Head (*783 feet above sea-level, ASL*), then more slowly from Elleray (*400 feet approx.*) to the Lake shore at Bowness (*135 feet*). Much of Windermere village lies at about 350 feet ASL, less than half the height of Orrest Head.

By 1820 the southern route around Orrest Head, as the principle artery through central Lakeland, had been engineered to turnpike standard. It wound its way around the hill, passing below Elleray and swinging north to Cook's Corner, Troutbeck Bridge and Ambleside. It was often called *'the old coach road'*, a metalled road linking Kendal to

Keswick, Cockermouth, and the west coast. From our starting point at Orrest Head Farm a narrow side track, known then as Orrest Lane, dropped steeply south, more or less straight, to join the Bowness Road near Oldfield Bridge. Orrest Lane is known today as Thwaites Lane,[36] but has been partly submerged beneath modern housing south of the railway, to re-emerge as Woodland Road.

From a second junction on the turnpike, opposite Elleray gate, another lane descended more gently southwards, known at that time as the Bowness Road. It defined the line of what is now Elleray Road, Main Road, Ellerthwaite Road, and finally Lake Road, before descending for a mile or more to Bowness Bay. The triangle of these three roads – Orrest Lane, the Ambleside turnpike, and the old Bowness Road – embraces the geographic centre of the commercial and residential village of Windermere today.

Further west of this domain a notoriously rough track, sometimes called Low Bowness Road, linked the ferry and Bowness village with the turnpike to the north. After climbing steeply from Rayrigg and Millerground, it intersected the Ambleside turnpike at Cook's Corner. The cottage which is so tightly clasped in the apex of this intersection today, previously known as Styebarrow Cottage,[37] probably served as an unofficial gatehouse for both roads. Low Bowness Road was notorious for the atrocious state of its roadway and bridges, and a determined attempt was made to raise it to turnpike standard in 1828.

Before that time the paying traffic on these routes amounted daily to little more than a dozen vehicles – horse-drawn wagons, the occasional gentleman's gig, and the mail coach running once a day in each direction. But the traffic increased weekly with farmers' carts going to flesh and produce markets at Bowness, Ambleside and Kendal. Trains of packhorses, drovers with their animals and foot travellers, often evaded tolls by using side lanes, some of which survive today as bridleways and footpaths.[38]

2.1   Orrest Head House & John Braithwaite

Until the early 1800s the road from Ings to Orrest Head Farm was ill-defined, rocky and boggy by turns, not yet engineered to turnpike standard.[39] It wandered aimlessly as a goat across two mires – Mislett Common Field and Applethwaite Common – changing course with the weather. A traveller using this southerly route would have passed a handful of humble tenanted farms – Heaning, Bannerigg, Grove, Alice Howe and Orrest Head. With the exception of Heaning and Grove, by 1828 these farms were all in the ownership of John Braithwaite, together with the gentrified yeoman's residence of Orrest Head House on the uphill side of the road, opposite to Orrest Head Farmhouse. He was the last of a line of Braithwaite men who had farmed there for a century past. In 1717 his great-grandfather from Colton[40] purchased Droomer Stile farm, adjacent to Alice Howe. Over the intervening years successive generations of Braithwaites acquired six more farming properties, and rebuilt Orrest Head House:

1717	Droomer Stile[41]	John Braithwaite (I)	(1687-1757)
1735	Droomer	John Braithwaite (I)	" "
1743	Alice Howe	William Braithwaite	(1715-1802)
1754	Ghyll	William Braithwaite	" "
1770	Orrest Head House	John Braithwaite (II)	(1749-1818)
1776	Bannerigg	John Braithwaite (II)	" "
1779	Causy (Causeway)[42]	John Braithwaite (II)	" "
1828	Orrest Head Farm	John Braithwaite (III)	(1782-1854).

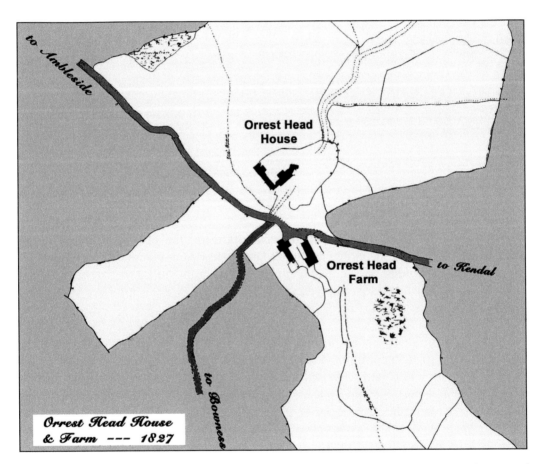

7. *At a long forgotten intersection of packhorse routes stand Orrest Head House, the seat of Braithwaite yeomen since 1770, and Orrest Head Farm, acquired by John Braithwaite in 1828.[43] The old coach road from Ings and Kendal (right) was properly engineered before 1820. A steep sidetrack named Orrest Lane descends from the farm, directly southwards for 1½ miles to Bowness; and on the uphill side of the turnpike an ancient track continues north towards Troutbeck, ultimately linking with Garburn Pass and High Street. Is it fanciful to speculate that this track might also have had Roman roots?*

Courtesy of Cumbria Archive Centre, Kendal

8. Orrest Head House, the statesman's residence of John Braithwaite, the earliest part of which may date from the 1600s.

These estates had long been leased to tenant farmers, the last two generations of Braithwaites occupying the more prestigious Orrest Head House with its own 45 acres of land. Although the oldest part of the building may date from the 1600s,[44] most of it dates from around 1770 when it was enlarged and gentrified to provide an attractive *statesman's* residence, with early Georgian features and six bedrooms.

By 1830 John Braithwaite's estates totalled some 1500 acres, making his land holding one of the largest in the area, and ranking alongside those of Curwen, Fleming, and Bishop Watson of Calgarth. He previously held the posts of agent to the Earl of Lonsdale, High Constable and Treasurer of the Kendal Ward, and Bridgemaster.[45] His duties required periodic inspections of the principal highways and bridges, stretching from Beetham in the south to Grasmere in the north, to oversee their maintenance and repair.[46] And in a related occupation he was Clerk to the Trustees of the Ambleside turnpike, with responsibility for letting the tollgate business at Plumgarths, Staveley, Ambleside and Grasmere. As a native-born Westmerian, baptised at the parish church of Windermere in Bowness, he came from a different mould to that of the in-comers who later populated the infant village. However, with great foresight, his contribution to the institutions of the village of Windermere was considerable at the critical time of its inception, as we shall presently see *(3.13)*.

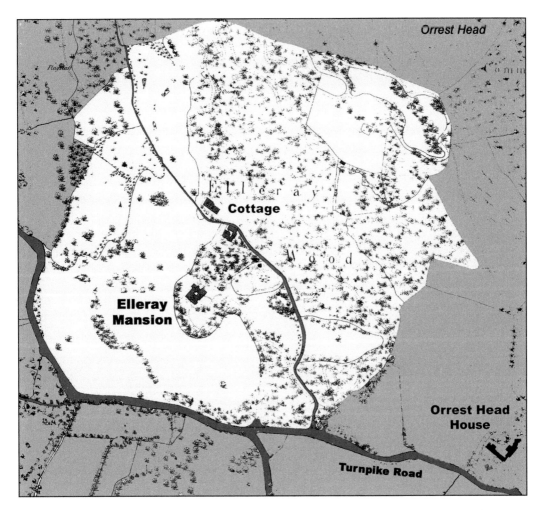

9. *The 60-acre Elleray estate purchased by young John Wilson in 1806, showing old Elleray Cottage and the site of the picturesque villa built to Wilson's own design. Also shown is a narrow track, a public footpath today, following a more direct line north towards Troutbeck Valley, passing between the pleasure ground and stable of Wilson's villa and Elleray Cottage.*

2.2   Elleray & Professor Wilson

Leaving Orrest Head House, next we see a heavily wooded rambling estate named Elleray, which was offered for sale in 1805 by the Rector of St Martin's Church, the Reverend William Barton. It was bought by an energetic and charismatic young Scotsman named John Wilson, a 20-year old gentleman-commoner at Magdalen College, Oxford. Fired by youthful exuberance and

   '--– *drawn thither by the brilliance of the intellectual community'*,[47]

29

he determined to reside in the Lake District, close to Wordsworth who was already ensconced at Grasmere, and to join his circle of Lakes poets and intellectuals.

At the age of 11 years, John Wilson had inherited a considerable fortune when his father, a Paisley gauze manufacturer, died unexpectedly in 1796. Unusually, John Wilson completed his school-age education at Glasgow University, lodging from 1797 at the home of an *'intellectual father'*, Professor Jardine, in whose household he developed a lifelong passion for poetry. On reading Wordsworth's *Lyrical Ballads*, he wrote a long and skilfully crafted fan letter to him, the first the bard had ever received, and Wilson was favoured with a lengthy reply. At Oxford, he achieved fame as the finest athlete of his day, leaping the Cherwell at a point where it was 23 feet wide, and walking the 57 miles to London in 8½ hours. Academically he excelled, becoming the first winner of the now prestigious Newdigate Prize for English verse. Wilson completed his studies at Oxford with a brilliance that was long remembered, the examiners proclaiming his final papers as

'--- the most illustrious examination within the memory of man'.

10. *Old Elleray Cottage, known today as Christopher North's Cottage, overhung by Wilson's favourite sycamore tree. Just visible in the centre are floor-to-ceiling windows which he installed in 1807; and the barn on the right, which he converted as a living room opening on to the garden.*
© *Ian Jones*

In 1807 Wilson came to live at Elleray, an estate of 60 acres tucked under the southern shoulder of Orrest Head, and extending from Orrest Head House half way to Cook's Corner. The only building then standing on the estate was a simple rustic cottage constructed of common stone and rubble, probably dating from around 1700, and later known as Old Elleray, or *Christopher North's Cottage*. It was thickly clothed in jasmine, clematis, honeysuckle and roses, and shaded by a majestic sycamore tree. In Wilson's words

> *'Never in this well-wooded world, not even in the days of the Druids, could there have been such another tree ! It would be easier to suppose two Shakespeares. Yet I have heard people say it is far from being a large tree. A small one it cannot be, with a house in its shadow —– an unawakened house that looks as if it were dreaming. True, 'tis but a cottage, a Windermere cottage. But then it has several roofs shelving away there in the lustre of loveliest lichens; each roof with its own assortment of doves and pigeons preening their pinions in the morning pleasantness. Oh, sweetest and shadiest of all sycamores, we love thee beyond all other trees!'*[48]

Wilson fell in love with this rustic abode and made it amenable to his needs *'—– with the addition of a drawingroom thrown out at one end —–'*, a converted barn with high French windows to bring light and views into the house.

In the following year, 1808, John Wilson began to plan a mansion of more substantial and picturesque proportions, *'after plans of his own'*, a larger and very individualistic gentleman's residence,[49] partly single storeyed to sit low and unobtrusively within the landscape.

> *'I abhor stairs. There is no peace of mind in a mansion where heavy footsteps may be heard overhead. —– You approach the front by a fine serpentine avenue, and enter slap-bang through a wide glass door into a green-house, a conservatory of everything rich and rare in the world of flowers. Folding doors are drawn noiselessly into the walls as if by magic, and lo ! drawing-room and dining-room stretching east and west in dim and distant perspective.*
> *Shrubs and trees and a productive garden shut me in from behind, while a ring fence enclosing about five acres, just sufficient for my nag and cow, form a magical circle into which nothing vile or profane can intrude.'*

This is his description of the most unusual feature of the house, a large conservatory room with ceiling-high bay windows opening directly to the garden and exploiting its magnificent panoramic views of Windermere Lake and the western fells. Surprisingly, for many years the room was unfinished, having only turf on the floor.[50] Here, Wilson hosted cockfighting mains to entertain his sporting friends and neighbours, and his prowess became legendary in all manner of outdoor pursuits.

11. The mansion house and garden room designed by John Wilson himself in 1808 in the picturesque style. For many years this room contained a turf floor and was used for cockfighting. Thereafter it reverted to its intended role as a living and dining room, which he filled with plants and flowers.

Courtesy of Cumbria Archive Centre, Kendal

As a young man, John Wilson and his many friends led a gay and riotous life of country sport, hunting, drinking, and socialising at Brathay soirées. Besides poetry and cock-fighting, his sporting passions extended to Cumbrian wrestling, bull-taunting, climbing, swimming, fishing – and most of all, sailing on the Lake. For many years he owned a fleet of seven boats and a ten-oared Oxford barge.[51] To maintain this fleet he employed, at considerable expense, a crew of professional boatmen led by one, Billy Balmer, who not only became his loyal boatman but also his lifelong friend.

One dark and dismal December evening, with great bravado and probably emboldened by liquor, they embarked in a small boat from Millerground in the midst of a blizzard. Within seconds they lost all sight of the shore and for several hours they drifted helplessly about, hopelessly lost, wrapped in a silent cocoon of gently falling snow. With Billy at the point of despair, and both men sodden and frozen to the bone, the boat suddenly and quite gently touched bottom and they were able to wade ashore in the ice-cold water.

> *'They had been beating about Millerground all the time, scarcely a stone's throw from their starting point ––– master was well nigh frozen to death, and had icicles a finger-length hanging from his hair and beard.'*

A nearby toll-keeper was roused from his bed and they spent the night wrapped in blankets by a roaring log-fire, supping ale and recounting many adventures.

Surprisingly, it was almost two years after his arrival at Elleray before John Wilson gathered courage to call on Wordsworth. At Allan Bank he found the bard in company with poet Hartley Coleridge and essayist Thomas de Quincey. With each of these he subsequently formed lifelong friendships, but especially with his physical antithesis, the diminutive de Quincey. Wilson's friendship with Wordsworth was less close, delighting in teasing the bard. On one occasion he repeatedly tumbled from a boat, fully clothed, feigning drowning. On another occasion when the party was returning from Keswick, they stopped for refreshments at Wythburn. Whilst the innkeeper was fetching a lantern, Wilson crept unobserved to the fireplace and blasted a shotgun up the chimney – a prank of infantile hilarity which frightened the party half to death, covering everyone with soot.

But when scarlet fever struck the village of Grasmere in 1810, with great compassion Wilson generously offered old Elleray Cottage to the Wordsworth family, where they gratefully took refuge for six weeks until the danger receded.

12. 'Girt, yalla haired Wilson of Elleray.'

At various times he wrote for, and edited, Blackwood's Edinburgh Magazine under the pseudonyms of 'The Leopard' and 'Christopher North'.

In stature Wilson presented a fine figure of a man, broad shouldered, tall and athletic, sure-footed, but with unusually tiny feet, and an unruly shock of sandy Scottish hair. In early manhood he was much given to drinking, and wild youthful pranks such as bull-baiting on horseback, with anyone who would accompany him in the middle of the night.

All of his wildness was soon to abate, *'he left off wine and many other follies'* in pursuit of a lady. In May of 1811 he and Miss Jane Penny, the belle of Lakeland society, were married by the Reverend John Fleming, minister of Troutbeck.[52] The lady was the opposite of Wilson in many ways – refined, pretty, and petite in stature – a perfect foil.

She was a daughter of James Penny, a Liverpool merchant and slaver. After her father's death, Jane Penny and her sister took up residence at Gale House in Ambleside, from where Jane and Wilson frequently attended balls at nearby Brathay Hall during their courtship. For four years following their marriage the couple lived a blissfully happy and simple existence, preferring to occupy the old cottage at Elleray where their first three children were born.

It was John Wilson's long-held ambition to be accepted on equal terms by the literary world, and to be recognised as one of the Lakes poets and writers. He began to assemble his poetical jottings from earlier years and a volume was published in 1812, a narrative poem entitled *'The Isle of Palms and Other Poems'*. At first it failed to receive the popular acclaim he fervently desired, and he condemned the critique in the Edinburgh Review as *'beggarly'*. Nevertheless, the book succeeded in bringing Wilson to the notice of the literary world, Sir Walter Scott proclaiming him as *'an eccentric genius'*.

Disaster struck the Wilsons in 1815. Their financial trustee, an incompetent and dishonest uncle, lost most of the combined fortunes of Wilson and his wife in a speculative and reckless investment. For the first time in his life John Wilson was bereft of financial means, and was forced to earn a living. Elleray was hastily closed up, and the family decamped by coach to Edinburgh, in the foulest of weather, where they took up residence with Wilson's widowed mother. She persuaded him to seek a legal career in Edinburgh where he qualified as *'Writer to the Signet'* (a type of Scottish solicitor), but it soon became clear that he was temperamentally unsuited to the law. Instead, John Wilson found work at which he excelled, covertly writing literary and political critiques for Blackwood's Edinburgh Magazine under several pseudonyms, the best known of which was *Christopher North*. But the remuneration was never sufficient to support a wife and growing family of five children for long.

In 1820 he quite audaciously applied for the most prestigious chair at Edinburgh University. Despite knowing almost nothing of the subject, but encouraged by Scott, John Wilson impressed the selection panel sufficiently to be appointed as Professor of Moral Philosophy – a position he held for the next 30 years.[53] His vigorous and rumbustious style of delivery was extremely popular with students – and scorned by many more conventional academics.

With improving fortunes, the Wilsons returned to Elleray for summer vacations. In 1825, Professor Wilson organised the most spectacular and colourful regatta ever beheld on Windermere, *a Festival of the Lake*. The guests included the novelist, Sir Walter Scott, with whom he was now well acquainted; and George Canning MP, the Foreign Secretary of the day. The meeting was contrived by John Bolton of Storrs Hall, Canning's mentor and political agent, and Tory party financier in Liverpool. He aimed to bring together Scott, who was gathering material for his book, *'A Life of Napoleon'*, and Canning, who had been at the centre of politics throughout the war with France. The grand pageant earned Wilson the accolade from Canning of *'Lord High Admiral of the Lake'* when his boat triumphantly led a flotilla of 50 yachts and barges, gaily streaming flags and bunting. They formed a magnificent procession around the islands of the Lake, accompanied by bells and cannon on shore,[54] a spectacle that has never been surpassed on Windermere.

13. The Rt Hon. George Canning, Foreign Secretary,[55] and Sir Walter Scott, novelist, guests of honour at the Windermere regatta organised by Professor Wilson in 1825.
Courtesy of Cumbria Archive Centre, Kendal

Sadly, Mrs Wilson died in 1837, an emotional hammer blow from which the Professor never recovered, and his visits to their beloved Elleray became increasingly melancholy and rare. He returned only twice more to Windermere before Elleray was sold in 1849.

During the following decade the mansion was let to wealthy visitors when the opportunity arose; as in 1841, to Lady Farquhar, the widow of Sir Thomas Townsend Farquhar MP, retired Governor of Mauritius and Director of the East India Company.

One of Wilson's faithful servants, and a frequent companion on fishing and camping expeditions, was Thomas Newby who lived at one end of Old Elleray Cottage. He told of one of Wilson's exploits which almost brought his end. Newby was with the Professor when he fought four pugilist brothers at Bowness. He recounted how they fell in with each other quite accidentally. The brothers' name was Varey, and owing to some recent fighting successes their brag and bearing became so intolerable that John Wilson, then and there, offered to fight all four in succession, locked in a room at the inn. It was at once agreed, and as soon as the door was locked Newby and several others listened intently outside. They heard Wilson knock each of them down in succession, as fast as they came up. But after a time, hearing the Professor call out, they knew foul play must be afoot, and burst open the door. They found all four brothers had set upon him together, kicking him senseless on the floor, and would surely have killed him. Wilson soon came round and told how the brothers, on finding they were each no match for him with fists, got savage. They set upon him together, threw him down by pulling his leg up behind, and began kicking. In the encounter the Professor sprained his wrist, which was never again quite strong.

Wilson and Wordsworth both objected to the proposed railway link from Kendal, but for different reasons. In October 1844, at a time when the initial plan was to terminate the line near Ambleside, the Professor chaired a protest meeting held at Low Wood Hotel, a gathering of landowners and others whose estates would be most assaulted. The proposed railway was to follow the line of a public footpath through the grounds of Elleray mansion, within yards of his front door. It was then to pass directly in front of old Elleray Cottage, cleaving his estate in two and devastating the privacy of both houses.

Even after the Bill before Parliament was amended to terminate the line at Birthwaite, Wordsworth continued his campaign against a rumoured, but absurd, extension north of Ambleside, where it would have passed close to the poet's home at Rydal Mount and violate the dale.

Failing health now curtailed all travel by Wilson beyond the limits of Edinburgh, and in 1850 – the year in which his old friend Wordsworth died – Elleray estate was finally conveyed to William Eastted, a property developer from Malvern.

More than any other man in the years before the railway, John Wilson left his mark on the village of Windermere. He is still remembered with romantic affection as a giant of a man in every way, the most flamboyant, charismatic and paradoxical personality ever to have lived here. He was blessed with an intellect – when he chose to employ it – which challenged that of Wordsworth himself; and a physique which was capable of challenging the best of Cumbrian wrestlers. He died in 1854 in Edinburgh where a larger-than-life-size statue now occupies a prominent place of honour in Princes Street Gardens[56] – in the shadow of the gothic monument to his great friend, Sir Walter Scott.

14. Statue of Professor John Wilson, alias 'Christopher North',
in Edinburgh's Princes Street Gardens, adjacent to the Scott Monument.

2.3 The Wood

Walking north on the turnpike road, a house and small estate known as The Wood occupy most of the land on the east side between the Elleray boundary and Cook's Corner. The oldest part of the house may date from the 1600s. In 1756 a farm on the site was occupied by members of the long established Dixon family,[57] of Bowness and Troutbeck. As with many small estates in the Lake District, part of its income derived from the sale of coppiced timber for bobbin mills at Troutbeck Bridge, Thick Holme and Staveley.[58] The house sits on a shelf of land adjacent to Winlass Beck, and originally enjoyed fine uninterrupted views of the Lake, before maturing garden trees intervened.[59]

15. The Wood pictured in 1925, gentrified probably in the early 1800s for Mrs Anne Parker of Hornby Hall. [60]

Courtesy of Cumbria Archive Centre, Kendal

The Wood estate was acquired in 1798 by Timothy Parker, a yeoman farmer from Hornby Hall in the Lune Valley, partly for its woodland value, but mainly for its amenity. Around this time, Ambleside and Bowness were beginning to stir with tourists in summer months, and the building of second homes around the Lake by wealthy people was slowly beginning. In 1780 a teenage heiress, Isabella Curwen of Workington Hall *(Appendix 1),* began the purchase of the island known then as Long Holme, and later as Belle Isle. She and John Christian of Eunerigg Hall in Maryport, who she married in 1782, completed the half-finished Round House on the island as their summer retreat.[61] The Christian and Curwen seats in the west of Cumberland were close to Mrs Parker's roots at Great Broughton.[62] These people had been well acquainted since childhood, and were followed to Windermere in 1805 by Isabella Taylor, née Fleming of Rydal. She was the widow of Peter Taylor, a West-Indies merchant from Whitehaven, guardian of Isabella Curwen during her minority, and executor of her father's will. At Bowness Bay Mrs Taylor also built an attractive villa named Bellfield[63] on a commanding site overlooking the Lake.

Following Timothy Parker's untimely death in January 1805 his widow, Anne Parker, who had borne him 16 children, moved from Hornby Hall to The Wood with several of her infants. There she lived close to her childhood friends until her own death in 1819.[64]

Probably in the early 1800s Mrs Parker *gentrified* the south side of The Wood for her own occupation, by the addition of a symmetric double-bayed frontage. She would certainly have been acquainted with John Wilson and his young wife Jane Penny of nearby Elleray, whose father had been a Liverpool ship owner engaged in the slave trade.

Clearly the Lancashire off-comers who increasingly arrived in the Lake District from 1850 onwards, were not the first to be attracted to Windermere. They were preceded by a significant and exclusive group of affluent and politically influential people, mine owners, merchant traders and landowners from west Cumberland. Their wealth and power derived mainly from the export of minerals – coal to Ireland and iron ore to Wales – and from the West-Indies trade through Whitehaven, Workington and Maryport. The developing social cluster included the Right Reverend Richard Watson, Bishop of Llandaff, who built nearby Calgarth Park in 1788. Even in the years before 1800 the shores of Windermere were sought as desirable building sites, taken up by a few wealthy Cumbrians acquainted with its picturesque and scenic charm.

In 1819 Anne Parker bequeathed The Wood estate to her third daughter, Isabella, the wife of John Sherbrooke Gell. He subsequently entered the legal profession as an attorney in Nottingham, but retained The Wood for a further decade. Their son was born at there in 1820 and attained the rank of Major-General in the Indian Army.

In the mid-1830s The Wood was rented by James Pennington,[65] a Kendal solicitor and friend of George Harrison Gardner. In failing health, he lived there for five years before his untimely and painful death in 1845.[66] Two months earlier, Pennington had prudently purchased the property to provide a home and security for his wife, Mary. Over the next 80 years the house descended progressively to their grandsons, Herbert and Hugh Pennington, both of whom became barristers at Lincolns Inn. The Wood remained with members of the Pennington family until 1925, during which time parcels of land were occasionally sold off to owners of adjacent houses.

In the 1840s the Gardners of Birthwaite Hall *(2.10)* were the only other permanent residents, and neighbours of James Pennington. It was Pennington's great-uncle in Kendal who was foster carer for Gardner's father during the latter's boyhood years. It is not surprising then that the bonds of friendship established at that time, and their practice in the legal profession, should bring the younger generation together at Windermere.

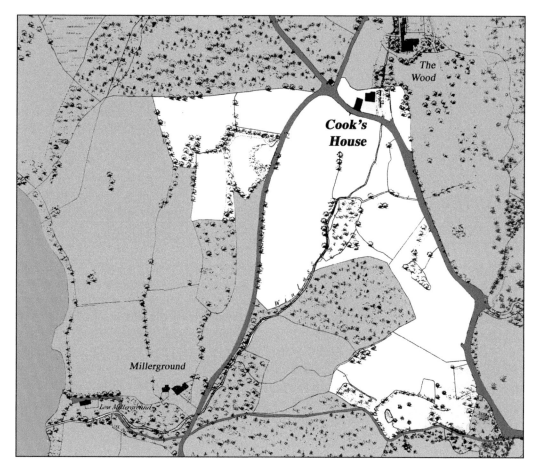

16. Cook's House Estate

2.4 Cook's House Estate

Returning to the turnpike road at a point where St Mary's Church now stands, it swings sharply north around the south-west corner of Elleray estate, opposite to the northern tip of the Birthwaite estate. At this bend there is also an intersection with the packhorse lane from Millerground Landing and an ancient ferry crossing of the Lake. In the early 1800s, between this junction and Cook's Corner there was little else but rough grazing land. On the west side of the road lay most of the land of Cook's House Farm, bounded further west by Rayrigg Wood and the Low Bowness Road.[67] Travelling north for half a mile, we reach the old Cook's Farmhouse on the right, adjacent to The Wood.

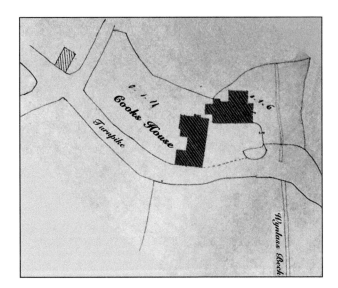

17. *Footprint of Cook's Farmhouse and adjacent barn ca.1840. At least since the early 1600s this farmhouse was the home of successive generations of Robinsons.*

Cumbria Archive Centre, Kendal

Cook's House[68] is recorded in the Windermere Parish Register at least since 1623 when the wife of Christopher Robinson died. The farmhouse seems to have stood close against the road, with a bank-barn set further back. The only surviving outline of these buildings appears on the Tithe map of 1841, and on title deeds of the estate ca.1850. They show a classic H-shaped plan, consisting of two symmetrically disposed wings, linked by a central hall, a typical vernacular layout for many Cumbrian farmhouses.[69] A second building of irregular plan, probably a barn, extended many times with lean-to sheds, sat back from the road adjacent to the Winlass Beck. Harriet Martineau described how the house contained a fine old fireplace, with alcoves to sit within, typical of the district. Here, a good man was forced to protect his shoulders from the soot washed down by rain.

With only 36 acres of land, the farm was similar in size to many of its neighbours, as large as could comfortably be worked by a single family, too small to scratch more than a meagre living from the land.

In 1691 Cook's House was occupied by William Robinson, who supplemented his farming income by carrying on the business of shoemaker. On the death of his son James Robinson, an inventory dated 1719 put the value of his goods and chattels at £41.[70]

These were certainly not wealthy people, as their few possessions, furniture and wearing apparel demonstrate. Farming implements, beasts and fodder were their most valuable possessions. Since the inventory was made in the month of October, the relatively high valuation of oats probably signifies a harvest recently gathered in, a stock of grain for man and beast to last the winter through. Oats and barley were the main crops grown in Westmorland at this time, and the staple grain of rural folk. A frequent vehicle of farm transportation was the horse-drawn sled or hand-sled, since the roads were often too narrow and steep for wheeled vehicles.

	£ s d
His personal apparrell	2 – 0 – 0
In John Loft two chists one bedstead	8 – 0
In ye Great Loft one table one chest	12 – 0
In ye Parlour a bedstead table a chest and forms	10 – 0
In ye back chamber a bedstead a chiest	2 – 6
A meal cheist	3 – 0
All the Bed Cloaths and Curtains	16 – 6
All the Wood vessel	11 – 0
Brass and Pewter	1 – 6 – 0
An iron pott frying ban gridle	1 – 4 – 0
Chairs and stools and forms	2 – 8
Earthen potts & plaits	1 – 8
Biggs[71] and Oats	6 – 0 – 0
Hay and Straw	3 – 0 – 0
Husbandry gear	8 – 0
Black Chattell 8	13 – 0 – 0
A Horse	2 – 6 – 0[72]
Sheep 'young and old' 59	8 –16 – 6
	-----------
	41 – 7 – 10[73]
Funeral expenses	3 – 0 – 0

At his death in 1719 James Robinson owed debts to 18 people totalling £24.

After 150 years, the last of the Robinson line to occupy Cook's House expired when Matilda Robinson died in 1840, at the advanced age of 91 years. A few years later Henry Robinson, a chemist and druggist in Ulverston, advertised Cook's House estate as *'eligible building sites'*, a mark of changing times and opportunities.[74]

Stybarrow Cottage

Stybarrow Cottage was the original name of the cottage, confusingly known today as Cook's Cottage, or Cook's House.[75] It sat tightly clasped in the northern apex of Cook's Corner between the Ambleside and Troutbeck Roads, where, in the early 1800s it may have served as a gatehouse. In 1840 the cottage was occupied by Richard Clapham, a gardener at The Wood. He and his wife Jane raised nine children in this small abode, one of whom married Edward Speight, the Windermere butcher, in 1872 *(5.6)*.

2.5 St Catherine's

Next, we will make a short deviation to St Catherine's, the first property beyond The Wood on the Troutbeck Road. Landholdings totalling about 100 acres were acquired by Timothy Parker in 1788, a decade before he purchased The Wood. At this time St Catherine's consisted of several small hillside holdings, none of which had any significant agricultural value apart from grazing for sheep and light timber. But they possessed good views and considerable attraction as building sites for residences:

Low Gate Mill How,	High Gate Mill How,	St Catherine's Brow Head,[76]
Brow Head,	Knotts,	Chapel Ridding.

In 1804 these properties were conveyed to Timothy Parker's second daughter, Anne Agnes Parker, who took up residence with her mother at The Wood. During the next quarter of a century she let the land of St Catherine's to various tenant farmers, yielding a comfortable living for a single lady. Around 1811 she built a small villa, featuring on the first floor

> '— a sitting parlour, which commands nearly the whole of the Lake, and opens by glass French doors upon a balcony, extending along the front and one end of the house, and overhung by a projecting roof.'[77]

In 1829 Miss Parker agreed the sale of her property to the Earl of Bradford[78] for a consideration of £8,000. The final settlement took many months of painstaking enquiry and wrangling between their respective attorneys, regarding liability for payment of tithes, fines, moduses and Easter dues. However, since payment of tithes in that part of Applethwaite had long since lapsed,[79] and only trifling payments were due to the Lord of the Manor, the Earl of Bradford eventually took possession of St Catherine's in 1831.

Miss Parker retained several paddocks and *housesteads* at Knotts, an ancient farmhouse on the Troutbeck Road with a total of 18 acres, but by early 1834 she had died in Kent.[80]

The origin of the name St Catherine's dates back many centuries, to a little chapel that is believed to have been the earliest place of Christian worship in Windermere, Bowness or Troutbeck. It once stood at the intersection of the two old trading routes, the Troutbeck Road from Cook's Corner, and the very steep and narrow ascent from Troutbeck Bridge to Causey and Ings. The intersection of the two tracks would have been a natural place for men and packhorses to pause for breath on the hard ascent from Troutbeck Bridge, to exchange gossip and haggle deals. The chapel was about 20 feet square, little more than a shelter or chantry, usually served by two monks from Furness who may have exacted tolls. Remains of a building still survived in 1777, but by 1829 it had been converted into a rustic dwelling, with the east window completely walled up. Today, not even this survives, its stone plundered for other use.

2.6 Millerground

Now we must back-track to Cook's Corner where, to the right, the Ambleside turnpike descends towards Troutbeck Bridge and Calgarth estate, purchased in 1788 by the Right Reverend Richard Watson, Bishop of Llandaff. There he built an impressive Georgian mansion named Calgarth Park. But it lies beyond Applethwaite and to go there would deviate too far off our route around the site of the new village of Windermere.

Continuing straight across the intersection at Cook's Corner, the bye-road from Troutbeck crosses the Kendal-to-Ambleside turnpike, to become the notoriously bad Low Bowness Road. It runs for a mile to Bowness and the Windermere ferry,[81] initially passing through rough pasture land on both sides belonging to Cook's House Farm. An open paddock on the right, High Fold affords splendid panoramic views of the Lake, a portent of later use. The track descends increasingly steeply through woodland towards Millerground and Rayrigg Bank,[82] until it plunges to re-cross the Winlass Beck at Miller Bridge.

18. The view looking south from Highfield towards Bowness Bay, drawn by Joseph Farington ca.1786. It reveals the notoriously rough Low Bowness Road near Millerground Farm. Rayrigg Hall is just visible in the middle distance, with the glacial hump of Rayrigg Bank (sometimes known as Oakbank) right of centre, and the narrow finger of Ferry Nab projecting into the Lake towards Long Holme and the newly constructed Round House.

© Jean Norgate; courtesy of Dove Cottage

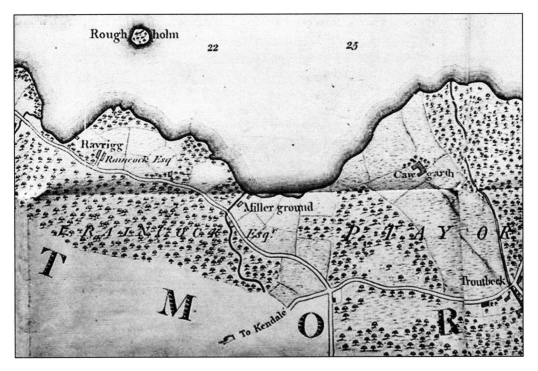

19. *'Clarke's Survey of the Lakes' of 1789 shows Rayrigg and Calgarth estates bordering the Lake. John Raincock and his father-in-law Peter Taylor are named as landowners.[83] Raincock inherited Rayrigg in 1779 via his mother, Agnes Fleming, when he adopted the Fleming surname. Whitehaven merchant Peter Taylor gained a pecuniary interest through Agnes Fleming's sister, Isabella, his wife.*

Courtesy of Cumbria Archive Centre, Kendal

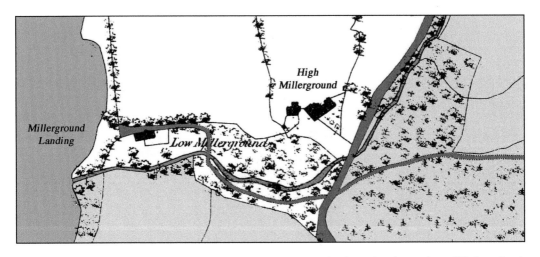

20. *Low Millerground and the ferryman's cottage near the boat landing where Winlass Beck empties into the Lake. The old packhorse track to Birthwaite and Kendal crosses the beck at the site of an ancient water corn mill that gave Millerground its name.*

Here, the old farmhouse of High Millerground was occupied since the 1500s by another line of the Robinson family, probably related to their neighbours at Cook's House. In 1840 Robert Wilson became tenant of Millerground, farming 55 acres of mixed grazing and woodland along the Lake shore between Rayrigg and Calgarth estates. He was an in-comer, born in Cartmel into another branch of the widespread Wilson clan. His wife Betty was also an in-comer, from Workington on the far west coast of Cumberland.

21. Millerground House, part of which probably dates from the 1690s, now a substantial yeoman's residence with well proportioned Georgian sash windows. Part of the interior may be older, possibly dating from medieval times.

Millerground takes its name from a watermill which once stood above the ferryman's cottage, near the stone footbridge where the trail crosses Winlass Beck.[84] The mill is variously described as a water corn mill or as a bloomery (i.e. a forge mill producing blooms of wrought iron).[85]

Take the track to Low Millerground, an ancient cottage where the gushing Winlass Beck has cut a rocky channel before spilling into the Lake. Around 1840 the cottage was occupied by a widow lady, Jane Kirkbride from Cartmel, and her family of five children.

She earned a grindingly hard living as a servant at the nearby Millerground farm, and her son George earned pence from fishing on the Lake. In former times this cottage served as a ferryman's house, with a bell mounted high on the gable to summon the wherry[86] from across the Lake at Belle Grange. The ferry conveyed travellers from Hawkshead and Wray, to the packhorse track which climbs steeply eastward from the shore. It crosses the Low Bowness Road at Miller Bridge and continues to climb directly for half a mile to join the turnpike road again, near Birthwaite and Elleray. This track once served as a trade route linking the important wool towns of Hawkshead and Kendal.[87]

> 'Hawkshead and Kendal are bound up together
> Firstly by Wool and lastly by Leather.
> Both live by their Trade in fair and foul Weather,
> And pay scanty heed to Mighty Folk's Blether.' [88]

22. The ancient Ferryman's cottage at Low Millerground, with its bell mounted high on the apex of a stepped gable. It was rung to summon the wherry from across the Lake at Belle Grange.

23. Gushing Winlass Beck beside the packhorse trail on the left. Together they descend towards the Lake and the old ferry landing. The footbridge crossing the beck is all that remains on the site of a watermill, hence the name Millerground.

Now, we should retrace our steps from the boat-landing and climb back to the Low Bowness Road. Here at Miller Bridge we turn right and proceed in the direction of Bowness. Shortly we reach Rayrigg Hall, the seat of the Revd Fletcher Fleming, which sits a little way to the south of the glacial hump known variously as Rayrigg Bank or Oakbank, obscuring the Lake from view.

2.7 Rayrigg Hall

First, a sawpit appears on the left, standing two storeys high in Rayrigg Wood, where logs were laboriously sawn by hand to provide planks for building work.[89] Opposite to the sawpit stands Rayrigg Hall, seat of a prominent line of the Fleming family. The hall is probably the most interesting building of antiquity in Applethwaite,[90] with its several faces of different date, Elizabethan and Georgian.

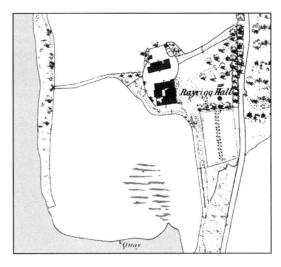

Slightly unkindly, Rayrigg was described by Harriett Martineau as a

> '--- *rather low, rambling, grey house, standing on the grass near a little bay of the lake. It is a charming old-fashioned house, and its position has every advantage, except that it stands too low.*'

The house stands two storeys high, approximately square in plan. The older north and west elevations betray an earlier yeoman's hall, which may date from the 1600s or earlier, when Rayrigg was in Dixon hands. [91]

25. Philipson armorial at Rayrigg Hall

They were succeeded by the Philipsons of Calgarth whose armorial enhances the main entrance, bearing crown, three boars' heads with tusks, and five small crosses on a chevron. Part of Rayrigg Hall may date from 1729 when Fletcher Fleming, the youngest son of Sir Daniel Fleming of Rydal Hall, acquired the estate.[92] The north and east elevations were later improved with more modern oak-mullioned windows and leaded glass. The main entrance, a gabled Cumbrian porch, is protected from the elements by a handsome door. A formal carriage drive circles impressively in front of the entrance, and a large pleasure ground slopes gently southwards to the lake shore at Rayrigg Wyke.

From a southerly aspect the house presents a wide and handsome face, topped with clusters of rounded chimneys in a traditional Lakeland style. At each of two levels there are well proportioned Georgian sash windows, asymmetrically disposed. Two triple-light windows on the left and one on the right, frame the central façade. In all, there are 12 south-facing windows of classic Georgian proportions.[93] The windows provide fine panoramic views just above lake level, reaching out to the isles of Lady Holme and Hen Holme, and as far as Long Holme in the distance. Unlike contemporary houses at Bowness Bay which perch high above the Lake, Rayrigg Hall sits low on its lawns in the picturesque manner. It is certainly not Palladian in style nor intrusive in the landscape.

In the early 1800s Rayrigg was the seat of the Reverend John (Raincock) Fleming (1768-1835), who in 1814 became rector at Bootle in west Cumberland. Born at Penrith of the Raincock line, he succeeded to the Rayrigg estate through his mother, Agnes Fleming. When the male line expired on the death of her brother in 1777, the young John Raincock adopted the Fleming surname to secure the inheritance, in accordance with tradition.

26. *In the 1800s Rayrigg Hall presented an asymmetric south aspect, set low on the margin of Windermere Lake*

(illustration by Arthur Tucker in 'Wordsworthshire')

The Flemings of Rayrigg Hall were *de facto* lords of the manor of Applethwaite, landed gentry and a cut above the middling yeomen of the area. The Fleming name has been associated with Cumberland and Westmorland since Norman times, and over the centuries clusters of this prolific and influential family had their seats at Whitehaven, Coniston, Little Langdale, Penrith, Rydal and Rayrigg. On at least three occasions the name was all-but extinguished when the male line died out; but in each case succession was secured by the female line when their spouses adopted the Fleming surname.

John (Raincock) Fleming was educated at Hawkshead Grammar School where he was contemporary with, and a close friend of young William Wordsworth – and also at St John's College, Cambridge. He married a cousin, Jane Taylor of Whitehaven, whose merchant father had plantations in South Carolina, worked by 116 slaves.[94] Their eldest son, Fletcher Fleming (b.1795), was rector first at Rydal and then at Grasmere.[95] In 1835 he succeeded to the Rayrigg estate on the death of his father. Confusingly, the rector of Windermere parish was a distant relation, Sir Richard le Fleming[96] of Rydal Hall – who was also incumbent at Grasmere.

During John (Raincock) Fleming's minority, in 1780 '--- *Mr Raincock has let Rayrigg to farm to one Mr Wilberforce'*. Here at Rayrigg Hall, in the 1780s young William Wilberforce, recently graduated from Cambridge, and MP for Hull, spent summer months absorbing the beauties of the Lake District. This assisted his convalescence from a painful intestinal ailment, and to experiment with an opium dose (short of addiction), to relieve the pain. He could frequently be seen rowing to the nearby island of St Mary Holme where he spent many hours amongst the ruins of an ancient chantry of the same name.[97] The experience may have contributed to his deep religious awakening in 1785, usually attributed to two continental trips in company with the Dean of Carlisle.

He began planning a campaign against the iniquitous trade in human slaves from Africa to the Americas. But his Slavery Abolition Bill took two decades to gain sufficient support in Parliament. It finally passed in 1807, after Wilberforce had laid much of the early groundwork at Rayrigg Hall.

It is ironic that his landlady, Isabella (Fleming) Taylor, was the wife of a slave owner. At least three other large houses were later built on the shores of Windermere from the proceeds of this brutal business.[98]

27. William Wilberforce, MP for Hull and anti-slavery campaigner, as a young man.

28. The pleasingly balanced east elevation of Rayrigg Hall today, with circular driveway and large sentry-box porch. The Hall was renovated in the early 1900s by G.H. Pattinson, builder of much of Windermere and Bowness, for his own use.

Rayrigg hall estate was purchased in 1729 by Sir William Fleming of Rydal for his brother, the first Fletcher Fleming (1675-1753). It remained in Fleming ownership until the death of Miss Jane Isabella Fleming in 1902.

2.8 Millbeck Stock

Leaving Rayrigg Hall, we continue south towards Bowness on a gently descending road past the high fern-clad wall of the kitchen garden, but with the sombre Rayrigg Wood louring over from the left. Shortly the road crosses another gushing stream which rushes relentlessly towards the Lake, the Myln Beck. In 1816 the roadway at this point was reported to be in a ruinous state

> *'Presentment that Millbeck Stock Bridge is one of the public bridges and that the said bridge and the 300 feet of the road at each of the ends is in great decay, and ought to be repaired at the expense of the County.'* [99]

Near the intersection of road and stream stands a cluster of cottages know as Millbeck Stock,[100] housing labourers and their families. The force of the beck was sufficient to power a number of mills along its two-mile length, as it tumbled down from Applethwaite Common to the Lake. Conveniently, the beck marks the geographic boundary between the ancient rural townships of Applethwaite to the north and Undermillbeck to the south.

29. Ancient cottage at Mill Beck Stock above the Myln Beck, built of undressed stone and rubble.

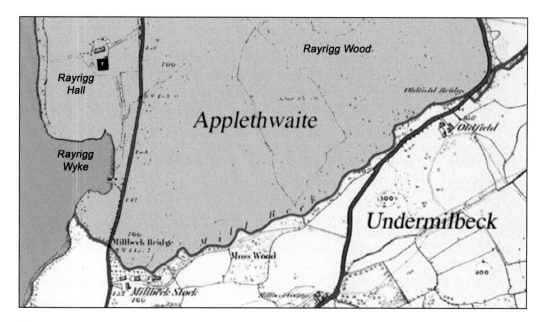

30. The Mill Beck, or sometimes Myln Beck, along the southern edge of Rayrigg Wood, marks the boundary between the ancient rural townships of Applethwaite and Undermillbeck.

Applethwaite once possessed many fine, mature and handsome trees from which a useful income was taken by estate owners and tenants. Coppiced timber was harvested at intervals, usually in regular cycles of 12 to 16 years. Ash shafts shooting skywards in search of light were harvested for bobbin turning; beech and birch for swill making; oak and elm for furniture and building work; and bark for tanning of leather. In former times, large quantities of charcoal were '*burned*' to provide fuel for the smelting of iron at Cunsey, on the west side of the Lake. The harvesting of timber from otherwise difficult land yielded a steady and useful income for the owners of Rayrigg and other estates in the area.

2.9 Birthwaite in Antiquity

Next, we need to back-track past Rayrigg Hall to Miller Bridge, turn right and follow the packhorse trail uphill to meet the turnpike road at a bend below Elleray. Turn immediately right here and follow the narrow path to arrive at Birthwaite.

The enigma that is Birthwaite[101] is central to the birth of Windermere since much of the village was built upon its land and initially took its name from the farm. The village was later renamed Windermere, following protracted squabbling between new residents of Birthwaite and Bowness, both claiming proprietorial rights to the name 'Windermere'.

For centuries the small Birthwaite estate lay on the south side of the Kendal-to-Ambleside road below Elleray, and was empty of habitation except for a solitary primitive farmhouse. At that time the estate covered less than 50 acres, a triangle of rough and rocky, un-enclosed common pasture, clasped between Rayrigg Wood to the west, Orrest Lane to the east, and the old coach road on its northern boundary. Long before that road was upgraded to turnpike standard it was little more than a section of the packhorse track between the wool towns of Hawkshead and Kendal. The Birthwaite estate extended from a point adjacent to Orrest Head Farm at its eastern extremity, to the intersection where St Mary's Church now stands, approximately a quarter mile. From this boundary the farm dropped gently southwards for a similar distance, roughly triangular in outline, and bisected by the old Bowness Road from Elleray Gate.

Birthwaite was never a prosperous property of any great consequence. The surviving deeds (Appendix 2) hint at the struggle experienced by its incumbents trying to extract a living from a typical small Westmorland farm.

Philipson – Knipe – Cowperthwaite

The earliest record of Birthwaite dates from before 1650 when its tenement and land were in the hands of John Philipson, the elder.[102] It is possible that he built the farmhouse in the early years of the century, during the *'rebuilding of rural England'*.[103] The old farmhouse survives today as Low Birthwaite Cottages. He was succeeded in 1654 by his second son, Christopher Philipson, both of them described as yeomen, who inherited all the ploughs, harrows, iron gear, and axes, etc. The first son, John Philipson the younger, was bequeathed a farm named Orrest.[104]

By 1708 the Birthwaite holding had been acquired by Thomas Knipe, who may have been related.[105] On Knipe's death in 1741 the property devolved through his sister Dinah[106] by assignment to her husband, Richard Cowperthwaite. He died in 1757 at the age of 45, which suggests a hard existence. The property then reverted back to Dinah for a further decade while she raised six children. Even with their help, she seems to have struggled to wrest a meagre living, typically from a few sheep, a cow, possibly a pig, hens and ducks.

In 1767 Dinah released her *widowright* in return for an annuity to be provided by their second son, James Cowperthwaite.[107] At the age of 27, and at the behest of his father's will, James attempted to establish himself as a farmer, but within three years he quit his mother's annuity and took a mortgage on Birthwaite from Gawen Braithwaite of Brathay.[108] Three years later James encountered more financial trouble when he failed to redeem the mortgage. And so in 1774, after three generations in the Knipe and Cowperthwaite family, Birthwaite was sold. For whatever reason, James Cowperthwaite seems to have failed to make a living from the farm, sufficient to support his mother and to repay the mortgage. What subsequently became of them is not recorded, but such an outcome is commonplace in the annals of Cumbria. More prosperous '*statesmen*' accumulated land and modest wealth from the financial difficulties of their neighbours,[109] who sometimes suffered the humiliation of becoming tenants of property which they had previously owned.

31. Low Birthwaite today conveys the tranquillity of the small farming property as it originally existed. The cottages (left) and converted barn (right) probably date from the early 1600s.

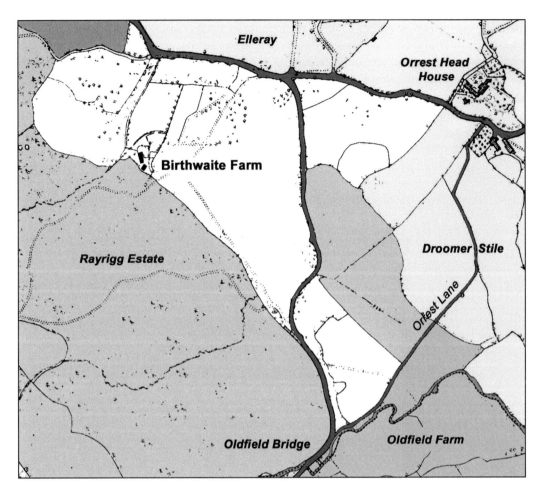

32. In the absence of a definitive ground plan, this map reveals the location of Birthwaite farm as it may have existed around 1800, based on the known boundaries of neighbouring farms and estates. In 1828 a villa named Birthwaite Hall was built beside the old farmhouse by barrister George Gardner, for his retirement. Ownership of the farmhouse appears to have transferred at this time to Thomas Crosthwaite, who divided the old building into a row of three small cottages known today as Low Birthwaite.

Thomas English

In 1774 the Birthwaite estate was purchased by Thomas English, an affluent tea and coffee merchant from London, the first of many off-comers who later came to Lakeland. English was described by Wordsworth as the

> '-— *first man to settle in the Lake District for the sake of the beauty of the country.'*

In his brief connection with Windermere, Thomas English acquired the rank of Lieutenant in the Westmorland Militia, a volunteer force established before the Napoleonic wars for civil protection against possible French or American invasion. It was English who, in 1774, also purchased from Robert Philipson the island known variously as Great Island, or Long Holme, and later as Belle Isle.[110] With great aplomb, English commissioned a talented young architect, John Plaw from London, to design a summer residence in a grand flamboyant style. It boldly took the form of a unique round house, complete with neo-classical portico, and built of local stone shipped down the Lake from a small quarry at Ecclerigg Crag.[111] Understandably, not everyone thought that this radical architectural innovation would grace its prominent location in the middle of Windermere Lake. John F. Curwen and others[112] describe how English first

'--- pulled down the old house and built the present bastard classic structure. The remains of a Roman pavement composed of small pebbles and many Roman antiquities were discovered during the excavations.'

33. The Round House on the island of Long Holme (renamed Belle Isle), with Orrest Head and Birthwaite village near the skyline.

Why Thomas English should also have acquired Birthwaite can only be conjectured.[113] If the Round House on the island was intended solely as a romantic summer residence, a small estate on the mainland connected more directly to Kendal and ultimately to London by stagecoach, would certainly have been attractive. Perhaps he planned to build a second villa, or a dowerhouse, below Orrest Head, with more elevated views than those available at lake level where there was also the risk of flooding. But before the Round House was completed English encountered financial difficulties of his own. After four years, having already expended £6,000, a great sum of money in those days, he was forced to raise a mortgage for a further sum of £2,000 with a view to completing the villa.[114] But even that was not sufficient, and in 1779 he had to abandon the partially completed project.

In May of 1780, the island of Longholme and the unfinished Round House were purchased by a mining heiress aged 14 years, Isabella Curwen from Workington, through Peter Taylor (2.3), executor of her father's will.[115] In 1779 the sale of Birthwaite was agreed by English and his solicitor, Steven Lushington, who seems to have provided the mortgage capital for English. The buyer was Daniel Gardner, a London-based portrait painter. But significantly, Gardner was born and raised in Kendal.

2.10 The Gardners of Birthwaite

Concurrently with the change of Birthwaite ownership, the Applethwaite Inclosure Act became law, and in the hands of Daniel Gardner the estate began slowly to be improved.

Daniel Gardner was born in Kendal ca.1753, the son of a baker, and nephew of Alderman Redman.[116] At an early age he showed considerable promise as an artist and briefly learned the art of portraiture from George Romney, a boyhood friend in Kendal. Around 1770 Gardner followed Romney to London where he studied at the Royal Academy School, and assisted in the studio of Joshua Reynolds for a while. He quickly gained a reputation for portraiture amongst London society, painting in pastel and gouache, and attracted wealthy and well-connected clients who paid him well. Perhaps his best known sitter was the great John Constable himself, a personal friend who Gardner introduced to the Lake District and its scenery.

In 1774 Daniel Gardner married Ann Haward of Lambeth who bore him a son named George in 1778, complaining bitterly of her husband's absence in Cheshire during her confinement. Sadly, three years later Ann and a second son both died in childbirth, leaving Gardner with the difficult task of raising young George. He began to resent the boy's presence near his studio in New Bond Street whilst serving his wealthy clients.

The solution was to remove the lad completely from the London scene by placing him in the hands of friends, the Pennington family in Kendal, 270 miles to the north. Daniel Gardner had formed a close boyhood friendship with three brothers, William, James and

Joseph Pennington. At the age of five, young George was generously accepted into their family circle as one of their own. For over a decade, from 1783 to 1794, they acted as the boy's surrogate parents, attending to his worldly needs and supervising his education at Hawkshead[117] and Sedbergh Schools, financed by his father.

34. Self portrait by Daniel Gardner (far left) with boyhood friends Joseph Pennington, Kendal solicitor; and probably William Pennington, stationer and paper maker.[118] The Penningtons acted as surrogate parents for Gardner's son, George, during his education at Hawkshead and Sedbergh Schools.
Cumbria Archive Centre, Kendal

By 1779 Daniel Gardner had accumulated sufficient wealth to embark on property investments in London, and also in his home town of Kendal:

• the Elephant Inn, attached shops, and its out-buildings within the Elephant Yard;
• burgage property in Redman's Yard (on the opposite side of Highgate);
• several houses in Lowther Street;
• a newly built house in New Street;
• land near the Sedbergh Road.

But most significantly for the history of Windermere, the small farm of Birthwaite was conveyed to him from Thomas English on 8 July 1780.[119]

Known to be a strong-willed, argumentative and parsimonious man with few close friends, Daniel Gardner became increasingly obsessed with property dealing. He moved from his comfortable rooms in New Bond Street, London, to less prestigious lodgings in Beak Street, Soho. As a contemporary noted, he

> '--- gave up the pursuit of every art, except that of improving his fortune, in which he is said to have been adept, not without a degree of penury which injured his health'.

On his death from liver disease in July 1805 Daniel Gardner's considerable property portfolio was valued at £8,429 [120] including a stake in the newly built Kendal Canal.

The passing of the Inclosure Acts[121] gave landowners the right, and sometimes forced them, to fence their open or common lands, often an expensive undertaking. And so it was with Birthwaite, especially as the practice in Westmorland and the north of England was generally to employ dry stone walls, a permanent but labour intensive construction.

Daniel Gardner's friend and agent in Kendal was William Pennington, who wrote to him in 1780 as the initial work at Birthwaite was nearing completion

> *'You may think the expense of fencing &c. rather high but there has been no more done than myself and others thought absolutely and immediately necessary: indeed there are still many other improvements that might be made in the estate, but these may be done at any time, and you may sometime come to see it.'*

Daniel Gardner owned the Birthwaite estate for a quarter of a century, making gradual improvements with further fencing, hedging and tree planting. Yet it could not be said that he *enjoyed* the estate, for throughout this time he remained aloof, an absentee landlord making only occasional trips to the north of England to consult with Pennington, and inspect his Kendal properties. Indeed, it appears that he sometimes did not see George for more than a year at a time. Birthwaite was let from 1779 to Thomas Elleray, a farmer and local man of Applethwaite, until his death in 1827.

In 1805 Daniel Gardner's properties in Westmorland and London passed by inheritance to George, his only son, then aged 27. By all accounts the boy had done very well at school in the north of England, eventually graduating in law from Trinity College, Cambridge, in 1801. Before his father's death George was called to the Bar, and occupied chambers at the prestigious Lincoln's Inn. He frequently served as a barrister on the Northern Circuit, which took him to familiar places in Kendal and Westmorland. Accompanying the circuit judges on their provincial duties required considerable stamina and time away from London, with much uncomfortable travelling on the poorly maintained roads of the time, in all weathers. Nevertheless it was a sought-after and varied practice, enabling young attorneys to increase their income – for those who could endure the travelling and indifferent accommodation of country inns.

George Gardner married Harriet Ann Harpley, a London lady, at St Pancras in 1808. They moved from his father's rooms in Beak Street to more appropriate accommodation in Burton Street, convenient to Lincoln's Inn. There they had two children, George Harrison Gardner and Ann Elizabeth. Like his father before him, George Gardner was an absentee landlord as far as the northern properties were concerned – until 1828. In that year he had accumulated sufficient wealth to invest £5,000[122] in Bank of England consoles, enough to provide a retirement annuity for himself, and later for his widow. In the same year he purchased from the Earl of Lonsdale the freehold of the estate at Birthwaite, previously copyhold.[123] By the end of 1828 we find him

'--- residing at Birthwaite in my new built messuage [124] --- a modern mansion peeping from finely wooded grounds' [125]

named Birthwaite Hall, accompanied by Harriet Ann and their two teenage children. It seems that around this time they may have sold the old Birthwaite farmhouse (Low Birthwaite) and part of the estate to a neighbouring farmer, Thomas Crosthwaite, but retained the Hall and most of its land.

35. Graphical reconstruction of Birthwaite Hall, built as the retirement home for London barrister George Gardner in 1828, two decades before construction of the village began. [126]
Cumbria Archive Centre, Kendal

Although they retained the house at Burton Street in London, as city dwellers the pastoral quietude and cooler northern climate of the Lake District must have been a considerable transformation from the over-crowding, smoke and grime of the capital. Nevertheless, travel to Kendal, Lancaster and further afield could not have been more accessible at that time, with coaches passing their gate twice daily on the newly metallised turnpike road.

By then, Ambleside and Bowness were stirring with tourists in the summer months, and the nucleus of a genteel society was slowly emerging, as we have already seen. A handful of merchant princes from Liverpool,[127] and other in-comers, acquired sites for summer seats around the Lake. And Bowness counted retired officers from the Indian Army and the Napoleonic wars as residents.[128] Inevitably, the Gardners were acquainted with their neighbour, Professor Wilson of Elleray, and through him with Wordsworth[129] and the Lake Poets.

It was the wish of George Gardner that William Pennington, his contemporary in the Kendal household where he had been so generously housed during childhood, should receive a bequest of Birthwaite Farm. If this gift had taken effect, the history of the village of Birthwaite may have been quite different. However, the strictures of land tenure intervened to frustrate the transfer of ownership from the Gardner family.[130]

36. Monumental Inscription to George Gardner at St Martin's Church, Bowness.

> *'Sacred to the memory of George Gardner, Esquire, of Birthwaite in this parish;*
> *who died 20th May 1837, aged 59 years. Also of Harriet Anna his widow who died*
> *at Castlewood, Durrow in Ireland April 3rd 1853, aged 68 years.'*

And so in 1837 the Birthwaite estate devolved by inheritance in the normal way to George Harrison Gardner, George Gardner's only son. Following his father's death G.H. Gardner, grandson of the painter, succeeded to the now freehold Birthwaite Hall and estate. In 1839 he married Jane Thompson of Lancaster, and their friend, Hartley Coleridge, wrote a charming poem to mark the occasion.

Over the coming years, until her own death in 1853, Mrs Anna Gardner shuttled between Birthwaite and their St Pancras residence. Even after the advent of the railway this continued to be a long and nauseating journey, three days by coach, or 10-12 hours by train, with steam and soot billowing about the carriage.

Like his father before him, G.H. Gardner entered the legal profession, and established a practice in Bowness with Staveley-born John Hirst Taylor. So by 1840 the Gardners were well settled at Birthwaite Hall. Although the elder George Gardner was born in London, the time he spent in Kendal and the Lake District during his formative years had clearly left a deep-seated affection for the home of his ancestors, and the properties bequeathed by Daniel Gardner provided succeeding generations with a northern seat.

Little is known of the appearance and particulars of Birthwaite Hall apart from an indistinct photograph printed in a prospectus for the Old College in 1910. Originally, the building appears to have been a modest two-storey villa of simple but pleasing style *(previous page)*, not unlike some of the Webster houses in Kendal. Its tall windows would have captured good light and views across the Lake to the western fells; and a first floor veranda offered elevated views of Fairfield and the Langdale Pikes to the north. A rather incongruous top floor seems to have been added later for The College, not part of George Gardner's 1828 house. Birthwaite Hall was absorbed into the much larger gothic-style College complex, built in 1853 for Reverend Addison.

37. Two charming drawings from a sketchbook belonging to Jane, wife of G.H. Gardner, possibly depicting herself (artist unknown). [131] Courtesy of Cumbria Archive Centre, Kendal

2.11 Return to Orrest via Droomer Stile

Continuing south beyond Birthwaite for a quarter of a mile along the edge of Rayrigg Wood, we join the Bowness Road, and shortly there is a junction with Orrest lane near Oldfield Bridge. Turn hard left here and begin the long trudge uphill towards the south-facing wooded slope of Orrest Head, high above.

Along the way we pass through the rough land of Droomer Stile, with the old farmhouse just visible far to the right. This is a large hill farm of 100 acres, another tenanted property belonging to John Braithwaite. Finally the lane meets the turnpike road at a steep junction where Orrest Head Farm and Orrest Head House are juxtaposed on opposite sides of the road,[132] where we first embarked upon this perambulation.

Orrest Head Farm of 62 acres spreads across Applethwaite Common, between Droomer Stile and Alice Howe farms. It straddles the turnpike road, spreading north along an ancient trackway beyond Mr Braithwaite's seat. From 1596, the farm devolved by customary inheritance through generations of Dixon, Brown, Fisher and Soulbys.

In 1770 part of the estate on the north side of the road was sold to John Braithwaite's father, and there he built a substantial yeoman's residence, Orrest Head House, as we saw at the start of the tour *(2.1)*.

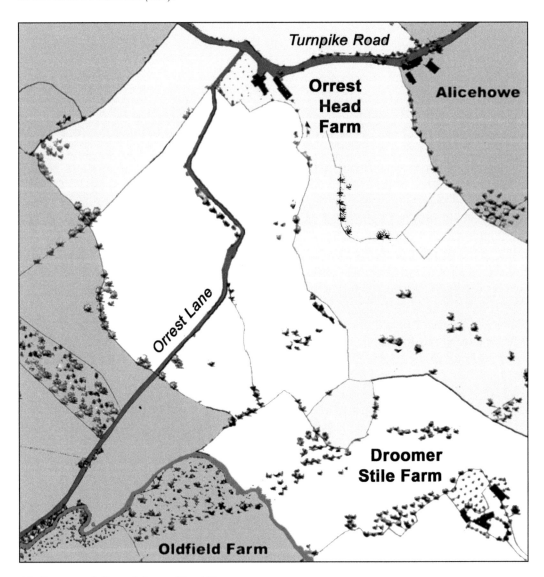

38. Droomer Stile and Orrest Head Farms

The Soulbys were stationers in Ulverston and do not appear to have occupied Orrest Farm, but leased it to tenants. In 1824 they took a mortgage for £1200 from John Braithwaite, and two years later for a further sum of £250, apparently using the farm as collateral. But their income seems not to have been sufficient to redeem the debt and so in 1828 ownership of the farm passed to John Braithwaite.

When John Braithwaite's elder brother William pre-deceased their father, all of the family's estates demised to the younger brother, nearly 1500 acres in all, accumulated in Applethwaite since 1717 by three generations of Braithwaite statesmen.

2.12 End of the First Tour

We have now completed one tour around the sleepy and unsuspecting domain in Applethwaite, situated to the south and west of Orrest Head where the fashionable village of Windermere will soon rise. In 1840 it is still a sparsely populated place with barely a dozen permanent residents along the turnpike road. They are a hardy and independent folk, mostly scratching a difficult and uncertain living from the thin and rock strewn soil; or coppicing timber in the woods in the wet and often inhospitable climate.[133] There is little cultivation of land aside from barley, oats and hay for winter feed. Coppiced wood for the bobbin mills at Troutbeck Bridge and Staveley is the main productive crop. The diminutive Herdwick sheep, unique to Cumbria, produce coarse grey wool for Kendal mills, and a little meat for those who can afford it. Perhaps surprisingly, we have also found a handful of early in-comers from west Cumberland and from Scotland, intermittent visitors to villas secreted picturesquely within the landscape.

Our route has circumnavigated the domain that is to host the new village, an area that will be utterly transformed forever before 1900. It consists mainly of three small farms, Cook's House in the north; Birthwaite to the south; and a large enclosure in the centre named Sossgills, part of the Rayrigg estate.

We shall return here next to witness the coming of the railway. But first we will visit Kendal to reveal the events and the men responsible for the railway.

Chapter 3 – Genesis 1845-1860

3.1 Thrust of a Railway

In the annals of Windermere the signal event of seismic proportions which begat the infant village was the irresistible thrust of iron way into the virgin landscape of Applethwaite. It is difficult to exaggerate the transformation wrought within two generations; yet it would be wrong to suggest that the tiny indigenous population was unaware of its coming. Proposals to include Kendal in the approaching railway network had been aired in the press for a decade or more. Mining, industry and commerce were the usual driving forces behind other lines, with the commercial prospect of mass movement of raw materials, finished goods, increased trade and unprecedented returns for manufacturers, merchants and investors. Paradoxically, the prospect of the mass conveyance of passengers was the principle reason for the branch line to Windermere.

To understand the historical context and its importance to the Lake District we must briefly deviate from our perambulations in Windermere, and look farther afield to trace the growth of railways in England generally. The first steam-powered, passenger-carrying railway was the 26-mile Stockton & Darlington line which opened in 1825. The Act of Parliament which authorised its construction was accompanied by familiar arguments between entrepreneurs, protesting residents, and politicians. They ranged over the engineering practicality, financial viability, disruption to town and country, operational safety – and unalloyed prejudice borne of ignorance. By the 1820s the industrial revolution was well advanced in the north of England. Coal was routinely carried by canal barge, and sometimes by rail, hauled by horse power or stationary steam engines. Cotton and woollen mills employed armies of lowly paid workers, delivering unprecedented profit to mill owners and investors. Even in Kendal, for a century or more the River Kent had been lined with woollen mills and dye works.

Mechanical invention was key to success. Early steam pioneers such as the Stephensons and Trevithick brimmed with energy and invention. They built monstrous self-propelled goliaths in pursuit of the competing requirements of motive power and boiler safety. On a good day these early locomotives could barely sustain a fast walking pace on a level track. But such was the progress in construction of the iron way and technological advances in steam locomotion, that grand plans emerged weekly for new railways. The whole country was seemingly to be wrapped in a vast network of metal rail connecting the principal cities and ports, centres of industry and commerce. Economies of scale resulting from the newfound speed of moving raw materials from mine to mill, coal in particular, were confidently predicted.

Opened in 1830, the most important railway the world had yet seen was the Liverpool & Manchester. It was designed from the outset for steam locomotion, hauling coal to Manchester and returning finished goods to waiting ships in Liverpool, in direct competition with the Bridgewater Canal. But its pioneering innovation was the scheduled carriage of passengers between the two conurbations, according to a published timetable. The L&M Railway was commercially successful and by 1845 it was linked to the arterial London & North Western Railway, with all the advantages of national connectivity to the north and south. London could now be reached in 12 hours by rail, where the stage took up to six days, and plodding ponderous packhorse lines took as long as two weeks.

In Westmorland, a tireless campaigner for a railway to be routed through Kendal was Cornelius Nicholson. A clever and energetic self-made man of humble origin, he was born in 1804 in Ambleside, the fifth of twelve children of the Postmaster.[134] He started from small beginnings, apprenticed as a compositor to the proprietor of the *Kendal Chronicle* newspaper. He read voraciously in his spare time and at the age of 21 was already part-owner of his own bookselling and printing business, Hudson & Nicholson. Some years later he married Mary Ann Hudson, his partner's sister. As a member of Kendal Town Council, Cornelius Nicholson took a keen interest in civic affairs,[135] mixing with the town's most influential and wealthy merchants and businessmen of the day – mill owners, hosiers, woollen manufacturers and bankers. By 1833 the high regard in which he was held in the town enabled a partnership, Messrs Hudson, Nicholson & Foster, to borrow capital from Wakefield's Bank. With this they purchased machinery for a water-powered paper manufactory at Burneside; and to modernise an older *'hand make'* enterprise at Cowan Head.[136] With Cornelius Nicholson residing on site, firstly at Burneside and then at Cowan Head, by 1845 the partnership had built a successful business employing 120 hands. Following this it was first leased, and subsequently sold, as a going concern to a young Liverpool gentleman, James Cropper.

From 1835, a plethora of routes was proposed for a rail line linking Lancaster to Carlisle, leading to protracted argument as to the merits of each route.[137] Two competing proposals from Stephenson and Hague both advocated lines crossing Morecambe Bay by barrage,[138] and following a coastal route via Whitehaven to circumnavigate the mountainous core of Lakeland. Due to their greater length these routes were more expensive to construct and maintain, compared with more direct inland routes (a difference of 22 miles). But they had the considerable advantage of almost level gradients, and promised a pay-back of farmland to be won from the sea.[139] Unfortunately, both routes by-passed Kendal.

Of the more direct routes northwards, one skirted around Kendal to Longsleddale, passing through a lengthy tunnel to Haweswater, and on to Penrith and Carlisle. A more easterly proposal followed the Lune Valley to Kirkby Lonsdale, Sedbergh, and the Eden Valley to Penrith. Variants of this latter route climbed over, or tunnelled under, Shap Fell. Although they were the most direct lines, they were difficult and expensive to engineer, with gradients which challenged the limited power of early locomotives.[140]

In 1837 Cornelius Nicholson grew increasingly alarmed that Kendal would be left isolated by every proposal. He attempted to mobilise the Kendal business community with a pamphlet published at his own expense, entitled

In this he argued a case for the town to be included on the direct line of a Caledonian railway, with the benefits that would flow from easier access to Lancashire coal, raw materials and fresh food; whilst greatly expanding the marketing reach of Kendal's commerce and manufacture. Previously, sea-fish arrived at Kendal *'tainted —— by the tedious conveyance of horse and cart'*. Even in that condition it commanded high prices, beyond the purse of many ordinary folk.

The matter of Kendal's connectivity became compellingly urgent in June of 1840 when construction of the London & North Western Railway reached Lancaster. Finally, a Royal Commission considered, and rejected, both Morecambe Bay coastal routes. A contour-hugging line through the hamlet of Oxenholme, skirting Grayrigg Fell[141] to Tebay, and passing close to Shap Fell, was chosen despite energetic representations from the Kendal Committee. Unfortunately, Kendal's burgers had no engineering solution to the excessive climb of 450 feet in the short distance from Kendal to Grayrigg. The Lancaster & Carlisle Railway Act was passed by Parliament and received Royal assent on 6 June 1844, leaving Kendal effectively isolated, two miles from the Caledonian line.

Cornelius Nicholson turned his attention to the possibility of linking the town by a short branch line from Oxenholme. It was immediately apparent that if this line could be extended beyond Kendal into central Lakeland, it would attract the burgeoning tourist traffic.[142] The prospect found favour amongst the wealthier business and banking community of the town, sufficient for a privately funded survey to be commissioned. On 20 August 1844 a prospectus was issued, seeking investors for a single-track railway from Kendal, through Burneside and Staveley,[143] and passing south around Orrest Head

> *'—— through Droomer Style, Birthwaite and Troutbeck Bridge Mill to the side of Windermere beyond the woods of Rayrigg and Calgarth, about one mile short of Ambleside ——'*,

that is, terminating at Low Wood.[144] Eighteen gentlemen of good repute formed a provisional steering committee *(Appendix 3)*, with Cornelius Nicholson as its Secretary. They included the most prominent Kendal families and businessmen; bankers like Wakefield, Crewdson, Wilson and Gandy; and mill-owners such as John and James Gandy of Dockray Mill, Isaac Braithwaite and his sons. At the time of publication these gentlemen had already subscribed £50,000 towards the required capital of £125,000, *(see Appendix 9)* and *'—— the scheme was at once taken up with great enthusiasm'*.

Cornelius Nicholson claimed that the railway would be

> *'—— signally useful to the working classes in drawing them away from the haunts of vice and intemperance, and opening out to them the beauties of nature, by which their minds would be enlarged and their hearts expanded'*.

But only one month later powerful opposition to the K&W Railway surfaced from an influential minority, landowners whose estates were to be violated by the proposed line; the Reverend Fletcher Fleming of Rayrigg Hall; the Earl of Bradford, whose summer seat was St Catherines; Henry Curwen of Workington and Belle Isle; George Harrison Gardner, owner of the Birthwaite estate; and Thomas Ullock, hotel proprietor from Bowness who feared competition from rival hotels at Birthwaite and Low Wood. On 2 October 1844, the ailing Professor Wilson of Elleray travelled from Edinburgh to chair a meeting of objectors at Low Wood Inn, at which they formed a committee to oppose the railway. Wilson, more than most, had reason to be aggrieved. His Elleray estate was about to be cleft in two. The proposed track was to cut directly across his formal garden, within yards of the front door of his mansion and close to the little rustic cottage where he and Jane had spent their honeymoon, his favourite place in all the world.

This group of men was reinforced from an unexpected and eloquent quarter, the poet laureate himself, William Wordsworth. Although his abode at Rydal Mount was far removed from the planned railway and not under immediate threat, speculation arose that the line might be extended through the vales of Rydal and Grasmere, to pass over or under Dunmail Raise to Keswick. His objections were expressed on a loftier plane, fearing that the peace and solitude of his beloved Lake District would be inundated by cheap excursions of working people. The group claimed these simple souls would be

'––– *incapable of appreciating the grandeur of the scenery* ––– *would destroy the solitude of their betters and* ––– *undermine the morals of the local inhabitants.*' [145], [146]

Wordsworth continued a solo – and ridiculous – campaign of opposition to the railway, writing again to the national press, and even to Prime Minister Gladstone himself. In October of 1844 he composed two lengthy letters to the *Morning Post* in prose and sonnet form. [147]

'*Is there no nook of English ground secure*
From rash assault ? Schemes of retirement sown
In youth, and 'mid the busy world kept pure
As when their earliest flow'rs of hope were blown,
Must perish; how can they this blight endure ?
And must he, too, the ruthless change bemoan
Who scorns a false utilitarian lure
'Mid his paternal fields at random thrown ?
Baffle the threat, bright scene from Orrest Head !
Given to the pausing traveller's rapturous glance;
Plead for thy peace, thou beautiful romance
Of nature; and, if human hearts be dead,
Speak, passing winds; ye torrents, with your strong
And constant voice, protest against the wrong !'

His views, whether intended or misunderstood, were deeply unpopular and widely perceived as offensive to working people. They attracted considerable ridicule from all sides. Sadly, the bard made such a fool of himself that he was left isolated, devoid of all support. Even the Board of Trade felt obliged to respond in withering terms:

> '--- *we must state that an argument which goes to deprive the artisan of the offered means of changing his narrow abode, his crowded streets, his unwholesome toil, for the fresh air and the healthy holiday, which sends him back to his work refreshed and invigorated, simply that some individuals may retain to themselves the exclusive enjoyment of scenes which should be open alike to all, appears to us to be an argument wholly untenable.'*[148]

Against this background a meeting of railway shareholders held in Kendal on 5 November 1844 considered a report from Mr J.E. Errington, at that time the consulting engineer for the railway. He stressed the high cost of the northern section of line to Low Wood. In particular, expenditure of £12,000[149] for a viaduct to span the Trout Beck would be unavoidable and excessive. He recommended that the line should be shortened by three miles to terminate at Birthwaite, a change that satisfied most objectors. The Kendal & Windermere Railway Bill was promptly withdrawn from Parliament for amendment and resubmission. The amended Railway Act was brought before Parliament on 19 February 1845, when it passed into law '--- *without a breath of opposition*'.[150]

So confident of success were the provisional directors that they had already awarded an engineering contract in April to Stephenson, Brassey & Co., with the aim of completing construction of the line within a single year. Three weeks later the first sod was ceremoniously cut by the Mayor of Kendal, most appropriately Cornelius Nicholson himself, and construction began on 16 July 1845. Parliament had permitted that additional capital of £40,000 could be raised, thus enabling the line to be upgraded to double-track from its inception. As things transpired, the construction schedule failed to anticipate the exceptionally wet spring of 1846, and the work took nine months longer than planned. Despite the unexpected delay and a necessary increase in the wage bill for navvies, the final cost was less than the total share capital authorised by Parliament, a remarkable achievement, one of which the directors and engineers were justifiably proud.

Before Christmas in 1846 a Preston newspaper carried the following progress report[151]

> '*Great alacrity is now displayed in forwarding the completion of this line. For this purpose, a great additional number of labourers have been put to work; and, on fine days, nearly the whole length of the line is thickly studded with workmen, waggons and horses. The contracts for the erection of the station at the terminus, at Birthwaite, near Bowness, were last week let, which was immediately afterwards commenced with. The erection of the new hotel is fast progressing; and to all appearances, if no untoward event occurs, it is very probable that this "gem of railways" will be opened for the public in June or July next.*'

In fact the Directors of the Kendal & Windermere Railway bravely chose to open the line for public use on Tuesday, 20 April, 1847, following successful completion of the necessary inspection by Captain Simmons, R.E., but before completion of the terminus.

'The terminus at Birthwaite is in most chaotic confusion, and blasting is still going on for the purpose of making a road from the line to the new hotel. The erection of station houses along the route is also a long way in arrear. ––– As an inducement for greater exertion on the part of navvies several casks of nut-brown ale were made available to be daily quaffed by them, a circumstance which has had a great effect'.[152]

It was a fine and sunny spring morning.[153] In Kendal, crowds queued to board two special trains. The first was due to leave at 10.00 a.m., the other at 12.00 noon, each carrying a band of music and gaily decorated with flags and bunting. The trains consisted of 16 and 18 carriages, each hauled by three locomotives[154] to cope with the gradient between Bowston and Blackmoss. Together they conveyed upwards of 800 passengers to Birthwaite amidst scenes of great gaiety and jubilation. Through Burneside, Staveley, Ings and Blackmoss crowds of local people emerged from the sparsely populated countryside to wave and cheer in wonderment at the spectacle, *'the concourse of spectators on the surrounding heights and along the line for some distance was immense.'*

'Each train, as it approaches, is preceded for many seconds by a sound as if a legion of winged horses were cleaving the air at a distance; and as they advance, they are seen furiously panting and clapping their pinions against their sides, whizzing along like skyrockets.'

Predictably, a group of youths bragged that they could race the train to Birthwaite on horseback. But due to its delayed departure from Kendal the race was an anti-climax. The riders departed at the appointed hour with victory assured, almost an hour before the train left Kendal Station – and without stampeding the animals.

The last section of the rail journey required a novel procedure. At Blackmoss the locomotive and tender were uncoupled from the train and ran the last mile downhill to a siding.[155] The carriages were left to coast gently a little way behind, propelled by gravity, but under braking control of the guard, to the main platform at the Station. The locomotive was then turned on a turntable, and reunited with the opposite end of the train for the return journey to Kendal. The novelty of this operation was a great source of fascination and excitment to adults and children alike – and tinged with not a little danger.[156]

39. For the excursion trains on opening day in April 1847 the K&W Railway Company hired additional carriages and locomotives from the London & North Western Railway, similar to the train illustrated here standing at Lancaster Station.

With kind permission of Lancaster City Council

Arriving at the terminus on the opening day travellers found the unfinished Windermere station, lacking its roof and much of its stonework, partly due to a strike of masons. In glorious isolation, across the nearby turnpike road stood the impressive new Birthwaite Hotel,[157] three weeks from completion and unable yet to assuage the thirst of travellers. Crowds, the like of which had never been seen before in these parts, surged down the quiet country lanes on foot and carriage to Bowness, with little to mask the view of lake and mountain scenery but occasional tree-tufted knolls and Rayrigg Wood. Every hostelry in the little lakeside village flung open its doors and '--- *great was the run on refreshment of the inns'*.

For many visitors the spectacular scenery around the Lake was the primary attraction. They boarded the waiting paddle steamers, *Lady of the Lake* and *Lord of the Isles*, plying to Ambleside and to Newby Bridge. A few determined souls reached Rydal where they peered inquisitively over Wordsworth's wall. The trippers he feared would *'destroy the solitude of their betters'* had indeed arrived – tactfully, the bard was not at home.

A party of 37 dignitaries and directors of the railway company sat down to luncheon at the Royal Hotel in Bowness, welcomed by John Gandy, Chairman of the Railway Board. Responding to one of many toasts, drunk as bumpers, Cornelius Nicholson declared

'--- we propose that the merchant princes of Liverpool, and the cottonlords of Manchester, should be enabled to exchange in a few hours the smoke of their factories, and the miasmata of their towns, for the salubrious airs and silvery mists that float around the hills we are now among.'[158]

How prophetic this prediction subsequently proved to be. With a side-swipe at the poet-laureate and a little patronising of the working man, he said he knew

'--- the operative classes as intelligent beings, capable of appreciating and being moved by those beauties which the district unfolded, and that they have hearts accessible to the elevating influences which the contemplation of such scenes is calculated to exert.'

Later that afternoon the railway engineers, Mr Watson and Mr Branthwaite Atkinson,[159] together with representatives of their Board and shareholders, eighteen men in all, were wined and dined at the nearby Crown Hotel. The stamina of Cornelius Nicholson must be admired as he presided over both these celebrations,[160] and thanked the engineers for

'--- the gem of railways. It is a nice line in an engineering point of view, it is a cheap line in an economical point of view, it is a beautiful line in a picturesque point of view, and I have no doubt it will yield a handsome return, and be rendered beautiful in a commercial point of view in the eyes of those who have the honour and pleasure of holding shares.'

The festivities rightly marked the day on which the Lake District was abruptly connected to the outside world by the umbilical of tourism – a day which heralded the onset of an unprecedented surge of building work and begat the village, initially named Birthwaite (pronounced *burr-tit* by local people) but later renamed Windermere.

By the end of June special excursion trains had carried almost 54,000 passengers of all classes to Windermere, and during the second half of the year there were 82,000 visitors, or about 5,000 per week during the first year. The masses predicted by Wordsworth had arrived – and were delighted with the experience.

Enlightened employers began to charter special trains for weekend picnic excursions for their workers. In June of 1857 Hodgkinson & Co., cotton spinners of Bolton, brought 450 of their workers, along with the owners and invited guests, to Windermere by special train for a day's recreation amongst the scenery of the Lakes.

On arrival *'--- they sat down to breakfast at Windermere Hotel where Mr Rigg did his worthy name justice in ably providing for such a stream of visitors.'*

The ticket entitled each holder to a steamboat trip around the Lake for a shilling, and few neglected to avail themselves of this attractive part of the treat.

'At four o'clock the whole company again collected, and sat down to an excellent tea in the goods warehouse at Birthwaite station.'

After which they walked to the top of the hill behind the hotel for the singing of hymns, in gratitude to a benevolent employer.

As a result of the successful introduction of the railway, Cornelius Nicholson's reputation spread far beyond Kendal and his organisational skills were in considerable demand beyond the town. He spent the next three years domiciled in Bury as Managing Director of the East Lancashire Railway, supervising its construction. During this period he also found time to serve as chief magistrate in Kendal. There followed eight years in London as Superintending Director of the Great Indian Peninsula Railway Company.[161]

Cornelius Nicholson was clearly a remarkably capable man, a self-made man who rose from humble beginnings in Ambleside. He ended his days in comfortable and honourable retirement at Ventnor on the Isle of Wight,[162] and rightly deserves the accolade of

'--- father of the Kendal & Windermere Railway'.

40. Cornelius Nicholson

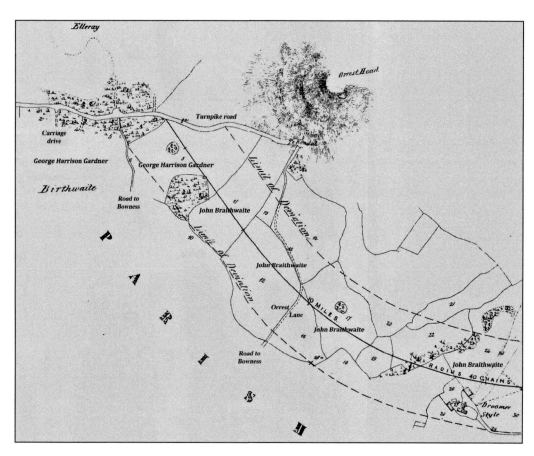

41. Plan of the railway's approach to Birthwaite.[163] *The solid line defines the centre-line of the planned track. The dashed lines define a swathe of land, the maximum permitted deviation from the planned line, and hence the area allowed for compulsory acquisition. The 1845 K&W Railway Act gave the company the usual draconian powers to acquire and clear land, houses and other buildings, that might impede construction of the railway.*

Courtesy of Cumbria Archive Centre, Kendal

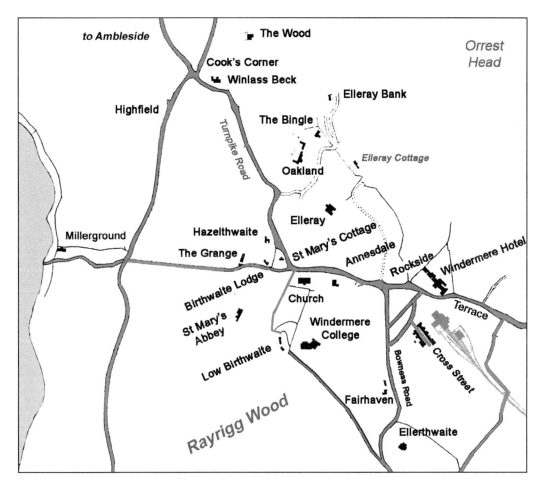

42. *This map shows places to be visited during our second walking tour, buildings mainly constructed between 1840 and 1860; and the location of the railway terminus. The last mile of line passed through farmland belonging to John Braithwaite, close to houses at Droomer Stile and Gill. It terminated within the Birthwaite estate of George Harrison Gardner where the Station and sidings were built (bottom right). These two gentlemen received compensation for the loss of 14 acres and 6 acres of land respectively.*

For our second walk we will take a similar route around the roads and tracks of the emerging village, still called Birthwaite by some people, to observe the many new villas and institutions built in the twenty-years from 1840 to 1860. We shall see the beginnings of an off-comer society, comprising both leisured folk and working peoples; and the laying out of the first new streets.

3.2 Dismemberment of Birthwaite Estate

Before we begin to trace the birth of the village of Windermere, we need to step briefly back in time once more to complete the early canvas. Following the passage through Parliament of the Kendal & Windermere Railway Act in 1845, the Company began the task of compulsory and rapid acquisition of land along the planned route. The last mile or so approaching the terminus at Birthwaite cut a swathe through farmland in the ownership of John Braithwaite. A total of 14 acres was taken, for which he received compensation of approximately £5,600.[164] Astutely, he reinvested the bounty in the Railway Company itself, becoming a substantial shareholder and one of its first directors. As we shall see later, that investment provided the fund for a most important and far-reaching personal gift to the schoolchildren, which took effect a decade later *(3.13)*.

The final few yards of railway terminated in the Birthwaite estate of solicitor George Harrison Gardner, around six acres of which were requisitioned for the Station and sidings.

As mentioned previously *(2.10)*, correspondence of his father, George Gardner senior, revealed that by 1828 he was '--- *residing at Birthwaite in my new built messuage*'. Although details of this dwelling have long since disappeared, it seems to have been a villa residence of good quality, possibly designed by George Webster of Kendal. It was erected adjacent to the ancient Birthwaite farmhouse which survives today as Low Birthwaite cottages. In the same year George Gardner purchased the freehold of the Birthwaite estate from the Earl of Lonsdale. Following his death in 1837 the new house, stables, woods and farmland passed by inheritance to his only son, George Harrison Gardner, lately qualified in law and practicing in Bowness.

As we have seen, the initial prospectus for the railway attracted powerful opposition. Three miles longer than that which was finally built, it was planned to pass through the estates of Birthwaite, Elleray and St Catherines, cross the Trout Beck on a substantial viaduct, and terminate at Low Wood. Understandably, G.H. Gardner opposed the plan, joining the committee of aggrieved landowners. Whilst the decision to drop the northern section of line from Elleray to Low Wood calmed the fears of the more influential landowners, it had the unfortunate consequence of increasing the acreage to be taken from Gardner's estate in order to accommodate the relocated terminus at Birthwaite. He was now faced with a dilemma of whether to live with a significant reduction of his acreage, or to be first in the market offering building land for sale. Not widely known at the time, the Birthwaite estate had been mortgaged for the substantial sum of £1,600. The opportunity to pay off the debt would certainly have been attractive to Gardner.

In February of 1845 he sold Birthwaite Hall and 31 acres of land[165] for the goodly sum of £5,000[166] to the directors of the Railway Company, who annexed the 6 acres they required for the terminus and sidings. Gardner retained approximately 14 acres at the southern end of Birthwaite estate furthest from the Station, as his site for a new residence.

At an auction in August 1845, held in Ullock's Royal Hotel at Bowness, the Railway Company attempted unsuccessfully to dispose of the remaining portion of their acquisition. Birthwaite Hall and its park of 24 acres, sandwiched between Rayrigg Wood and the Bowness Road, were advertised attractively:

> '--- a genteel residence, with all its Outbuildings, Offices, Gardens, and Shrubberies, together with Twenty-four Acres of Land, undulating in lines of beauty and exact proportions of taste, interspersed with tufts of Larch and other Wood. As to access, and facilities of communication, no property was ever so fortunate, or so well placed. It is bounded by the Ambleside and Kendal road on one hand, and by the Bowness road on the other. The Kendal and Windermere Railway Station will be at the distance of perfection --- conferring all conveniences, and yet removed from all that may be disagreeable to the eye or ear. The Steam Yacht passes within ten minutes walk four times a day; and the London Mail close by the Entrance Gates, twice a day, giving time for reply by return.'[167]

With the signing of the K&W Railway Act the Company wasted no time, as we have seen. Armed with the power of compulsory purchase, it had embarked on a buying spree to acquire an eight-mile corridor of land, nine chains wide,[168] between Kendal and Birthwaite. By January 1846 the Chairman of the company, John Gandy, was able to report that

> '--- nearly all the land required for the line is now in possession of the contractors'.

The last section formed a broad fan of land to accommodate the Station buildings and sidings. It made good commercial sense for the directors to speculate on the unneeded part of Birthwaite estate, bounded by Orrest Head Farm and Low Birthwaite,

> '--- a large plot of land which, after they had used what they wanted for the purposes of the Company, might no doubt be disposed of at a handsome profit'.[169]

By 1847 the Railway Company owned all of the land on the south side of the turnpike road, 31 acres[170] of prime building land stretching a quarter mile from the Station to the bend near Birthwaite Hall, where the road swings north towards Cook's Corner. Their land extended a similar distance south, comprising much of the sylvan hillside on which the village of Windermere was later to rise. There, with the assistance of architect Miles Thompson,[171] the directors of the railway had

> '--- plans made, for the purpose of laying out the ground in building lots'.

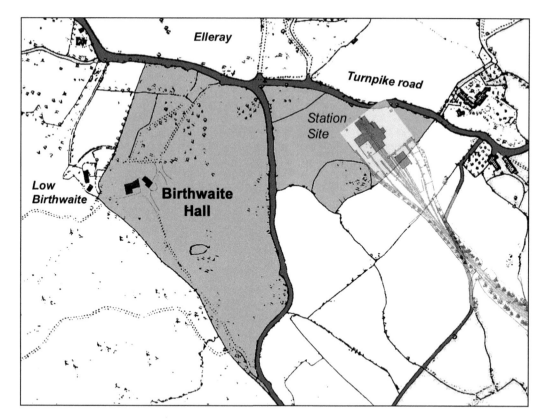

43. Part of Birthwaite Hall estate purchased by the K&W Railway Company from George Harrison Gardner in 1845. A total of 31 acres, including Birthwaite Hall, was purchased from Gardner by the directors, partly as a speculative venture. Six acres were acquired by compulsory purchase for the Station, as was land of John Braithwaite stretching south-east along the line.

G.H. Gardner and his young wife, Jane Thompson of Lancaster, moved to Bowness in 1845 where they took up residence near his legal practice, pending construction of a new villa at Ellerthwaite. This was a sad time for the Gardners. Their first two children died during the following year, Jane at the age of 19 months and George aged just two days.

Other landowners were now alerted to the rising value of their property. In September 1849 Cook's House estate and its ancient farmhouse were offered for sale by the owner, Henry Robinson, a chemist in Ulverston.[172] He seems to have inherited the place three years earlier, following the death of a relative, Matilda Robinson of Cook's House. The time was ripe, and most of the land was perfectly placed along the west side of the turnpike road, within half-a-mile of the new Station and Post Office, being '— *particularly eligible for building purposes*'.

One of the agents named in the sale particulars was the Kendal architect Miles Thompson. He recognised the commercial potential of the land and acquired the full 36 acres as a business venture, dividing it into lots of 1-4 acres for villa residences,

'–– *nearly all command fair views of the Lake, and several of the sites are not to be surpassed ––– with the stupendous Langdale Pikes, Coniston Old Man, and the distant mountains of Cumberland and Westmorland'.*

44. *View over the lofty rooftops of Elleray Bank in the 1860s to Calgarth Park, Windermere Lake and the Langdale Pikes.*

© *Ian Jones*

45. Windermere Hotel, begun early in 1846 for the Railway Company, and opened for business on 12 May 1847, three weeks after the railway. It occupies a magnificent elevated site, opposite to the Station and turnpike, for the benefit of travellers by rail and by road. [173]

Courtesy of Cumbria Archive Centre, Kendal

3.3 Windermere Hotel

Continuing our second tour across the turnpike road from the Station, there stands the impressive Windermere Hotel,[174] designed by architects George Webster and Miles Thompson of Kendal[175] and built for the Railway Company[176] by Abraham Pattinson in solid local stone, its footings hewn into the southern slope of Orrest on land of its neighbour, John Braithwaite. The hotel stands three storeys high, boldly announcing its presence to the world, quite unlike the picturesque and inconspicuous Elleray mansion on its other side, seat of Professor Wilson. At one end, a tower houses water storage, supplied from springs and ponds on the hillside above, a necessary facility for such a large establishment two decades before mains water came to Windermere. With commanding views of the Lake from all its front-facing windows, the hotel is visible from afar. Its many comfortable rooms were taken up from the beginning by tourists and travellers alike, arriving by rail at the terminus opposite the hotel, and by road.

Richard Rigg (1814-1866) its first proprietor and tenant, was an energetic and enterprising young in-comer.[177] He and his wife, Sarah Bownass, were descended from long established farming stock of Middleton in Lonsdale.[178] They were preceded to area by Sarah's brother William Bownass, who was already established as innkeeper at Thomas Ullock's Royal Hotel, in Bowness. Together, the popular couple have built a thriving hotel business at Birthwaite.

In its commodious stables we will later see that Richard Rigg took over a far famed business of liveried coaches, transporting visitors onward from the rail terminus to destinations in Bowness, Ambleside and deeper into Lakeland. Around 1855 he secured the mail contract,[179] serving Keswick and towns to the north, a contract which two of his sons will retain continuously until the 1920s.

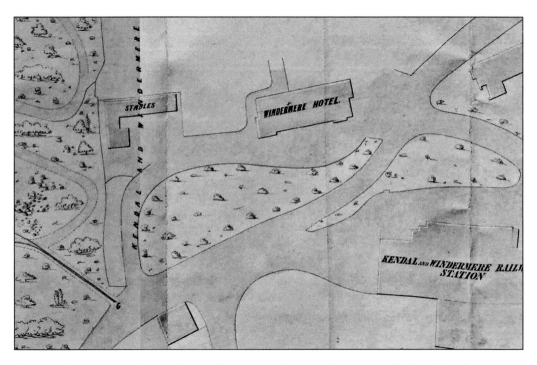

46. Keyplan showing the stables at Windermere Hotel which served Richard Rigg's coaching service for almost 70 years from 1855.[180]

Courtesy of Cumbria Archive Centre, Kendal

In 1851 Richard Rigg leased Orrest Head Farm from his neighbour, John Braithwaite, there to graze horses and grow fodder – and barley for brewing ale. The farmland also provided a site for disposal of night soil from the many rooms of the hotel – the convenience of deep sewerage in Windermere not being available for many years yet.

In 1855, eight years after the hotel first opened its doors, the Railway Company, which owns the property, approved expenditure for a sizeable expansion of its accommodation:

'—the occupier of the Windermere Hotel having applied for further accommodation, the directors after careful consideration, decided to sanction an addition to the building, and the new rooms have been occupied as speedily as the contractors from time to time could give them up for use. The directors do not doubt that the outlay will have the approbation of the shareholders.' [181]

Contrary to early concerns, the business of the hotel grew steadily from the beginning. On the night of 31 March 1851, before the tourist season had begun, visitors to the hotel included a young couple from Bermuda, three commercial travellers and the new owner of Elleray estate, William Eastted, accompanied by a land surveyor. In addition to the hotel proprietor, the Rigg family and seven servants were residing on the premises. Ten years later, in April 1861, the business had grown considerably. The Riggs now employed 20 live-in servants and maids, a children's nurse and a coachman. Several other domestic staff, coachmen and ostlers lived or lodged nearby in the village. The guest list reflected a largely commercial clientele at this early stage of the season – four merchants, four commercial travellers, one gentleman, one gentlewoman, a manufacturer, and five ladies accompanying their men-folk.

Harriet Martineau wrote in glowing terms of Rigg's Windermere Hotel in 1854:

'At this establishment, families and others visiting the Lakes' District will meet with every accommodation and attention, combined with moderate charges. The hotel is on an eminence immediately above the terminus of the Kendal and Windermere Railway, and is so situated as to prevent the least inconvenience or annoyance from the traffic. The views of lake and mountain scenery commanded from the windows of the hotel are unsurpassed by any in the district —– the Lake Windermere, with its numerous islands, being seen nearly to its utmost extent. Open and close carriages, cars, and post-horses always in readiness.'

We shall return to visit the Rigg family again and the business of the hotel, during a later walk in the village (4.1).

47. Rigg's Windermere Hotel showing, on the left of the tower, a sizable extension of accommodation added in 1855 by the Kendal & Windermere Railway Company, Mr Rigg's landlord. (From an engraving printed by John Garnett)

Courtesy of Kendal Local Studies Library

48. *Professor Wilson's self-designed Elleray mansion, ca.1865.*

© Ian Jones

3.4 Elleray for Development

Leaving the hotel, a few steps down the turnpike road, in 1842 Elleray estate was advertised for sale by Professor Wilson,[182] and again in August 1849.[183] Coming near the end of his long and eventful life, and suffering increasing infirmity, he could no longer make the long and arduous journey by stagecoach from Edinburgh to Windermere and his beloved Elleray. His final visit in 1848 had evoked such feelings of melancholy that he could not bear to be alone at night, but lodged at Mrs Ullock's hotel at Bowness,

> '--- *the silence and loneliness of myself at night not being to be borne, though during the day I was tranquil enough.*'

During the four years before 1851 Elleray mansion was let to William Dillworth Crewdson,[184] a partner in Wakefield, Crewdson & Co., bankers in Kendal, and probably the first businessman to commute daily on the newly opened railway. He was born into a Quaker family, but was now in transition from the Society of Friends to the Anglican church, along with many younger members in England and abroad who renounced the older Quaker strictures and dress convention.[185] He became known as an eloquent and evangelical preacher, conducting religious services at Elleray,[186] probably the first to be held in Birthwaite prior to the opening of St Mary's Church in 1848. His wife, Sarah Fox from Plymouth, described their time at Elleray as

'--- four years of deep enjoyment of beauty and poetry, of scenery and of mind ---'.[187]

Whether the sale of Elleray was the reason we cannot tell, but the Professor's faithful old servant and boatman, Billy Balmer, trudged his way to Edinburgh to be with his master, a journey that took him several months to complete on foot, shunning the railway.

'Billy was re-established in his master's service, dressed after the fashion of his early days, in sailor guise, with pleasant work to do, and a glass of ale daily to cheer his old soul.'[188]

But sadly, old Billy began to ail. After several weeks he gently slipped away in August of 1850, with John Wilson by his bedside, '--- *so quietly, that we scarcely knew when he was gone'.* During those last hours Billy clutched a black silk handkerchief in a weather beaten hand that had so often pulled an oar or tied a rope on Windermere. His wife was called from Bowness and his body was interred in Warriston Cemetery in Edinburgh, the Professor walking with pride and dignity at the head of the coffin to lay Billy to rest. Such was the huge affection between these two old friends of very different status.

After 40 years of ownership of Elleray, through times of great joy and hardship, it must have been a heart-rending decision for Professor Wilson to sell his Windermere home, which was largely his own design. The auction was widely advertised through agents in London, Edinburgh and Kendal, and at all the principal hotels in the Lake District

'--- comprising a mansion suitable for the residence of a gentleman of station, pleasure grounds and land adjoining, containing in all 82a. 3r. 27p.'[189]

By the beginning of 1850, all of the land along both sides of the turnpike road between Orrest Head Farm and Cook's Corner was available for building purposes, apart from a short frontage at The Wood.

In September 1849 Elleray failed initially to sell at auction in Mr Ullock's Royal Hotel at Bowness,[190] when the reserve price of £8,000 failed to be reached. The eventual buyer was a property speculator and railway contractor named William Eastted from Great Malvern, another Victorian town which owed its existence largely to the coming of a railway. Eastted proceeded to draw up plans to dispose of the estate as building lots.[191] He laid out a private roadway within the grounds, providing access to eleven building sites intended for villa residences, most of them overlooking the turnpike road and St Mary's Church. They were in addition to the mansion house itself, which was offered with its own 9 acres. Building plots varied in size from ½ to 2 acres, semi-detached villas being permitted on the larger blocks, all intended to attract buyers of quality in line with Revd Addison's ideals. But only three large plots found buyers.

William Eastted was much praised in 1851 for a scenic carriageway 2½ miles in length, engineered by 40 men to allow carriages to ascend by a serpentine route to the higher slopes of the estate, almost to the summit of Orrest Head.[192] During the ownership of Professor Wilson the public had been allowed free use of two footpaths through the estate, with a preference for the back entrance beside the Windermere Hotel. But these were denied before and after the sale of Elleray. Following an abortive court case Mr Eastted relented and reinstated permission for public access. However those wishing to reach the summit by either of the two routes were now requested to purchase a ticket from Mr Garnett at the Post Office,[193] the price being a donation in favour of Birthwaite school, at least one shilling for a party of six.

At Christmas in 1852 a violent storm hit the Lake District and Birthwaite sustained extensive damage when 200 fine trees in Elleray Wood were brought down, blocking the new carriage driveway. The front door of neighbouring Windermere Hotel was shaken so violently that the bolts gave way and it was blown in, causing a marble table in the foyer to be overturned.

In August 1855 building plots at Elleray amounting to 22 acres were widely advertised for sale from Edinburgh to London by William Eastted, as

> '--- sites of peculiar beauty --- villa residences only are to be erected --- the whole is so abundantly timbered that each lot will be enriched with large ornamental trees.'[194]

But most of this land remained stubbornly unsold for the next ten years – until 1865.

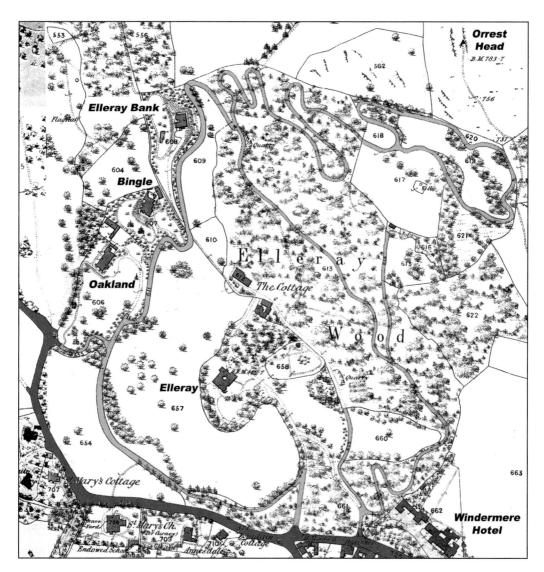

49. *The spectacular winding carriage drive laid out in 1851 for William Eastted, through the pleasure ground of his Elleray estate, which also gave access to Oakland, The Bingle and Elleray Bank. The drive was planned as an amenity for owners of the intended villas, who might wish to ascend to the summit of Orrest Head with the help of a sturdy pony and light carriage, there to enjoy the views of four counties. The metalled driveway climbed from the rear of Rigg's stables at Windermere Hotel, on a long traverse through Elleray Wood, followed by a serpentine ascent almost to the top. It returned past Elleray Bank, The Bingle and Oakland, to sweep close to the Ambleside turnpike and finish near Elleray gate, a total distance of 2½ miles, and a rise and fall of 800 feet.* [195]

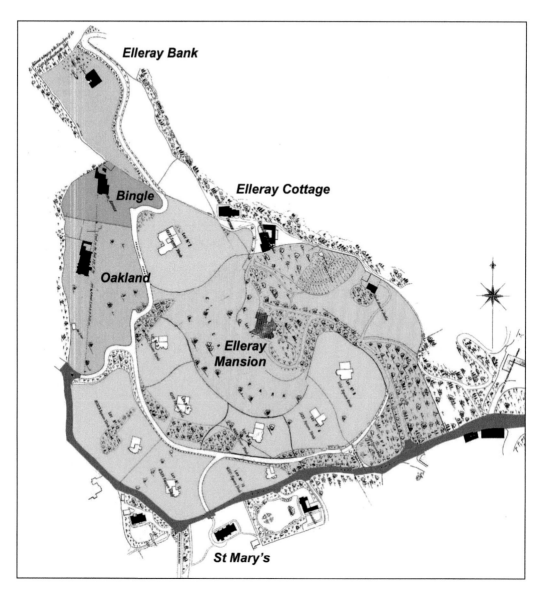

Elleray Bank

Bingle

Elleray Cottage

Oakland

Elleray Mansion

St Mary's

50. *Lower part of the Elleray estate divided into nine building lots for villa residences, and advertised for sale by William Eastted in 1855. The plan shows a new carriage road cut through the grounds providing access to the building sites (green); and Wilson's Elleray mansion with its own 9 acres.*

'*Views from the sites --- embrace nearly the whole extent of the enchanting Lake of Windermere, and the noble Lake Mountains.*'

Courtesy of Cumbria Archive Centre, Kendal.

Neighbouring properties of Oakland, The Bingle (pink) and Elleray Bank were built in 1853-1855 on the north-western boundary of the estate, the only sites that were sold.

St Mary's Ecclesiastical Campus

3.5 The Reverend John Aspinall Addison – Father of Windermere

Stepping down the turnpike road from Elleray gate we quickly reach the gateway to Birthwaite Hall on the left, and the site of Revd Addison's future ecclesiastical campus, built in seven short years.

For many, the publicity and excitement surrounding the announcement of a passenger-carrying railway to a little-known terminus named Birthwaite, near Windermere Lake, promised to transform access to the Lake District for folk of every age and every class. Even before its commencement, a few more intrepid visitors were travelling by the turnpike road to Bowness and to Ambleside, to enjoy the lake and mountain scenery, clear air – and above all, the tranquillity of the place. One of the first of these off-comers was an energetic, and charismatic young cleric with a vision, the Reverend John Aspinall Addison, at that time the incumbent of Mitton near Clitheroe. He arrived in 1845 brimming with missionary zeal and youthful confidence, propounding lofty ideals of social order and aspiration. He envisaged a hierarchical community based on the established Church, ministering to the spiritual needs of a god-fearing and deferential populace. He saw Birthwaite as a unique opportunity, a fertile ground in which to implant an ecclesiastical community centred on his church, surrounded by prestigious institutions of learning, and dwellings of quality for devout and genteel parishioners. Importantly he possessed sufficient personal wealth to launch the enterprise.

As his name implies, John Aspinall Addison sprang from a pedigree rooted in the commerce and enterprise of maritime Liverpool. His father, Richard Addison, had been a moderately wealthy merchant. But his maternal grandfather, John Bridge Aspinall, was a merchant prince of the West Indies trade, Mayor of Liverpool in 1803, related by marriage to the Brancker sugar kings, and to the Tobins of the West Africa trade. Together they were three of the wealthiest and most influential families in Liverpool.

John Addison was born in 1813, the eldest of seven children of Betty Aspinall and Richard Addison. He attended St John's College, Cambridge, and was ordained in Chester as an Anglican priest in 1838. His first appointment was as *'perpetual curate'* to the rural parish of Middleton and Barbon, in Lonsdale. In that quiet rural idyll, backing on to the Yorkshire Dales, he found unexpected inspiration from the Reverend William Carus Wilson, at that time incumbent of neighbouring Casterton. It was Carus Wilson who pioneered the Clergy Daughters School, attended briefly by the Brontë sisters.[196] As we shall see later, this acquaintance profoundly influenced the fertile mind of the younger man. In 1840 John Addison married Mary Wilkinson of the rural parish of Slaidburn in Bowland; and two years later he was elevated as vicar of nearby Mitton, under the patronage of a name-sake, John Aspinall of Standen Hall.[197]

During Revd Addison's early career it was proposed to route the Lancaster & Carlisle Railway through the Vale of Lune, close to Middleton and Barbon.[198]

In August of 1845, whilst attending a convention of the Church Missionary Society at Bowness, on finding that land was to be auctioned by the Railway Company during the following week *(3.2)*, John Addison enthusiastically and somewhat hurriedly entered into negotiations for the purchase of Birthwaite Hall estate. The newspapers reported that

> '--- *a gentleman now sojourning at Bowness who is anxious to purchase Birthwaite, the intended terminus of the above line, late the residence of G.H. Gardner, Esq., solicitor, and now advertised for sale. Should he succeed, it is his intention to build a church, and lay the foundation of a town ---. A church in that locality would be a great accommodation to the country, as providing room for the farmers and the increased population scattered over that side of the parish ---.*
> *Since writing the above, we learn for a fact that the treaty for Mr Gardner's late residence at Birthwaite, is at an end, by the gentleman's purchasing a part of the adjoining estate, belonging to Mr Thomas Crosthwaite. The site for Church, Parsonage House and School is pitched upon and the work is to be proceeded with immediately.'* [199]

A week later the buyer was revealed to be Revd J.A. Addison, the incumbent of Mitton.

There can be little doubt that he travelled on the first train, a never-to-be-repeated opportunity for a man who aspired to be the founder of the infant township. In July of 1847, referring again to Mr Addison, a meeting of the K&W Railway was informed that

> '--- *a clergyman near Birthwaite had submitted to the bishop of the diocese a plan for the building of a new church there, and the bishop had approved of the site.* [200]
> *This would no doubt be another inducement for gentlemen to buy land and build villas in the neighbourhood.'* [201]

John Addison purchased land in three stages from Thomas Crosthwaite and the Railway Company, enabling him to launch impressive and ambitious building projects spread over the following seven years – an ecclesiastical campus with few rivals.[202] It comprised

- a grand villa residence for himself, which he named St Mary's Abbey;
- a chapel, also named St Mary's, with seating for 220 worshipers;
- a two-roomed school   '--- *for the benefit of the children of the poorer classes';*
- a college   '--- *for the sons of clergymen principally';*
- a middle school   '--- *for the sons of tradesmen, farmers and others';*
- two small villas

--- all to be built at his own expense.

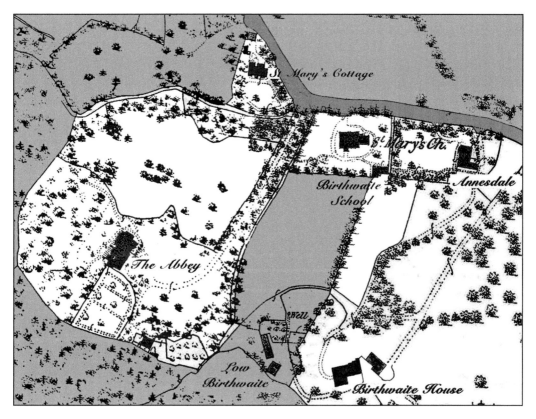

51. Revd Addison's ecclesiastical campus in 1852, before commencement of the College.

Mr Addison's first residence, St Mary's Abbey, sits in its own nine-acre park of private pleasure grounds; close to his second home, St Mary's Cottage, both adjacent to the church. Annesdale overlooks the chancel and his little school for the poorer classes. A decade later Annesdale was acquired by the diocese to become St Mary's Vicarage. Also shown is the original Birthwaite farmhouse, now named Low Birthwaite, which remained the property of farmer Thomas Crosthwaite along with some adjacent land. Before Birthwaite Hall was built in 1828 this farmhouse was the only building on the south side of the turnpike road. In 1852 Mr Addison acquired Birthwaite Hall and 8 acres of land from the K&W Railway Company as the site on which to build his prestigious Birthwaite College for the sons of clergymen, farmers and tradesmen.

52. *St Mary's Abbey, a grand gothic-style villa residence, described as being "in the style of the fourteenth century". Unashamedly ostentatious, it was built for Revd Addison in 1847-1848 by Abraham Pattinson, probably to the design of Kendal architect Miles Thompson.* [203] *Complete with Watch Tower, it was intended to impress, and to command high respect for its owner.*

© Ian Jones

3.6 St Mary's Abbey

Somewhat grandiosely, Revd Addison named his residence St Mary's Abbey.[204] Like no other mansion seen before in the area, it was boldly ostentatious in the gothic revival style, an architectural phenomenon that was sweeping Victorian Britain in the wake of the Westminster masterpiece of Charles Barry and Augustus Pugin. Construction was begun in 1847 by Abraham Pattinson, almost certainly designed by architect Miles Thompson, and was completed the following year.

The mansion was graced by 6½ acres of garden, approached by an impressive carriage driveway from the turnpike road, with a terrace, shrubberies, pleasure ground, coach house and stable. The internal arrangements were commodious, with all living and bedrooms heated by hot air apparatus. The building possessed magnificent views of the Lake and surrounding mountain scenery, incorporating a prominent 'watch tower' housing water tanks to supply domestic water to all floors.

The Addison family were now installed commandingly at the head of the embryonic village community and its in-coming residents, perfectly placed to minister to the spiritual and secular needs of the growing populace, and to shape its institutions. John Addison's passion for the pointed gothic style bordered on obsession, shaping all his buildings and also those of his neighbours. Such was his infectious enthusiasm that wealthy in-comers were persuaded to surround the little church with their villas, similarly fashioned in the pointed gothic style. His imprint endures even today, more than a century after his parting, endowing the architectural heritage of Windermere forever.

53. 'St Maries Church, Birthwaite' by Alfred T. Vardon.[205]

Courtesy of Cumbria Archive Centre, Kendal

Opened in October 1848, the pretty little chapel of St Mary, the first church in Applethwaite, was built for Revd Addison entirely at his own expense, consisting modestly of a simple nave and chancel, with unreserved seating for 220 souls.

3.7 St Mary's Chapel

Close by, he also built entirely at his own expense a handsome little chapel named St Mary's, the name recalling an ancient chantry that once stood on the island of Lady Holme in the Lake of Windermere.[206] His little church was perfectly placed at a bend of the Ambleside turnpike where the road swings north near Birthwaite Hall and St Mary's Abbey, enjoying easy access from all directions. It sat geographically within the old ecclesiastical Parish of Windermere, but as the private property of Mr Addison it remained un-consecrated for eight years, at arms length from diocesan jurisdiction. Baptisms, marriages and burials were not yet licensed, '– *without cure of souls*', which continued to be the responsibility of St Martin's at Bowness. Confusingly, St Martin's had long held the status of Parish Church of Windermere. But the *'quasi-parochial character'* of St Mary's was accepted by the Bishop, recognising that a centre of worship more convenient than those at Bowness and Troutbeck would be required for the growing population, and anticipating the future need for a separate parish.

For his little chapel, Revd Addison commissioned Miles Thompson of Kendal as architect[207] and Abraham Pattinson as builder. Mr Pattinson was to be employed almost without break on all of John Addison's construction projects for the next seven years. The building cost of the little church was a remarkably modest figure of £1,000; [208] and the church was '– *endowed with a like sum given by a friend of the worthy clergyman'*. [209]

The opening of the church on 4 October 1848 by a close friend, the Vicar of St Pauls in Liverpool, was marred by atrocious weather. Two special trains chartered to convey celebrants from Kendal, travelled almost empty, and collections from the morning and evening services suffered accordingly. Despite this setback, from those early days Revd Addison's enthusiasm, missionary zeal and infectious style filled his church on Sundays.

3.8 Birthwaite School

Hardly had Revd Addison and his family occupied The Abbey and completed the church when he embarked on the next step in his grand plan. In 1850 he founded a small two-roomed school in the shadow of the church, also built entirely at his own expense

> '--– *for the benefit of the children of the poorer classes at Birthwaite and in the neighbourhood'*.

The little school was a most valuable asset to the new village, with around 70 pupils enrolled from the start. It served the community without interruption for over a century in various forms, but at the outset

'--- like the chapel itself, it lacked anything in the shape of a reliable permanent source of income and was maintained by the bounty of the founder, supplemented by an occasional collection and by school pence.'

At the opening of the College in 1854 two collections were taken up for the benefit of the school, amounting to less than £16. However, in the same year a bequest of £1,000 from John Braithwaite of Orrest Head House provided the first *'settled endowment'* to augment the salary of a master.

Along with the church, the school was purchased by public subscription in 1855 during the winding up of Mr Addison's affairs. It was placed in the hands of a management committee of trustees comprised of local worthies, together with the new incumbent of St Mary's and the churchwardens. In addition, a committee of six ladies was formed *'--- to assist in the visitation and management of the girls' and infant schools'*.

Due to increasingly intolerable overcrowding of the little school, temporary arrangements had to be adopted for the teaching of infants in other premises. Some relief came in 1860 when the ladies' committee raised sufficient funds to begin construction of a third schoolroom for the infants, and also to engage a mistress. Three years later a new and much larger schoolroom was added, intended to relieve the pressure of village population for many years to come. This room was dedicated to the memory of one of the ladies, Miss Jane Yates, and gifted by her sister Mrs Sarah Hornby of Dalton Hall, near Burton.

In rapid succession there were three masters, James Ball, Mr Burt and William Briggs, the latter from St Mark's College, Chelsea. He was engaged at a salary of £70 per annum but died in 1859. He was succeeded at a lesser salary of £60 by a redoubtable young Lincolnshire man, Henry Robinson, who held the post of schoolmaster of the National School for 40 years, and also served as organist and choirmaster of St Mary's Church.

54. Annesdale was built in 1850 adjacent to St Mary's Church, a picturesque example of Mr Addison's taste, probably also designed by Miles Thompson.

Courtesy of Alan Marsh

3.9 Annesdale

Also in 1850, Mr Addison commenced construction of a pretty little *cottage ornée* named Annesdale,[210] on a site he had purchased in the previous year from the K&W Railway Company, overlooking the east window and chancel of the church. The house was intended as a letting property, aimed at attracting retired clergymen and clergy-widows to his ecclesiastical community to swell the flock of reverential and socially desirable residents.

This graphical reconstruction shows how the little villa would have appeared when first built, gothic but pretty, and smaller than today. It was topped with 'barley sugar' chimney pots and distinctive roofing slates.[211] These were pointed to form hexagonal, or fish-scale patterns, echoing those on the church, The Abbey and later on St Mary's Cottage.

During the disposal of Mr Addison's affairs in 1855, Annesdale was sold for £1,332 to John Ducker Beckitt, a Yorkshire iron manufacturer. However, in 1859 a gift of £1,000 from Miss Jane Yates, of The Wood, enabled the diocese to purchase Annesdale for a price of £1,400 to provide a vicarage for the living. However it was necessary to double the size the building in order to accommodate the incumbent, Revd Charles Clayton Lowndes and his family of seven children. When completed in 1860 it was renamed St Mary's Vicarage, and the original name of Annesdale subsequently migrating to a different house nearby.

3.10 St Mary's Cottage

In 1852, at a cost of £3,280 Revd Addison purchased from the K&W Railway Company an adjacent portion of the Birthwaite estate,[212] including Birthwaite Hall to the south of the Church, there to build his long-planned College for the sons of clergymen. To reduce the financial strain on his resources he let his grand residence, St Mary's Abbey, to a wealthy cotton heiress, Miss Anne Marriott of Liverpool. He built a much more modest house for himself, St Mary's Cottage,[213] on land he had acquired earlier close to the north-west side of the church. Possibly as a further cost saving measure, one account attributes the design of that house to Revd Addison himself, the style of which betrays an amateur hand. Once again Abraham Pattinson carried out the building work.

A local resident complained that Revd Addison had contrived to conceal the entrance to the packhorse track to Millerground by erecting a gateway to his new residence which blocked the public path.[214] Since the lane lay adjacent to his garden fence, the reverend gentleman apparently wished to secure the privacy of his home. Unfortunately, the practice of improperly closing footpaths was commonplace at the time, and not controlled by any authority. Nothing was done to rectify the matter until in 1858 Revd Fleming, owner of Rayrigg Wood, was forced by village activists to restore the *right of road*.[215]

After Mr Addison, his wife Mary and two young children departed from the village in 1855, St Mary's Cottage was sold to a wealthy cotton spinner, John Humber of Winckley Square in Preston. He owned cotton mills both in Preston and in Lancaster. As secretary to the Cotton Spinners Association, in 1854 he was at the centre of a protracted and bitter dispute between the masters and mill operatives, who were seeking a rise of 10% in their meagre wages. John Humber and his wife decamped to Birthwaite during this period of unrest, from where he commuted by train to Lancaster and Preston. He served as Mayor of Preston in 1857-58, opening the new Magistrates' Court and Police Station while in office. During the cotton famine of 1862 John Humber at first kept his mills working four days a week, at a time when other masters were closing their mills. But by 1863 he was forced to close the Preston mill completely. Following the death of his wife in the same year he sold St Mary's Cottage and left Windermere.

55. St Mary's Cottage, built in 1852 as a more modest residence for Revd Addison. It displays the familiar fish-scale pattern of roofing slates, similar to those at St Mary's Abbey, Annesdale and the Church. But the architectural style of the building betrays a different, possibly amateur hand, compared with any other villa in the village. One account suggests that it may have been styled by Revd Addison himself, a great advocate of the pointed gothic style of architecture.

56. St Mary's College engraving ca.1853.

Courtesy of Kendal Local Studies Library

3.11 St Mary's College

The true scale of John Addison's ambitious plan was revealed in 1852 when he acquired additional land from the Railway Company, together with Birthwaite Hall, as the site for St Mary's College, where

'--- *the sons of clergymen chiefly, though not exclusively,' would receive*
'--- *a cheap and thorough education on sound church principles'*.

Comparison with Revd Carus Wilson's Clergy Daughters School at Cowan Bridge is striking, which Wilson had opened for the daughters of poorer clergy.

But it was a further year without the benefit of fees before a sufficient part of St Mary's College was ready for occupation.[216] Despite many delays and difficulties it opened for the autumn term on 31 August 1853, amid a fanfare of publicity and under high patronage *(Appendix 4)*. However, by opening day only 25 boys had been enrolled, mainly the sons of laymen. In fact they were accommodated temporarily in Birthwaite Hall for '--- *the commencement of its pious and practical labours'*. But it was confidently predicted that when building work was completed all 200 places would quickly be taken up.

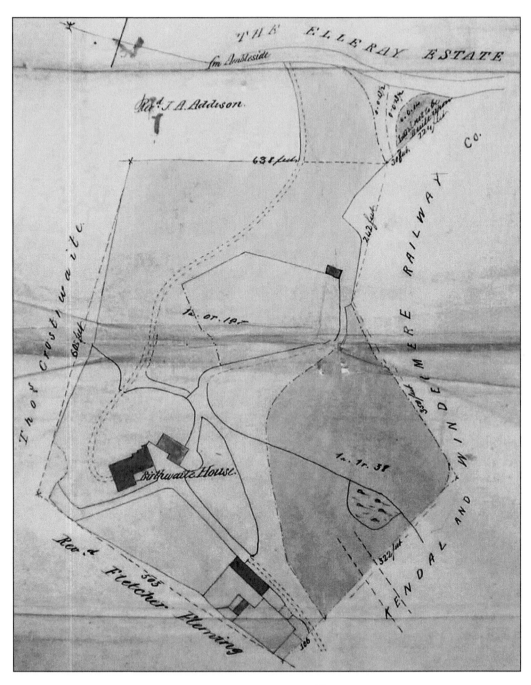

57. Keyplan of part of the Birthwaite Hall estate ca.1848.[217] It shows approximately nine acres of the estate, previously owned by three generations of Gardners from 1780 to 1845, and purchased from the Railway Company by Revd Addison in 1852 as the site for his College.

Courtesy of Cumbria Archive Centre, Kendal

There is no doubt that the opening of the College had been long and eagerly anticipated, and the boldness of its concept brought great acclaim to Revd Addison, the founder. The local press observed that

> '–-– the establishment of St Mary's College, Windermere, forms an important era not only in the annals of the district, but in the furtherance of the highest order of education in the country generally, –-– the high aims and the energy and taste with which the design has been instituted –-– are such as to command earnest attention –-– neither Cam nor Isis present a seat for an alma mater at all comparable in beauty to St Mary's College, Windermere.' [218]

The teaching staff were to be drawn from the very best of Oxford and Cambridge colleges, and meticulously selected by Mr Addison himself as Warden and owner of the establishment.

The fees to be charged for students were generously discounted in favour of the sons of impoverished clergymen

> '–-– from the surrounding districts of obtaining an education, sound and useful –-– at a cost which bears no proportion to the benefit received –--'.

The fees charged for boarders were remarkable value when converted to today's monetary values.

> 'The total charge for each pupil for Education, Maintenance and Lodging to be:
>   for the Sons of Clergy   30 guineas per annum,
>   and in special cases,   a much lower charge;
>   for the Sons of Laymen,   55 guineas per annum,
>
>   under which sum is included every charge for instruction, comprising:
>   Classics, Mathematics, Divinity, Fortification, Vocal Music, Drawing,
>   and such Modern Languages as the College may consider it desirable to teach.
>
> The charge for Day Boarders is:20 pounds per annum.' [219]

It was intended that two-thirds of the students would be sons of clergymen and one-third the sons of laymen; and a fund would be created for exhibitions and scholarships to universities, open to the whole college, and awarded according to merit.

3.12 St John's Middle School

Revd Addison's plan knew no bounds. To complete his grand scheme of social engineering he now planned a second college, a distinct establishment to be included within the College site at Birthwaite,

> '--- St John's Middle School will be founded for the benefit of the sons of tradesmen, farmers and others of the middle class, offering a complete commercial education upon a sound religious basis ---'. [220]

The Middle School was to be conducted by clergymen assisted by lay masters – strictly on the principles of the Church of England – and to teach such practical subjects as

> '--- divinity, reading, writing, spelling, history, geography, arithmetic, algebra, geometry, land and timber measuring, bookkeeping, the elements of natural philosophy, drawing and vocal music.
> Terms for tuition and board, including all expenses except books and washing, will be 25 guineas per annum.'

On 4 September the bells of St Mary's College and the Church rang out in counterpoint, summoning the students and masters for the first time to Sunday morning service.

> 'For this they wore the appropriate collegiate costume of caps and gowns,[221] and went in procession to the church, headed by the warden and fellows in the costume of their respective universities. On arriving at the church, which was filled by a highly respectable congregation comprising the influential families of the neighbourhood, the students took their seats on each side of the chancel.' [222]

With his personal fortune now completely expended, in 1854 Revd Addison and his family were forced to move from St Mary's Cottage, and take up residence at Birthwaite Hall within the college complex, close to his duties as Warden.

In July of that year he offered five properties for sale by auction at nearby Rigg's Hotel;

- St Mary's Abbey and adjacent building land were reportedly purchased by a gentleman from Cheltenham for £4,030; [223]
- Annesdale, St Mary's Cottage and St Mary's Church failed to reach their reserve prices,[224] piling more strain upon John Addison's now precarious finances.

As we shall see, the failure of his properties to sell at auction pushed him beyond breaking point and precipitated a most unfortunate event, with far-reaching consequences.

58. *Massive tower forming the College entrance, housed water tanks. With up to 200 boys, the demand for domestic water would have been great, prior to the availability of mains water in the village from 1878. On weekly bath days, the ration of water for each boy was probably limited to 4 inches in the bottom of the bath, unheated except in winter. This photograph is believed to date from ca.1870.*

© *Ian Jones*

59. South front of Windermere College, showing the gothic character of all parts.

Abraham Pattinson was almost certainly the builder, and Joseph Stretch Crowther the architect. When the College was under construction in 1852-53 they were working on the south aisle of St Mary's Church for Revd Addison, and on several nearby villas. Birthwaite Hall was incorporated into the college complex, and is obscured behind the three-storey wing on the left.

60. Entrance to the College for masters and visitors ca.1900

3.13 John Braithwaite's Bequest

By 1852 Mr Addison's little chapel was overflowing on Sundays and John Braithwaite of Orrest Head House generously donated £300 towards the cost of a new south aisle. Abraham Pattinson constructed the extension, with its distinctive semi-circular arches, with astonishing rapidity in four short months. Mr Braithwaite, a bachelor, died in March of 1854, one month before his neighbour of almost half a century, Professor Wilson, and four years after their friend William Wordsworth. John Braithwaite's estate was left in trust for a nephew, Joseph Crosthwaite of Bowness, at that time a slip of a lad aged four years.[225] But most of the compensation which John Braithwaite had received for his farmland requisitioned for the railway, was now put to great good use as a most generous and far-reaching bequest, to benefit future generations of schoolchildren.

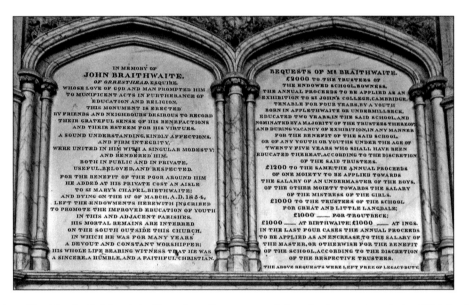

61. A wall tablet in St Martin's Church at Bowness explains the bequest made in 1854 by John Braithwaite for the benefit of five schools in the area.

> *'£2000 to the trustees of the Endowed School, Bowness, the annual proceeds to be applied as an exhibition to St John's College, Cambridge, tenable for four years by a youth born in Applethwaite or Undermillbeck —--.[226]*
>
> *£1200 to the same; the annual proceeds of one moiety to be applied towards the salary of an undermaster of the boys, of the other moiety towards the salary of the mistress of the girls.*
> > *£1000 to the trustees of the School for Great and Little Langdale;*
> > *£1000 —-- for Troutbeck;*
> > *£1000 —-- at Birthwaite;*
> > *£1000 —-- at Ings.*

107

In the last four cases the annual proceeds to be applied as an increase to the salary of the master, or otherwise for the benefit of the school, according to the discretion of the respective trustees.'

The effect of the scholarship was to provide local boys with an opportunity for higher education at Cambridge, on a par with the sons of wealthier gentlemen attending Windermere College, opened in the previous year with high patronage.

3.14 The Father of Windermere

John Aspinall Addison's infectious enthusiasm and pioneering zeal persuaded wealthy in-comers to surround his little church with their villas, mostly fashioned in his beloved gothic style. He aimed to attract sympathetic neighbours for his ecclesiastically led society – retired clergymen, clergy widows, people of culture and learning, and also wealthy, socially mobile, *nouveaux-riches* from the industrial conurbations. In this aim he was eminently successful. The building boom of villas in Birthwaite produced

- The Terrace (1854) above the Station, a row of five houses for the directors of the K&W Railway Company;

- The Bingle (1853) for Robert Braithwaite, a drysalter and mill owner from Kendal, related by marriage to Robert Somervell and John Harris (below);

- Oakland (1853) for John Gandy, banker and mill-owner from Kendal;

- Birthwaite Lodge (1853) for John Harris,[227] engineer of the K&W Railway, and brother-in-law of his neighbour Robert Somervell;

- Hazelthwaite (1853) for Robert Miller Somervell of Kendal, shoe manufacturer;

- Winlass Beck (1854) for Peter Kennedy, Scottish owner of cotton mills in Austria, who married into the Bolton bleaching and calico printing family of Ridgway;

- and Holehird (1854) for John Rowson Lingard of Manchester, a solicitor, canal and railway proprietor.

In a dramatic surge of building operations these villas were all completed by 1855, and survive today. For all these villas, including Hazelthwaite,[228] the architect was Joseph Stretch Crowther of Manchester, at the height of his prolific career and still in his mid-thirties. Architects Bowman & Crowther were recognised exponents of the gothic revival style, and Crowther designed many fine houses and churches in the cities and shires of the north of England, notably at Alderley Edge.[229] [230] He applied his architectural talent in great measure to Windermere, continuing the theme which Revd Addison and Miles Thompson had begun, enhancing the building fabric and architectural character of the growing township. There is no doubt that Crowther and Addison were of one mind, drawing inspiration from Charles Barry and A.N.W. Pugin.[231]

However, in striving to implant his grand design on the infant township, Revd Addison spent the whole of his personal fortune – and more – advancing his several projects. Unfortunately, he was forced to subsidize the launch and the running costs both of the school and particularly of the College. Collectively, his building projects are estimated to have cost his personal finances the equivalent today of at least £3 million.

Understandably, John Addison's already depleted resources were fatally exhausted soon after he commenced construction of the College in 1852, and by 1854 they were irretrievably encumbered by mortgage debt, with no way to repay. In June of that year he unsuccessfully attempted to sell all his properties at auction in Windermere Hotel.[232] So when John Braithwaite of Orrest Head House bequeathed £1,000 for the benefit of Birthwaite School *(3.13)*, it must have come like manna from heaven. Sadly, and in desperation, as trustee of the little school Mr Addison diverted half of the endowment capital away from the school to the College before the misdemeanour was revealed.

The mortgage debt was called in and the Victorian society of the day was unforgiving in its condemnation of the cleric. Following protracted negotiations lasting many months – which almost failed – an agreement was reached that St Mary's Church and Birthwaite School could be purchased from Revd Addison, their owner, by public subscription on behalf of the township. A committee of landowners and ratepayers was formed in April 1854, chaired by John Gandy of nearby Oakland, with G.H. Gardner of Ellerthwaite acting as secretary, and John Lingard of Holehird as treasurer and legal advisor. They negotiated a price of £1,400 with Mr Addison for church and school, and secured pledges from wealthy residents and landowners to meet the cost.[233] The committee insisted that the depleted funds of the Braithwaite endowment would be reinstated in full, and would remain with the school as intended by the benefactor. But the sale negotiations dragged on for many months and were only finalised on 27 April 1855. Humiliatingly, two days later all of the personal property and effects of the Addison family were publicly auctioned at their home St Mary's Cottage, next to the Church, and they left Windermere forever. It was a further year before all pledges of money were collected in from donors, mostly by the boundless energy of William Harrison. Purchase monies of £1,410 for church and school were finally paid on 20 January 1856.[234]

So how should we judge this man of God, so publicly disgraced ?

Undoubtedly, Revd Addison offended by misappropriating the Braithwaite bequest, intended solely as endowment for the school, and abusing his position as sole trustee of the fund. But he did quickly make financial restitution as promised. It seems fair to conclude that Mr Addison was an unrealistic romantic, whose pious and social ambition raced ahead of his worldly means and expertise. He lacked the project management and business skills required to control such large and complex projects, and to run his enterprises viably. In their absence, he quite naively over-stretched the resources available to him. Such a failing is not unknown !

In his favour, John Aspinall Addison had the grand creative vision which implanted on the infant village of Birthwaite enduring ecclesiastical and educational institutions of a high order, and an architectural style of villa residences which has enhanced the village of Windermere for 160 years. Ironically, much of Mr Addison's social blueprint later became reality – albeit in modified form. And he expended his entire personal fortune, the equivalent perhaps of £3 million today, striving to complete his grand design.

Following their departure from Birthwaite in 1855, Revd Addison and his family moved to Devon where he served quietly as curate of Plymouth and Brixton for seven years. In 1862 he was installed as vicar of Hound near Southampton, and finally became rector of Cowlam, near Beverley in Yorkshire in 1874. He died at Bridlington Quays in 1883 and was interred in Scarborough Cemetery – having never set foot in Windermere again.

In November 1882 the vicar of St Mary's Church, at that time the Reverend Henry Ainslie, was moved to install at his own expense a handsome memorial window in tribute to the founder, a fine gesture indeed. Perhaps the Reverend John Aspinall Addison should now be forgiven his human frailties, and finally recognised as the *'father of Windermere'*.

62. Revd John Aspinall Addison

63. The inscription below the Addison window in St Mary's Church reads

'Huic adi Christi sacrae condendae primus operam navavit, Ioannes A. Addison, A.D. MDCCCXLVIII Laus Deo'

which translates as

'John Addison was the first who devoted himself to the work of building this church of Christ, 1848. Praise be to God.'

64. Located in a quiet corner of Scarborough Cemetery, a simple memorial to Rev. John Aspinall Addison and his wife Mary.[235]

Following the departure of Revd Addison from Windermere, the Church was temporarily conveyed to Messrs Gandy and Lingard as joint trustees of the purchase fund, and subsequently to the diocese of Carlisle. [236] Since the Church had been the private property of Revd Addison, despite sitting geographically within the ancient Parish of Windermere (comprised of the townships of Undermillbeck, Applethwaite, Troutbeck and Ambleside-below-Stock), it was neither integrated within the parish nor consecrated.

Arrangements were now put in hand to create a separate ecclesiastical parish of Applethwaite, carved from the ancient Parish of Windermere by the church Commissioners, and officially created on 24 November 1856, as follows:—

> *'On the north-west the boundary separating the township of Troutbeck from the township of Applethwaite to a point in a direct line west of a farm called The Boot. On the north by an imaginary line proceeding from the above mentioned point easterly across Applethwaite Common to a bound-stone placed on the boundary line separating the parish of Windermere from the parish of Kendal. On the south by the boundary line separating the township of Applethwaite from the township of Undermillbeck, and on the west by the Lake of Windermere.'* [237]

St Mary's Church and churchyard were consecrated by Bishop Villiers of Carlisle in separate ceremonies on 8 and 9 August 1856, the weather being so foul on the first day, the formal consecration of the burial ground was delayed until the second.

Not everyone in the village had been in favour of a burial ground at the Church. Mr Eastted, whose building land for villas at Elleray overlooked the churchyard, felt it would '--- *interfere with the amenity of the place'*. But an order had been issued for the termination of interments at St Martin's churchyard, requiring new burial grounds to be found for the townships of Undermillbeck and Applethwaite. Since the average number of deaths within Birthwaite was only six per year, and half of those were buried at Troutbeck, St Mary's churchyard was finally approved by the residents, who wished to have an independent site within their township.

The Reverend Charles Clayton Lowndes, a young lecturer at St Cuthbert's in Carlisle, was recommended by the Bishop of Chester to be installed as the first incumbent of St Mary's, and took up duties officially on 22 August 1856. Shortly thereafter, it emerged that the living had been endowed with a gift of £1,000 from Matthew Dobson Lowndes, a Liverpool solicitor, his father.

Now, if we leave the site of St Mary's campus, the turnpike road bends north. We will shortly arrive at a formal carriage driveway on the right which leads to the sites of three impressive villa residences – The Bingle, Oakland, and Elleray Bank.

Villas and Grand Houses —-– the Arrival of Quality

3.15 The Bingle (Cleeve How) – Robert Braithwaite

Prior to Mr Eastted's sub-division of the Elleray estate and his attempt to sell building plots, two blocks of land bordering The Wood estate to the north-west, measuring 1.2 and 2.8 acres respectively, were sold privately to Kendal businessmen. Land from Elleray for the Bingle was acquired in February 1853 by Robert Braithwaite; and an adjacent site for Oakland was purchased two months later by John Gandy.

Robert Braithwaite was the son of Isaac Braithwaite of Highgate, mill-owner, drysalter,[238] engineer and manufacturer of woollens. They were descended from two well known Kendal Quaker families, Braithwaite and Wilson *(Appendix 5)*, although Robert Braithwaite espoused the Church of England from an early age. He and his brother, Isaac Braithwaite junior, married Quaker sisters Charlotte and Louisa Masterman from a wealthy banking family in the City of London. Robert Braithwaite and Charlotte Masterman were married in 1844 in London by her brother-in-law, the Reverend Benjamin Symons, who was Warden of Wadham College, Oxford. The Braithwaites lived initially in Highgate, Kendal, but following Robert's retirement from the woollen business before the age of 40, they moved to Birthwaite on completion of a gothic-style villa named The Bingle. His brother Isaac moved south to the City of London where he became a broker in the Stock Exchange, close to his Masterman in-laws.

A few months after acquiring the site for The Bingle, Robert Braithwaite purchased a further parcel of land adjacent to Elleray from Mary Pennington, owner of The Wood, to build a stable and coach house. Joseph Crowther was commissioned as architect for this attractive villa on the lower western slope of Orrest, a house whose gothic style and owner perfectly matched the preferences of Revd Addison's grand plan. It was the first of several villas to rise along the Ambleside turnpike road over the next three years, most of which were designed by Crowther.

In 1856 Robert Braithwaite became a founder trustee of Birthwaite School, after its purchase by public subscription from Mr Addison; and Mrs Braithwaite joined the committee of ladies charge with managing the girls' and infants' schools.

But the Braithwaites did not remain long in the new village. In the spring of 1859 Robert Braithwaite made a career change, following a long-held ambition to enter the ministry of the Church of England. It is likely that he was encouraged into an ecclesiastical career by Revd Symons, who led an evangelical reform movement at Wadham College. Like Revd Addison, Mr Braithwaite left Windermere for the south of England, but for entirely different reasons.

During the next 14 years he held a series of curacies in parishes across southern England, from Clifton in the west to Margate in the east, finally settling as vicar of Chipping Camden in the Cotswolds in 1873. There, he served the ancient parish of St James, which, like his home town of Kendal, had prospered for 500 years on the wool trade. Following his death in 1882 Robert Braithwaite was interred in the churchyard at Chipping Camden, below the impressive east window of the chancel.

65. Known as The Bingle when first erected in 1853, but now named Cleeve How, this pleasant gothic style villa presents its face to the Langdale Pikes and the northern fells. Around 1892 a billiard room and lantern shaped cupola were added on the south side of the building. On the far left of the picture, the coach house backs on to the narrow track that would have been the line of the Ambleside Railway. If the railway had been built, it would certainly have been a major intrusion into the privacy of this property.

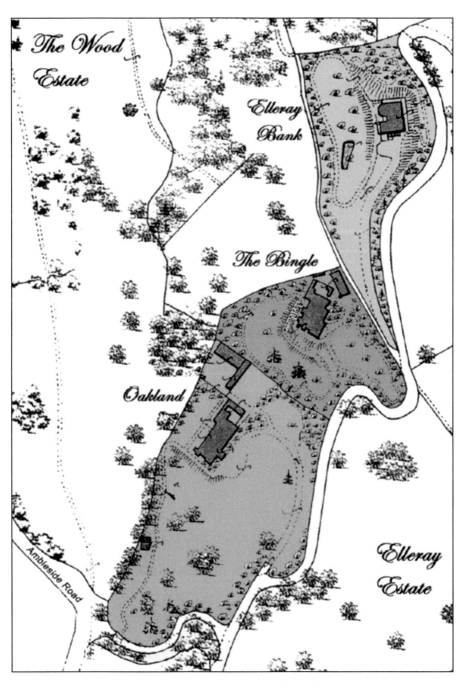

66. Sites of three elegant villa residences, built in 1853-1855 share a winding carriage driveway to the west of Elleray.

67. *In 1853 John Gandy, a Kendal banker and mill owner, acquired a site measuring almost 3 acres, on the western boundary of the Elleray estate. There he built this impressive gothic mansion named Oakland, designed by Joseph Crowther of Manchester.*

Courtesy of Colin Tyson

67a. Oakland today.

3.16 Oakland – John Gandy

The Gandy brothers, John and James, were partners in Dockwray Hall Mill in Kendal, built in 1816 for Gandy & Sons, described at that time as

'-– the largest manufacturing building ever erected in the county.'

Like so many enterprises in Kendal they were drysalters and dyers, producing woollens and carpets. Unlike many newer towns in industrial Lancashire, woollen manufacture was well established in Kendal and Hawkshead for five hundred years due to the proliferation of sheep in Westmorland, the hill-hardy Herdwick breed and the Leicester cross. In 1833 the Gandy brothers were instrumental in founding the Bank of Westmorland, one of the first joint stock banks in England, which proved to be a well respected and successful enterprise for the rest of the century.[239] Their father, James Gandy senior, was also a founding director of the Carlisle & Cumberland Bank in 1836.[240]

John Gandy, the elder of the two brothers, became chairman of the Kendal & Windermere Railway Company on its formation in 1845, a position which he held for the rest of his life. It was natural therefore that he would gravitate towards Birthwaite. In 1851 he and his wife, Magdalen Agnes Hunter, occupied Birthwaite Hall, a convenient result of its acquisition by the Railway Company from G.H. Gardner. This allowed John Gandy time to seek a permanent site for his retirement in the new village. In April 1853 he acquired nearly 3 acres of Elleray land from William Eastted, immediately below Robert Braithwaite's Bingle, sharing the same carriage drive. These two gentlemen were well acquainted as mill owners in Kendal. Gandy also engaged Joseph Crowther as architect for Oakland. It was an impressive gothic mansion and the largest private residence yet to appear in the village, befitting a successful businessman of his standing.

In 1855 John Gandy chaired the committee of ratepayers and land-owners for the purchase of St Mary's Church and school from Revd Addison, and was one of the trustees who conveyed the church to the Diocese of Carlisle *(3.13)*. The Braithwaite endowment was subsequently deposited at his Westmorland Bank and managed by a panel of five trustees, with John Gandy himself as treasurer.

John Gandy's contribution to the early success of the village was outstanding. A north aisle for St Mary's Church, to balance the Braithwaite south aisle, was added at his sole expense with a gift of £1000, to commemorate two of his sons who had died in the service of the Crown.[241] John Gandy himself died at Oakland in 1859 and, appropriately, his interment was one of the first in the newly consecrated churchyard at St Mary's.

3.17 Elleray Bank – George Godfrey Cunningham

Elleray Bank was built in 1855 for George Godfrey Cunningham, at the top of the shared driveway on the steep western slope of Orrest Head, high above The Bingle and Oakland. The design was commissioned from a young Liverpool-born architect, Alfred Waterhouse, who was then in the first decade of a prolific and prestigious professional career. He was later to gain fame and acclamation for his magnificent work on Manchester Town Hall and the Natural History Museum in London. At a time when Waterhouse was still experimenting with different styles, Elleray Bank was described as Londonesque, and is architecturally quite unlike the pointed gothic style of its neighbours. Unfortunately, the construction of Elleray Bank was marred by interminable delays, causing consternation for the client who found that three days before he

'--- was due to leave his old house --- Elleray Bank was not even glazed.' [242] [243]

The Scottish client for Elleray Bank was a Londoner by birth, but with strong Scottish ancestry. G.G. Cunningham (1803-1860) returned to Scotland as a young man and spent most of his working life in Glasgow and Edinburgh. He became a publisher, editor, and prolific historical writer – an authority on the *Lives of eminent and illustrious Englishmen from Alfred the Great to modern times'*, published in eight volumes from 1835 to 1837. His publications [244] were widely read and highly regarded, at a time when Edinburgh was awash with literary works [245] and writers, including the late Sir Walter Scott.

In 1843 G.G. Cunningham married Isabella Crawford Laurie, a Glasgow lady who bore him a son also named George Godfrey Cunningham. In 1854, following the death of John Braithwaite, the family rented Orrest Head House whilst Elleray Bank was under construction. The cost of the new villa was largely met from Isabella's inheritance, following her father's death two years earlier. She was the fourth daughter of James Laurie who had prospered as a Glasgow merchant and property developer, importing the finest timbers from the East and West Indies. In 1802 two Laurie brothers took the bold step of acquiring an area of riverfront land on the south side of the Clyde. There they laid out an impressive residential district which still bears the name of Laurieston today. [246] Two fine terraces of Georgian residences fronting the river, were built along Carlton Place for the burgeoning class of Glasgow merchants, importers and manufacturers. James Laurie and his family occupied an apartment over the portico. [247]

For six years the Cunninghams enjoyed Elleray Bank with its spectacular, uninterrupted views across Windermere to the western fells, [248] and their son attended nearby Windermere College [249] under Puckle and Irving. An early gravestone in St Mary's Churchyard records the death of G.G. Cunningham in 1860. Elleray Bank then reverted to his widow, Isabella, who continued to live in Windermere for a further decade until her son's marriage in 1871 to Mary Louisa le Fleming. She was the daughter of Major-General George Cumberland Hughes le Fleming of Rydal Hall.

68. *Elleray Bank was built in 1855 for George Godfrey Cunningham senior, a historical author and publisher in Glasgow and Edinburgh, and his wife Isabella Crawford Laurie. An early design of Alfred Waterhouse in the Londonesque style,[250] the house sits on a spectacular site, high on the steep western slope of Orrest Head. The site was selected for its magnificent views across Windermere towards Wetherlam and the Coniston Fells.*

69. The elegant little villa of Birthwaite Lodge bears the unmistakable hallmarks of Joseph Crowther. Built in 1853 for John Harris,[251] engineer to the K&W Railway, Harris' brother-in-law, Robert Miller Somervell built neighbouring Hazelthwaite in the same year.

3.18 Birthwaite Lodge – John Harris

Crossing the turnpike road, secreted behind St Mary's Cottage we find an elegant little villa named Birthwaite Lodge which bears the signature characteristics of architect J.S. Crowther. Its unique and glorious feature is a beautiful little overhung oriel window on the gable end, overlooking the garden of St Mary's Cottage and its magnificent cedar tree. In 1853 Crowther advertised in the local press seeking '--- *stone-masons, wallers, carpenters and plumbers*', and naming the owner as John Harris. [252]

John Harris was born in 1812 into a Quaker family from Maryport and Lamplugh.[253] He began an engineering apprenticeship in Co Durham, but a year later, at the age of 24 he took over as engineer of the Stockton and Darlington Railway, largely funded by Quaker money.

He worked initially on the maintenance of the line and later on various projects in Middlesborough Docks, including design of the Tees Bridge. He pioneered the use of wooden sleepers combined with cast-iron rail track, which became standard railway practice. He was engineer on several railways in the north of England in the 1840s, including the Lancaster to Carlisle. In 1844 he married Mary Wilson, of the Kendal Quaker family of woollen manufacturers, whose sister Anne married Robert Miller Somervell *(3.20)* five years later. In 1846 John Harris succeeded John Errington as site engineer on the Kendal & Windermere line during its construction phase.[254] With an eye to the future, he acquired 6 acres of Cook's House Estate from architect Miles Thompson, which became the site for Birthwaite Lodge and Hazelthwaite. But although the Lodge was completed in 1853, the Harris family never had the opportunity to take up residence, as his work drew him back to Darlington. There he built locomotives, a water works, a brick factory, and rose to be Vice-President of the Institution of Civil Engineers.

John Harris died in Kendal in 1869, worth £16,000.[255] Like his contemporary, Cornelius Nicholson, he was a self-made Cumbrian man who progressed rapidly in the early days of railway engineering, due to considerable energy, ability and Quaker family connections. Harris's time at Birthwaite was all too brief, but his legacy to the infant village in the form of Birthwaite Lodge, is one of the prettiest little villas ever to grace the area.

The house was occupied around 1854 for three years, by Joseph Greaves, a Liverpool merchant and broker. And from 1866-1878 it was the home of Mrs Margaret Morewood, widow of the Vicar of Burton-in-Kendal, who fitted Mr Addison's social blueprint well.

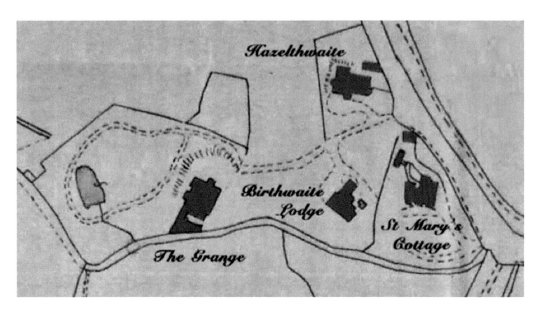

70. Keyplan of St Mary's Cottage, Birthwaite Lodge, Windermere Grange and Hazelthwaite

3.19 Windermere Grange – Dr Edward Bradley

Hidden behind St Mary's Cottage and Birthwaite Lodge is the site of Windermere Grange, usually shortened to The Grange. The building was sited on a large plot acquired from John Harris, below his Birthwaite Lodge and alongside the old packhorse track which descends towards Millerground. The house was built in 1857 for a Liverpool surgeon, Dr Edward Bradley, and shares a carriage drive with Birthwaite Lodge and with Hazelthwaite on the north side, all of which enjoy excellent views.

Edward Bradley qualified as a surgeon and practiced in the 1850s in the Mount Pleasant area of the teaming port of Liverpool, close to the Infirmary. He married Ann Hutchinson of Embleton near Cockermouth in 1826 and they had six children. Like so many industrial towns in the 1800s, Dr Bradley's native Liverpool was an unsanitary place in which to raise children. Cholera epidemics in 1832 and 1849 killed almost 7,000 people and infected four times that number, provoking riots. Even doctors and hospitals were not immune from attack. Edward Bradley became a member of Liverpool Council where he campaigned for the provision of a clean water supply and a properly designed underground sewerage system. He strenuously promoted the benefits of a continuous supply of piped water to replace the inadequate communal wells and occasional barrels of water, placed at intervals along the streets. In 1848 he wrote in the Liverpool Mercury

> '--- in the construction of our sewers great consideration should be given to the size of the bore; for if you have too much space in them, this great evil arises --- you do not get sufficient force of water to carry off deposits; hence you get the generation and accumulation of the most destructive and offensive gases --- the sewers becoming so many gasometers.'

In his mid-fifties Dr Bradley had accumulated sufficient wealth to escape the squalor and diseases of the port. He was the first of many professional men to retire to the Windermere area, escaping from the *miasmatta* of the industrial towns of Northern England, exactly what Cornelius Nicholson predicted the railway would make possible.

It is interesting that Windermere Grange incorporated a prominent tower, probably to house fresh water from springs on Orrest Head, or pumped spring water. Unsurprisingly, Dr Bradley supported the provision of mains water and sewerage for Windermere,

> 'All the sewage runs down the brook from the village through the extensive estate of Rev. Fletcher Fleming to Lake Windermere, near Rayrigg, polluting the water and forming a nuisance to his property.'

By 1870, shortly after Windermere Local Board was formed to introduce piped drinking water and thoroughgoing sewerage, the Bradleys departed from Windermere to reside successively in fashionable Cheltenham, Brighton and finally in Somerset.

71. Hazelthwaite, built in 1853 for Robert Miller Somervell, founder of K-Shoes in Kendal.

© Ian Jones

3.20 Hazelthwaite – Robert Miller Somervell

A few steps north of St Mary's Cottage on the turnpike road stands Hazelthwaite, a very different style of villa built on the remaining land purchased by John Harris. The lower pitch and greater overhang of its roof give the mansion an impressive appearance, which contrasts surprisingly harmoniously with its neighbours. Its windows lack any trace of Gothic style, and although the construction is of local greystone, the predominant effect is Italianate. A short central tower houses a belvedere for water storage, as seen on Belsfield at Bowness, St Mary's Abbey, The Grange, and later at Heywood's new Elleray mansion on the hillside opposite.

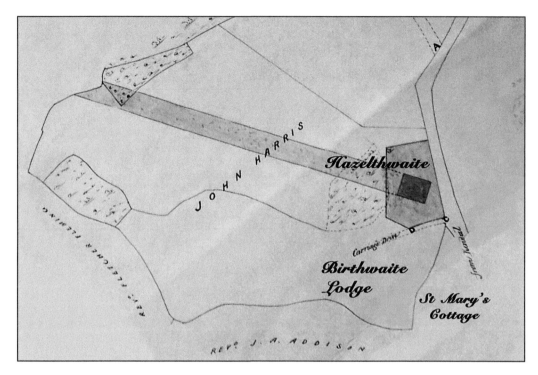

72. Keyplan of building land sold to Robert Miller Somervell for Hazelthwaite by John Harris, who built the neighbouring Birthwaite Lodge in 1853 on part of the land he purchased from Miles Thompson.[256] *The architect for both these houses of very different style was Joseph Crowther of Manchester.*

Courtesy of Cumbria Archive Centre, Kendal

In 1853 a large plot of land, perhaps 4 acres in all, originally part of Cook's House Estate, was conveyed to Robert Miller Somervell, his brother-in-law, by John Harris. Here, Hazelthwaite was built by Abraham Pattinson to a design of Joseph Crowther.[257] Its Italianate style is very different from most of Crowther's villas, although the large bay windows have similar proportions to those which he installed at Holehird for John Dunlop a decade later, and at Crowther's own villa in Alderley Edge. During building work the Somervell family moved temporarily from Kendal to Windermere Cottage near Elleray gate, to supervise proceedings.

Robert Miller Somervell (1821-1899) prospered by dint of his own prodigious energy and business acumen as a leather merchant in Kendal, where he pioneered large scale factory-based boot and shoe manufacturing. He was born in London, the grandson of a Scottish minister of the Presbyterian kirk, son of a London textile merchant, and the youngest of three brothers.[258] Robert Somervell joined his brother William in 1840 to learn the leather trade in London, supplying *findings*[259] to the many boot and shoemakers in the city. In 1843 he moved north to Kendal and, with funds borrowed from his mother and brothers, set up his own leather supply business in that town. In 1848 he took another brother, John Somervell, into partnership, and together they raised the business from small-scale outsourcing of cottage shoemakers, to one of the premier mechanised footwear manufactories in the country (*Appendix 6*).

In 1849 Robert Miller Somervell married Anne Wilson, of the long-established Kendal Quaker family of woollen mill owners and hosiery makers. Her sister Mary Wilson was already married to John Harris who built Birthwaite Lodge, provider of the land for Hazelthwaite. To compound the myriad family connections, in 1847 Robert's brother John Somervell had married Rachael Wilson, a cousin of Anne and Mary. And finally, to consolidate confusion and coincidence, the Wilson ladies shared common great-grand-parents with Robert Braithwaite of The Bingle, on the opposite side of the turnpike road; and with George Braithwaite Crewdson, who later took up residence at The Wood near Cook's Corner. Clearly, family ties, Kendal business interests, and non-conformist heritage created strong ties of kinship, leading to a cluster of villas in the emerging village of Birthwaite. They fulfilled admirably Revd Addison's plan for a reverential flock of wealthy residents living near his little chapel.

However, Robert Somervell came of Presbyterian stock and was baptised into the London Wall Scotch Church. When he moved north to Kendal in 1842 he became an ardent Congregationalist. Following his move to Birthwaite, Robert founded and supervised the construction in 1858 of the first non-conformist church in the Windermere area, the little Congregational Chapel at Troutbeck Bridge. And four years later he took charge of its enlargement. For over 40 years it was his constant place of worship, where he often led the service.

73. Overleaf, a panoramic view taken from Elleray Bank around 1880 shows Hazelthwaite (centre foreground), St Mary's Abbey (top left) and Windermere Grange (bottom right). Clearly visible are their towers for water storage. Belle Isle and Ferry Nab are also visible in the background.

The first villa built in Windermere after the opening of the railway was St Mary's Abbey, in 1847. It must have been a startling sight to local people in its majestic pointed gothic style, quite unlike anything most of them would have seen before. In contrast to the low and picturesque style of Professor Wilson's nearby Elleray mansion, it towered above the tree canopy and other buildings. By 1875 the Abbey had acquired a second tower, with observation rooms inserted at several levels in Revd Addison's 'Watch Tower', from which to enjoy the spectacular views.

In contrast, Hazelthwaite and the Grange, built in the 1850s, intrude less dramatically into the landscape, presenting a cleaner Italianate style with roofs of lower pitch and overhanging eaves.

© Ian Jones

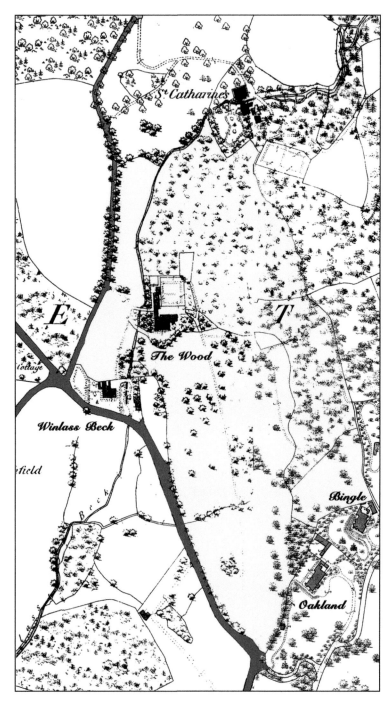

74. *The Wood estate of 20 acres adjacent to the Ambleside turnpike and the road to Troutbeck, extends from Oakland in the south to St Catherine's in the north.*

3.21 The Wood – Miss Jane Yates

A short walk north of Hazelthwaite and Oakland lies The Wood, which we visited during the first walk *(2.3)*. It consists of an elongated estate of some 20 acres in size, bounded on the east by the steep slope of Orrest head, to the north and west by St Catherine's estate and the Troutbeck Road, and to the west and south by the Kendal-to-Ambleside turnpike. The villa sits high above Cook's Corner, overlooking a parcel of Cook's House farm. Like Elleray, The Wood was contemporary with George Gardner's Birthwaite Hall, pre-dating almost every other villa in Windermere. Historically, the principle economic value of the estate was in the timber it yielded for bobbin-making and charcoal.

In the 1700s an ancient house on this site was occupied by the Dixon family, Troutbeck yeomen for centuries past. Around 1798 The Wood estate was acquired by Timothy Parker of Hornby Hall in the Lune Valley, and was enjoyed by him and his family as a summer retreat, until his untimely death in 1805. It then passed by descent through the Parker family until ca.1830, when the estate was rented by James Pennington, a Kendal solicitor. This is the same Pennington family of Kendal who acted as surrogate carers for Daniel Gardner's son George during the boy's education at Hawkshead and Sedbergh Schools, and as property agents following his acquisition of Birthwaite in 1780.

James Pennington (1797-1845) initially made The Wood his summer residence, and then his principle seat. He purchased the property just two months before his death in 1845, possibly to provide security for his wife Mary and their young family. James Pennington and George Harrison Gardner, childhood friends and both now practicing solicitors, were amongst the few permanent residents of the Birthwaite area before the building of the railway – and each died before his time.

Following his death in 1845 James Pennington was interred in the churchyard at St Martin's in Bowness. His widow Mary returned briefly to live at Kirkland in Kendal, but subsequently moved permanently to Sedbergh. She let The Wood to provide an income, occasionally selling parcels of land to neighbours. In 1853 she sold land to Robert Braithwaite for his stable and coach house at The Bingle, and a larger portion to Thomas Toulmin in 1859 for additional garden.

The first tenant to occupy the Wood in 1848, after the death of James Pennington, was **Miss Jane Yates** from Bury. She inherited considerable wealth from her family in industrial Lancashire. Her grandfather William Yates,[260] co-founded Haworth, Peel, Yates & Co. of Bury in the late 1700s, one of the first and most successful cotton spinning, calico printing and bleaching enterprises in early industrial Lancashire.[261] When her father, Thomas Yates, died in 1815 he left a considerable fortune for the benefit of six children, all of whom were then under the age of 21 years.[262] His will directed that a ⅗ part was to be divided amongst two sons, and ⅖ amongst four daughters. [263]

As an early arrival in the hamlet of Birthwaite, Miss Jane Yates became closely acquainted with Revd Addison and his little church. In 1854 she was among the first subscribers to pledge £100[264] towards the fund to purchase St Mary's Church and Birthwaite School on behalf of the community. In an even greater act of generosity, in 1859 she contributed £1,000 towards the purchase of the little villa of Annesdale to provide a Vicarage for St Mary's.[265]

When Jane Yates died at The Wood in July 1862 she possessed a considerable fortune of around £70,000,[266] and although she never owned The Wood, it served as her permanent residence with up to seven servants. Her interment was one of the early burials in the graveyard at St Mary's Church. As a fitting memorial to the lady

> '--- in view of her deep interest and involvement with the welfare of the school, it was felt by her family that to extend the small second classroom would be a fitting tribute to her memory.'

This classroom became a prominent feature of the little school behind the church, almost doubling the number of pupils it could accommodate, and enabling the school to serve the village of Windermere for more than a century.

George Braithwaite Crewdson, JP

In the spring of 1863 The Wood was advertised to be let on behalf of Mary Pennington:

> 'The property consists of a Mansion House in excellent repair, containing Drawing and Dining Rooms, Library, Servants' Hall, Butler's Pantry, Kitchen, Scullery, twelve Bedrooms; Coach House, Stable, and other requisite Outbuildings and Offices, and a large Garden and Orchard, and upwards of TWENTY ACRES of Meadow, Pasture and Woodland.'

The successful applicant was George Braithwaite Crewdson, a Kendal banker who was already residing with his family at The Terrace above the Station. From a long established Quaker family, he married Eleanor Fox of Falmouth, but had left the Society of Friends around 1840, crossing to the Church of England. Like Miss Yates, he supported the acquisition by public subscription of St Mary's Church and School from their founder, making a substantial donation to the appeal fund. Following consecration of the church in 1856 he took charge of the parish finances, and his two younger sons attended St Mary's College under the new ownership of Puckle and Irving. Three decades later his middle son became the incumbent at St Mary's Church.

George Braithwaite Crewdson was probably the first businessman to travel regularly by train to Kendal, commuting to his office in Highgate until his death in 1876.

75. *Winlass Beck, built in 1854 on the site of the original Cook's House for Peter Kennedy.*

3.22 Cook's House – Peter Kennedy

Immediately before we reach Cook's Corner, on the east side of the Ambleside turnpike stands another gothic villa designed by Joseph Crowther. Writing in 1854, Harriet Martineau tells us that

> '--- *Cook's House has only just disappeared, and a new residence, built by Peter Kennedy Esq. has taken its place.'*

Standing on a elevated site acquired from Miles Thompson, and previously occupied by the ancient farmhouse, the villa initially took the old name of Cook's House.[267] The new house is similar in size to Birthwaite Lodge, displaying the same signature styling characteristics of Joseph Crowther, seen on both these houses and at The Bingle.

Peter Kennedy (1799-1882) was descended from a family of Scottish hill farmers who scraped a difficult living from moorland at Knocknalling, north of New Galloway. When their father died in 1779 the eldest son, David Kennedy, succeeded to the property. It could not sustain all five brothers, and so the four younger siblings were forced to leave home and make their way in the world. They embarked on a remarkable journey, during which they rose by their own considerable abilities to become successful merchants and industrialists. The next three generations of Kennedys occupied a central place in the industrial revolution in Glasgow, Manchester, Leeds ––– and remarkably, in Austria !

John Kennedy (1769-1855), after an apprenticeship in Chowbent near Wigan, became an innovative machinery engineer. In 1791 he and a fellow Scot, James M'Connel, also from Kircudbrightshire, raised joint capital of £1,770 to form a manufacturing partnership that lasted for 30 years. M'Connel and Kennedy began as cotton spinners using their version of Crompton's *mule*,[268] but John Kennedy also built an experimental workshop in which he developed his own engineering improvements. His major innovation was a method for doubling the speed at which thread could reliably be spun, and for the first time successfully harnessing the power of steam to drive their spinning frames. Together these innovations multiplied many times the number of spindles that could be driven in a single mill, permitting mass production of fine yarn of the highest quality. John Kennedy was so successful that he was known as ' *one of the makers of industrial Manchester'*. When he retired in 1826 McConnel, Kennedy & Co. was the second largest cotton spinner in the whole of Manchester, with 125,000 spindles. Their principal markets in the 1790s were the Glasgow and Paisley weavers of fine muslin cloth, at a time when the Glasgow trade was in the hands of another brother, Robert Kennedy (1771-1820).

Peter Kennedy of Winlass Beck was born in Glasgow, the son of Robert. Peter and two brothers, followed their father into the silk and calico printing business, initially in Glasgow. But sponsored by his uncle John Kennedy in Manchester, young Peter Kennedy entered an partnership with a Swiss engineer named Albert Escher,[269] to build and operate cotton mills in Austria. In the period between 1826 and 1834 they built four mills, at that time the largest mills in post-Napoleonic Europe, equipped with the most advanced of John Kennedy's spinning mules. Three mills were located in Feldkirch, a small Austrian town on the Swiss border, where they harnessed the power of the fast-flowing River Ill. The first mill had two waterwheels and 24,000 spindles. A fourth mill was constructed in 1835 for Escher, Kennedy & Douglass[270] at nearby Thüringen.

Around 1839 Peter Kennedy gave evidence to the Factory Commissioners enquiring into industrial working practices in Britain and abroad. His evidence was quite revealing regarding the attitude of mill-owners on the Continent to their workers. In Austria, he was unable to employ children under the age of 12 years, since the law required them to be educated by a priest for at least two hours a day. The interruption to mill production made it uneconomic to employ young children, but teenagers were routinely worked for 12-16 hours/day. He knew of '– *no combinations'* (trades unions) in that country,

> '––– *such a thing is entirely unknown.' If such a thing did arise* '––– *I should very soon have them in prison. In Austria they do not like people who combine ––– the people are well contented, and the manufactories are prized and esteemed by them as a beneficial source of employment.'*

Peter Kennedy remained a partner with Escher in the Austrian mills until 1842, when he sold his interest and returned to England following his marriage to Ann Ridgway of Bolton. She was a daughter of Thomas Ridgway whose family, along with the Bridsons, had created the hugely important cotton bleaching empire at Bolton, Wallsuches and Horwich, said to be the largest calico printing and bleaching enterprise in the world.

Peter and Ann Kennedy had two sons[271] who briefly attended private school in Southport. But in 1854 the family took up residence at their newly built villa at Cook's Corner in Birthwaite, their residence for the next ten years. During this time Cook's House was renamed Winlass Beck, after the gushing stream which still tumbles through the grounds towards Millerground and the Lake. Appropriately, Peter Kennedy became a trustee of the Ambleside turnpike trust, a road which passed close beside his villa; and director of three railway companies, the Kendal & Windermere Railway, the Trent Valley, Midlands & Grand Junction Railway, and eventually the Manchester and Milford Haven Railway. Their second son James, who was born in Austria, attended nearby Windermere College, playing cricket for the school, and later becoming a Cavalry Officer in the Army.

Peter Kennedy's sister married his Swiss partner, Albert Escher, continuing the family link with Austria and Switzerland.[272] His eldest son, Thomas Kennedy, became a pioneering climber in the Alps. In 1862 he and another Englishman made the first ascent of *Dent Blanche* in the Swiss Alps, a peak of 14,000 feet. Thomas Kennedy went on to study engineering in Hanover, and subsequently joined the Leeds firm founded by his uncle, Sir Peter Fairbairn. There, he rose to be partner and a very successful manufacturer of mill machinery, employing over 1000 hands.

In 1863, a few months prior to the untimely death of Mrs Ann Kennedy in Heidelberg, Peter Kennedy sold Winlass Beck and all its contents at auction, and left Windermere. Accompanied by an Austrian butler, he moved to Regent's Park in London where he spent the rest of his life. His estate in 1882 was valued at £100,000.[273]

John Lawson Kennedy, son of the earlier John Kennedy of Manchester, and first cousin of Peter Kennedy of Windermere, became a wealthy calico printer and head of the firm of J.L. Kennedy & Co. of Manchester.[274] Succession to the remote family hill farm at Knocknalling passed to him in 1836, and he replaced the old farmhouse with a Scottish baronial mansion in 1840. It then passed directly down the male line for three generations, with many members of the extensive Kennedy clan citing Knocknalling as their seat. Collectively, the self-made and clever Kennedy men, springing from hard and humble beginnings in New Galloway, were responsible for much of the explosion of the cotton industry in the north of England and Glasgow in the 1800s.

In Windermere, Peter Kennedy's legacy is the attractive villa of Winlass Beck at Cook's Corner. Perhaps inevitably, a man of his energy and drive was destined not to remain long in Mr Addison's ecclesiastical campus.

76. Cook's Corner, seen from Hammar Bank, showing Stybarrow Cottage and the steep entry to the Troutbeck valley road to Kirkstone and Patterdale. Hidden from view, the Ambleside turnpike lies behind the line of conifer trees. On the right is part of the kitchen garden of Peter Kennedy's villa built on the site of the original Cook's farmhouse. In 1860 he adopted the name Winlass Beck for the villa, and the old Cook's House name later migrated to the cottage.

© *Ian Jones*

Stybarrow Cottage

In June of 1853 Richard Clapham, a gardener at the newly built Cook's House villa, was living at nearby Stybarrow Cottage. His wife's washing had been left out overnight to dry, but in the morning many items were found to be missing and suspicion fell upon four strangers who had been seen in the area. Two constables pursued them north through Troutbeck Valley to Kirkstone Pass, where they found one of the men wearing a missing shirt and in possession of a bundle of more missing items. The men were brought before the magistrates' court where two of them pleaded guilty to theft and

> '--- *were severally sentenced to be imprisoned and kept to hard labour for three calendar months*'!

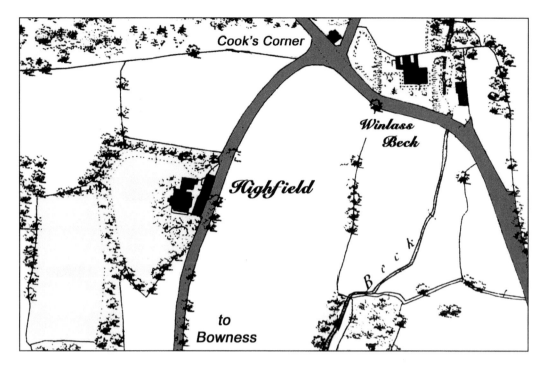

77. Highfield, near Cook's Corner and Winlass Beck ca.1860.

3.23 Highfield ––– William Sheldon

Leave Winlass Beck and turn left towards Bowness at Cook's Corner. After 100 yards there is a new house on the right where no house has stood before. This is Highfield, built on a paddock previously known as High Close, as its name implies. Harriet Martineau in 1854 described the site as

> '––– *a sort of table land from which there is a prospect magnificent beyond description, unsurpassed for beauty in the whole Lake District. The entire lake lies below, the white houses of Clappersgate being distinctly visible at the north end and the Beacon at the south: and the diversity of the framework of this sheet of water is here most striking. The Calgarth woods ––– rising and falling, spreading and contracting below, with green undulating meadows interposed, are a perfect treat to the eye; and so are the islands clustering in the centre of the lake. Wray Castle stands forth well above the promontory opposite; and at the head, the Langdale Pikes, and their surrounding mountains seem, in some states of the atmosphere, to approach and overshadow the waters; and in others to retire, and shroud themselves in soft haze and delicate hues peculiar to cloud land.*

There is a new house, built just below the ridge at Miller Brow by William Sheldon, which we have thought, from the time the foundation was laid, the most enviable abode in the country, commanding a view worthy of a mountain top, while sheltered by hill and wood, and with the main road so close at hand that the conveniences of life are as procurable as in a street.'

William Sheldon was a maverick character, lacking much of the polish of his wealthier neighbours in his early life. He was born in Preston in 1811 at a time when that town was growing fast as an industrial powerhouse of cotton manufacture. As a young man, he possessed both physical strength and the ability of a coachman to haggle for a fare. But more significantly for young William Sheldon, Preston straddled the main coach road between Manchester and Carlisle, and his father was a coach proprietor. Daily, the lad witnessed the drama and excitement of coaches clattering through the town, drawn variously by two, three or four sturdy horses. So it is not surprising to find that he followed in the family tradition, becoming a driver himself. He operated mainly on the coach routes from Lancaster through Kendal to Scotland, and also through the central Lake District to the more remote west coast towns of Keswick, Cockermouth, Workington and Whitehaven. Coaches with exciting names like *'The Locomotive'*, *'The Engineer'* and *'The Flying Machine'* were driven as much as 100 miles a day, stopping only to change horses at intervals of around eight miles.

Returning through Kendal late one Sunday evening in 1839, William Sheldon recklessly attempted to race another coach *'at a furious rate through Kirkland'*, but was apprehended by the constable on night patrol and brought before the magistrates. The constable described how *'--- I saw t' fire strike frae t' horses heels and I thought t' coach ligg'd over'*, with grave risk of death or serious injury to its passengers. Young Sheldon was fined 10 shillings, plus costs of 6 shillings. [275]

By 1842 Lancaster was the northern terminus of the new railway from London. Passengers travelling further north to Glasgow or Edinburgh had no choice but to take the stage. A typical fare for the 16-hour journey was 50 shillings,[276] lucrative business for a driver taking several passengers. It was customary to negotiate the fare with the first driver in the line outside the Station. But other drivers further back would intervene, loudly offering lower fares, often leading to physical conflict – *'give him a milling'* was the cry. Following such an event in 1842 William Sheldon was fined 53 shillings including costs, for brawling with a rival driver at Lancaster Railway Station.[277]

But coach operators like Sheldon were valued and employed by the magistrates, for the conveyance of prisoners to hulk ships moored in the docks at Liverpool. These men, and some women, had often been convicted of quite minor crimes and sentenced to transportation to the colonies. During one such *'conveyance of transports'* from Preston, William Sheldon was offered a huge bribe of £2,000 to allow the escape of a convicted armed robber – an offer which he properly declined.[278]

'PASSENGERS and PARCELS booked, at the Royal Hotel Coach Office, Market Street, only, at very REDUCED FARES, by Fast COACHES and ROYAL MAILS, from Lancaster to Glasgow and Edinburgh, twice daily.

		Inside	Outside
Lancaster to Glasgow, in	*16 hours*	---- 2– 1– 0	---1-10-0
Do. Edinburgh,	*16 hours*	---- 2-15-0	--- 1-15-0
Do. Carlisle,	*6½ hours*	---- 1– 5– 0	--- 0-15-0
Do. Dumfries,	*10 hours*	---- 1-18-0	--- 1– 4-0

To prevent mistakes on arrival at Lancaster, ask for SHELDON'S Coaches.'
(Manchester Courier, 19 Feb.1842)

The skill and physical stamina required to drive the heavy coaches on the many indifferent roads of Northern England were considerable, and William Sheldon possessed both. In one incident before the railway was extended north of Lancaster to Carlisle, he was introducing a new horse in a unicorn[279] to the steep climb over Shap Fell to Penrith. At a sudden increase in the gradient at Huck's Brow, a notorious black spot for coaching accidents,[280] the new horse baulked. A serious accident was only averted by Sheldon's skill and strength in deploying the newly introduced patent brake.

In 1842 a steadying influence entered William Sheldon's life when he married Esther Harris, by birth a Quaker lady from Lamplugh, a quiet farming village in the far west of Cumberland.[281] They lived first in Lancaster, then briefly in Kendal, before settling in Birthwaite. In 1847 he was already Superintendent of the Stations at Lancaster and Kendal, and added the newly opened Station at Windermere on 29 May; and the contract for the Royal Mail Coach service from Windermere Station to Cockermouth.[282] [283]

78. Esther Harris from Lamplugh.
Courtesy of Catherine Lazier

By 1850 he was prospering as a coach proprietor. Before Rigg's Coach Service was founded in 1855, Sheldon's Royal Mail and Coach Company held the contract for the mail from Windermere Station to Keswick, Penrith and Cockermouth, returning to Windermere in time for the evening train to the south.[284] He claimed this to be the fastest coach service on the road, carrying small numbers of passengers who were prepared to sacrifice personal comfort for speed of travel, and paying a premium fare for the privilege. For other more sedate travellers he offered a comprehensive network of scheduled services from stables located alongside the Windermere Station. These routes linked with Keswick, Cockermouth and Penrith Stations via Ambleside and Grasmere, Patterdale and Ullswater, Hawkshead and Coniston, Broughton-in-Furness, Furness Abbey and Bootle. His advertising boldly declared

'--- the fares by these coaches shall at all times be as low as the lowest on the road.'

A typical return journey from Windermere Station through Ambleside and Keswick to Cockermouth took 14 hours altogether, including the driver's lunch break of 80 minutes.

For a short time the Sheldon family occupied Birthwaite Hall while Highfield was building. In the autumn of 1850 construction of Highfield began on what had been a portion of Cook's House estate, around 3¾ acres. The house, with a simple symmetric plan, contained three reception rooms, nine bedrooms and the modern luxury of water closets. With so many rooms, it may have been intended as a hostelry for coach travellers. Inevitably, there was a coach house and a four-stalled stable. Highfield was probably the work of Kendal architect Miles Thompson, a pupil of Webster, who had so recently acquired Cook's House estate as a speculative venture for villa residences.

79. Graphical construction of Highfield as it is thought to have appeared in the 1850s, built for William Sheldon

By 1853 William Sheldon was established in the Windermere community as an entrepreneurial figure of some standing; and three years later he was Secretary to the Windermere Iron Steamboat Company, in which he became a shareholder following his transfer to Richard Rigg of the Royal Mail contract at Birthwaite. Sheldon was also at the forefront of a national campaign to abolish taxation on stagecoaches, a campaign which gave him national prominence.

In 1859 Highfield was sold and, with his wife and two young children, William Sheldon moved south to the rapidly expanding city of London. There he became director of the London General Omnibus Company, before developing tramway interests in Europe, initially in Bucharest and Madrid. The British and Foreign Tramways Company, of which he was now a director in 1870, won lucrative contracts to construct tramways in Brussels and Copenhagen.

80. William Sheldon, pictured in Denmark where he had tramway interests.

Courtesy of Catherine Lazier

When he left Windermere it was not completely the end of Sheldon's coaching interests in the Lake District. His younger brother Jack, based at the Crown Hotel in Bowness, briefly ran services to Patterdale and Keswick, before following his brother to London.

In 1869 William Sheldon was called as an expert witness to give evidence to a Parliamentary Committee enquiring into the safety of Metropolitan Street Tramways. His views were sought on various innovations and practices in tramway design in Europe, particularly the sunken, or grooved rail system, and its safety for other road users. Following his work on the design of tramways in Brussels and Copenhagen the number of passengers conveyed rose to 4,000,000 per year.

In 1870 he was elected as a director of the Metropolitan Tramways Company, with construction well under way in several parts of London, and carriages on order from New York. In the following year he also became a director of the newly formed Glasgow Tramway and Omnibus Company.

His son, Joseph William Sheldon, was married in Madrid in 1872 and spent several years in European cities managing his father's tramway contracts, before emigrating to Canada.

Following William Sheldon's death in 1884 at his London home, Clanranald Lodge, his estate was valued at £17,351,[285] a remarkable rise in personal fortune for a man of quite modest beginnings. Here was a self-made man who, from an unruly beginning in industrial Lancashire, by his own exertions built a successful career as a coach proprietor and then as director of prestigious tramway companies both at home and abroad. He successfully exploited expanding opportunities in London and later in Europe, and his knowledge was sought by Parliament.

William Sheldon was interred in the Quaker burial ground of the Society of Friends at Stoke Newington, alongside Esther his wife.

3.24 Birthwaite revisited

If we continue from Highfield to Miller Bridge, we can return to Birthwaite by way of the packhorse track through Rayrigg Wood. This takes us to St Mary's Church at the bend of the turnpike road. If we turn right along a path on the west side of the church, it takes us to Low Birthwaite. On the right side of this path is the garden and mansion of St Mary's Abbey, now occupying land that was originally part of Birthwaite estate, and sold by Thomas Crosthwaite to Revd Addison in 1845. Mr Crosthwaite moved a short way up the turnpike road above the Station to Alice Howe, where he was tenant farmer for 30 years. He retired back to Low Birthwaite around 1880, but his son Anthony Crosthwaite continued to farm at Alice Howe well into the following century.

During these years the old farmhouse at Low Birthwaite, in the shadow of the prestigious gothic buildings of the College, presented a rather run-down appearance. The farmhouse was divided into three cottages, and occupied by several Crosthwaite relatives. Here also, Birthwaite Hall is now embraced incongruously within the College complex *(2.10)*.

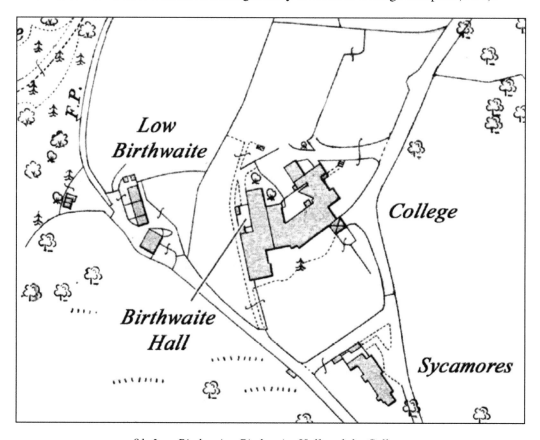

81. Low Birthwaite, Birthwaite Hall and the College.

141

82. Ellerthwaite villa as it was built for George Harrison Gardner in 1850, possibly designed by Miles Thompson and showing a mix of Georgian and Lakeland features. [286]

3.25 Ellerthwaite – George Harrison Gardner

Leaving Birthwaite and the College behind, if we walk south down the carriage drive of the College we will reach a gate on the Bowness Road, opposite to a new villa named Ellerthwaite.

In 1845, following the sale to the Railway Company of most of his Birthwaite estate, George Harrison Gardner began planning a new villa residence on a substantial part of land which he had retained. There he built an impressive house named Ellerthwaite, probably designed by Miles Thompson of Kendal who was working in Birthwaite and at Bowness before the railway. It had a simple symmetric T-shaped plan, built of dressed local stone with Georgian features, but not ponderous or Italianate as at Belsfield and Fairhaven. The new villa was built on raised ground above the Bowness Road,[287] with classic sash windows and two ground floor splayed bays at the front. Large interlocking slabs of

Honister blue slate were prominently employed as quoins, a traditional construction method seen on many Lakeland buildings prior to the importation of Lancashire and Yorkshire sandstone.

Unfortunately Robert Barrow, the joiner employed on the original build, died before his work was complete. Protracted litigation by Gardner sought unsuccessfully *(and unreasonably?)* to win compensation through the courts from the unfortunate executor of Barrow's estate, another joiner from Bowness named Joseph Crosthwaite, who eventually completed the work.[288]

G.H. Gardner faced recurring financial difficulties throughout his life. Beginning in 1849 he borrowed £500, probably to pay the joiner. In 1852 he increased his borrowing to £1800 from the Wakefield Crewdson Bank, offering as security the newly built villa itself and other properties in Kendal inherited from his father.[289] Both debts were repaid in 1855, but were closely followed by a succession of borrowings from various lenders in Kendal, Orton and Kirkby Stephen. It seems that Gardner overstretched his finances by taking second mortgages on Ellerthwaite villa and the remaining land. In December 1858 the creditors felt obliged to foreclose. The new villa and Kendal properties were sold, and the family moved in disarray to Burton-in-Kendal. When all the debts were settled they were left with a mere £670.

Sadly, within three weeks of their move to Burton, George Harrison Gardner died of consumption,[290] leaving his widow Jane to raise five young children. Tuberculosis is a debilitating infectious disease, and his ability to work seems to have been progressively impaired over previous years, leading to loss of income and mounting financial difficulties. Consumption in Victorian times was not confined to the working classes, nor to the industrial ghettos, but was prevalent in rural areas as well.

Through an ironic twist of fate, in 1855 G.H. Gardner had assisted in winding up the affairs in the new village of the unfortunate Revd Addison. He acted as secretary to the committee which raised the funds by public subscription for the purchase of St Mary's Church and school on behalf of the community. For very different reasons these two gentleman, so intimately connected with the birth of the village of Windermere, tragically suffered financial ruin during its earliest years.

George Harrison Gardner's contribution to the heritage of Windermere is important as the owner of Birthwaite estate when the railway project began, most of which was sold to the K&W Railway Co. and re-sold by them as building land for the village. Three decades later, around 1882,[291] the original villa was extended on the south side in a very different architectural style, to provide a new main entrance, morning room and an additional bedroom. A date stone mounted on the new extension bears the inscription 1850, the date of the original house. His villa of Ellerthwaite, one of the few grand houses on the south side of the village before 1900, survives today as the Windermere Public Library.

83. *Above, Ellerthwaite villa, built on an elevated site commanding excellent views to the western fells. On the left is the original villa built for George Harrison Gardner in 1850 on land retained from his Birthwaite estate. It was the first new villa on the south side of the village following the opening of the railway. This picture probably dates from around 1920, and displays a blend of early Lakeland and Georgian detail, alongside the rather uncoordinated Victorian addition on the right.[292]*

(courtesy of Colin Tyson)

84. *Right, a small obelisk standing in St James's churchyard at Burton-in-Kendal, bears inscriptions to George Harrison Gardner, his wife Jane and several members of their family.*

3.26 Fairhaven – Richard Wilson

If we turn now from Ellerthwaite and look across the Bowness Road, opposite there stands a large and imposing mansion named Fairhaven. In 1855 Richard Wilson, the County Coroner for Westmorland, built this impressive house on elevated ground. It possesses an extensive landscaped garden laid out in front of the house, and commands outstanding views to the west and south. Like Ellerthwaite, Fairhaven was probably the work of Kendal architect Miles Thompson, but of very different style. The marriage of Italianate and Georgian styles at Fairhaven imparts a clean and balanced appearance, similar to Belsfield mansion in Bowness Bay designed by Thompson's former employer and mentor George Webster.

Richard Wilson came of an influential family from Underbarrow in the Lyth Valley. His father, Smith Wilson, was an Alderman and Mayor of Kendal, and his grandfather was one of the Kendal hosiers. In 1819 Richard Wilson was articled for five years to Isaac Wilson, an uncle and attorney on the King's Bench of Common Pleas, and solicitor to the High Court of Chancery. For many years Richard Wilson lived at Thorns Hall, Underbarrow, and married Agnes Bolton of Linthwaite by whom he had four boys.

With a legal practice in Kendal and connections in London, Richard Wilson and his neighbour George Harrison Gardner were very well acquainted. He was appointed Coroner for Westmorland in 1835, and like his father served as Mayor of Kendal in 1839 and 1842. Unusually, towards the end of his second term he

> '--- gave an excellent dinner of roast beef and ale to the prisoners at the House of Correction'.[293]

In the politics of Kendal, Richard Wilson had a reputation as a robust and formidable man, notorious for violent tirades against his political opponents and the press, when vexed by their reports.[294] In the face of such a fearsome reputation, we can only wonder at the courage of a simple road worker who called at Fairhaven to claim payment he was owed by Wilson for work done at Underbarrow.

Richard Wilson died in November 1862 at the comparatively young age of 58, three years after his neighbour and legal colleague George Harrison Gardner; and only four months after his wife. The Wilsons were interred in a massive grave at All Saints Church in Underbarrow.

85. *Fairhaven, photographed in the 1860s, its recessed gateway opening on to New Street, almost empty of traffic apart from a bread van (far right). Crescent Road was cut through the open field*

in the foreground. Four cottages, shops with familiar curved arch windows, over-hung bays, and other houses (far right), are all recognisable in the street scene today.

© Ian Jones

147

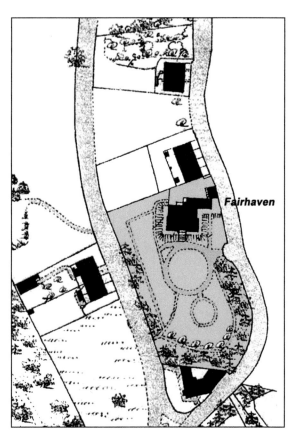

86. *1859 keyplan showing a circular driveway and landscaped garden at Fairhaven, sandwiched between the old road to Bowness (right), named New Street at this time, and the newly opened College Road (left). Also shown at this date are Hazelwood Cottage (bottom), St Mary's Terrace of three houses on College Road, and two short terraces of cottages above Fairhaven.*

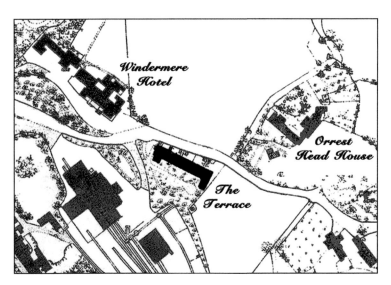

87. *The Terrace, built above the Station on an isolated corner of the old Birthwaite estate, in 1852-1854 for the K&W Railway Company.*

3.27 The Terrace

To complete the second tour, we will now climb back from Ellerthwaite to the Station by way of Orrest Lane. When the railway terminus was built, a parcel of land acquired with the Birthwaite estate was left isolated above the Station, bounded by the turnpike road and Orrest Head Farm. The directors of the Railway Company recognised the potential of this elevated site for residences of distinction, with its unsurpassed views of the southern half of the Lake. To attract potential residents to visit and settle in the village they commissioned Abraham Pattinson to build a terrace of five

'--- *commodious dwelling houses, of various sizes, suitable for genteel families'.* [295]

This was probably the first case of a developer following Mr Addison's preference for the gothic-revival style, and also the first of the villas and mansions in the village designed by architects Bowman & Crowther. Work commenced in 1853, and the houses were completed in May of 1854.[296] They proved to be popular with wealthy visitors from the start, both for short and longer term rental. At various times these houses were taken as weekend retreats by directors of the K&W Railway Company and their friends, often a step towards more permanent residence in the area – gentlemen like G.B. Crewdson, a partner in the Wakefield Crewdson Bank of Kendal, bankers to the Railway Company; and members of the Durning Holt family, cotton brokers and engineers from Liverpool.

George Holt (1790-1861) sprang to riches from a family dye works in Rochdale. He married well, Emma Durning, the daughter of a Liverpool merchant with influential Unitarian connections in that town.[297] With boundless energy and business acumen, George Holt rose rapidly to become one of the most successful cotton brokers in Liverpool.[298] In 1834 he built the original India Building on Water Street.[299]

Three generations of the Holt family came to Windermere, travelling almost door-to-door by rail. George Holt's daughter Annie rented part of The Terrace for several years, and the same house was shared at various times by his sons, Philip Henry and Sir Robert Durning Holt. They later purchased the nearby Heaning and High Borrans estates as weekend retreats.

The Holts were a most accomplished family. Philip Henry Holt (1830-1914), and third brother Alfred Holt (1829-1911), a clever and innovative marine and steam engineer, formed a partnership as shipowners, trading with China. Together they founded the Ocean Steamship Company in 1865, which later became the Blue Funnel line. The youngest brother Robert Durning Holt (1832-1908), was also a successful Liverpool cotton broker and elected as the first Lord Mayor of the city in 1892. Robert's second son Lawrence was Lord Mayor in 1929, while his eldest son Richard became an MP.

88. An elegant row of five gothic revival houses built above the Station, known as The Terrace. They were designed by Joseph Crowther, built by Abraham Pattinson for the directors of the K&W Railway Company, and completed in 1854 for letting to friends and genteel visitors of quality.

Courtesy of Alan Marsh

3.28 Turnpike Improvements

The stretch of turnpike road from Alice Howe and The Terrace to Cook's Corner was notoriously dangerous when driven fast, with two sharp and rocky bends. Then, as now, accidents occurred all too frequently. Near Hazelthwaite

> *'--- an omnibus --- met the Cockermouth mail, and although the mail was well lighted with lamps, so sharp is the curve the drivers could not see each other until the collision took place, when the mail pole was broken, a horse lamed, and the undercarriage of the omnibus broken to pieces. It is to be hoped that the trustees of the road will at once carry through their project of making the new road from Mr Somervell's to Cook's House, which has been surveyed for the purpose, and only waits the sanction of Mr Miles Thompson, architect, the owner of the land, who will, no doubt, as a friend to improvement, meet the trustees [300] on fair terms.' [301]*

An earlier, even more serious accident had occurred nearby when two clerks of the Highgate Bank were travelling to Elterwater in a gig, and the horse became unruly while descending the hill at Elleray Gate.

> *'The young men exerted themselves to manage the horse, till the front of the gig gave way, when they were both thrown out with considerable violence. Mr Huddlestone had his skull shockingly fractured, and is now lying in a dangerous state at Cook's House, near Troutbeck Bridge. His companion was only slightly injured in one arm, and is not considered in any danger.'* [302]

In 1857 the Ambleside Turnpike Trust made long overdue improvements to the road:

> *'The declivities between the Post Office and Oakland Gate were removed, very greatly to the comfort of travellers, and to the opening out of the view towards the Lake. An alteration is now in course of being made ––– on the road from Cook's House to Oakland, for about a third of a mile, which consists in widening, straightening and levelling the road. An avoidance of the sharp corner near the latter point would be a still further improvement; but difficulties exist in the way of arrangement with some of the neighbouring landowners, which it has not been found possible to overcome without litigation and expense. The outlay of the improvements now in course of progress will be about £400.*
>
> *Another year, we understand, it is in contemplation to widen the road beyond Cook's House, towards Troutbeck Bridge, and to form a parapet walk to join with that at Troutbeck Bridge. And when this is accomplished, there will be a footpath for pedestrians from Birthwaite all the way to Low Wood.'* [303]

3.29 Windermere Railway Station

We will finish this circuit of the village at the Station – the second and more durable terminus built on the site, the first having been spectacularly consumed by fire.

On a fine but windy Sunday morning in May of 1853 part of the first station, a timber construction, caught fire disastrously. Much of the populace was attending morning service in St Mary's Church when the alarm was raised. Revd Addison immediately *'advised the male portion of the congregation to hasten to assist'*. One was sent to Kendal on horseback to request assistance from the fire engine, while the others did whatever they could with buckets and ladders. But the intensity of the conflagration was too much for them, with burning brands flying far and wide in the wind. Great damage was done to William Harrison's joinery shop, Mitchell's smithy, and Sheldon's stables; but thankfully the horses were released and led to safety before they could be panicked.

A colourful theory was advanced in the *Westmorland Gazette*, claiming that wood shavings in the joiner's workshop of Mr Harrison may have been ignited by sparks blown in the breeze, after being raked from a locomotive boiler. He had a large quantity of good quality timber stored in the workshop, and completed work for nearby houses.[304]

> *'Next to the part occupied by Mr Harrison was a blacksmith's shop, let to Mr Mitchell, and at the north end were the stables of Mr Sheldon, coach proprietor.*
>
> *The fire was no sooner discovered than it became manifest that nothing could save the carpentry premises where it was first observed. The combustible nature of the interior, and the wind which prevailed, made it evident that this part of the building was doomed, and the efforts therefore of all were mainly directed towards saving the station side ––– by cutting away the timbers and throwing water in at the junction of the roofs.*
>
> *In the meantime a special messenger was despatched to Kendal for the fire-engines,[305] which were on the spot as soon as the horses could convey them, the steam not being ready at the time to afford the facility of a railway transit. The county police superintendent was soon on the spot and shortly afterwards an engine was despatched from Kendal ––– which turned out to be of great assistance, for the supply of water being scanty at Birthwaite, a supply was continually fetched by the engine in a waggon, full of large tubs, from the watering depot at Black Moss.*
>
> *By these means ––– the fire was effectually kept from extending to the other parts of the building, and Mr Sheldon's stables ––– were saved. But the carpenter's shop, the blacksmith's shop, and the room where furniture was deposited were reduced to a mere shell ––-. Burning embers were blown to a great distance, to the danger of houses in the neighbourhood. In one case a burning fragment was blown through the chamber window of a house ––– at the next house a fire brand was flung by the wind 100 or 150 yards from the station to the threshold of a shop door, where it burnt its way into the shop, charring the floor and the counter, and would have set the entire row of houses[306] on fire if it had not been extinguished.'[307]*

The village at that time did not have a fire service of any sort, the nearest fire brigade being in Kendal. It took two hours for three engines to arrive, one by rail, having been delayed while steam was raised in the locomotive boiler. The only water available in Birthwaite came from streams, hand-pumps and wells; and the month of May normally being the driest season of the year, the supply was low. Consequently the locomotive was employed in conveying water in hogsheads and puncheons[308] from the Railway's water storage tank at Black Moss, 1½ miles down the line towards Kendal. It was to be 15 years before a mains water supply reached Windermere village, and even then the head of water was insufficient for a supply at the Station.

Workshops along the east side of the Station building were almost completely gutted, although the main station building and the stables were saved by the efforts of the fire fighters. William Harrison suffered a considerable loss for which he was not insured, including all his valuable tools and those of his men, together with much fine timber and finished work in the workshop. The total loss, including buildings, was estimated at £1,500.[309]

3.30 Birthwaite or Windermere – What's in a Name?

In the early days there was considerable confusion and disagreement over the name of the new village. The children acquired a reputation for being rough and a little wild and the appellation 'Birthwut people' entered the common parlance in some quarters as a term of insult and contempt. In 1857, when the garden at Rydal Mount was invaded by some unruly children, the widowed Mrs Wordsworth uttered a derogatory condemnation of 'Boys from Birthwaite'. A chase was made, and embarrassingly, the centre of the party was found to be none other than the Prince of Wales !

It was not until 1860 that the name of the new village was finally settled in favour of Windermere.

For some years an undercurrent of discord surrounded the subject. In-coming new residents of the village favoured the name *Windermere*, whilst those of Bowness defiantly called it *Birthwaite*,[310] the name of the small estate around Birthwaite Hall where much of the village was starting to rise. But use of this name was considered provocative by village residents, despite several new buildings briefly having Birthwaite within their names – Birthwaite Hotel, Birthwaite Abbey, Birthwaite School, Birthwaite Lodge.

A complication arose in 1851 when the new Post Office was labelled officially as Windermere, since it served the whole district, much to the annoyance of some residents of Bowness. And the Station was published in official railway timetables as Windermere, despite its location 1½ miles from the Lake.

Ironically, both camps were comprised mainly of off-comers, speaking with self-appointed authority borne of wealth and station. The *Bownessonians* claimed that the name Windermere properly belonged to the ancient ecclesiastical parish based at St Martin's Church in Bowness, which was long established as the Parish Church of Windermere. The parish bordered much of the lake, and included Ambleside-below-Stock, Troutbeck, Applethwaite and Undermillbeck. The *Windermerians* asserted, correctly, that the whole of Windermere Lake lay within the ancient township of Applethwaite, including the infant village, and as independent residents of that township and village they were entitled to choose their own name.

Matters came to a head in the spring of 1860 when release of the first Ordnance Survey map was imminent. It emerged that following representation to the Board of Ordnance at Southampton from an unnamed person with influence in high places, the plates for the map had been altered to show *Windermere* as the name. Public meetings were held and a battle of words ensued, many of them puerile and trivial, and the ink on Kendal newsprint ran hot for many weeks.

But by the end of 1860, with the printing of the Ordnance Survey maps the will of wealthy residents of the new village prevailed, supported unanimously by traders who valued their more commercial and prestigious address. Gradually the name Birthwaite faded from official and private use, apart from some die-hards at Bowness.

Windermere it was, and Windermere it has remained.

Such was the calibre of wealthy people attracted to the new village of Windermere from its earliest days. By 1860 most of their grand houses had been built, spread mainly along the Kendal-to-Ambleside turnpike road between the Station and Cook's Corner. In the next two chapters we will tighten our route to explore the development of the centre of the village, and the arrival of the working and business people.

89. View across Windermere to the Langdale Pikes (top right), by J.B. Pyne, ca.1850. [311]

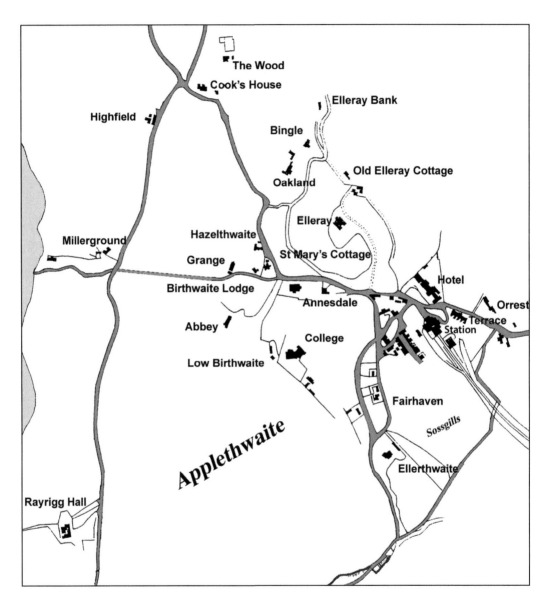

90. *As shown here, most of the villa residences scattered along the turnpike road between the Station and Cook's Corner had been built by 1860. But almost none of the tightly packed village development south of Cross Street had taken place. Fairhaven and adjacent cottages are isolated on New Street, along with Ellerthwaite on the old Bowness Road. But the grid of streets with several hundred low cost terraced houses for working people, had not yet been planned or laid out on the virgin farmland of Sossgills.*

Chapter 4 – Emerging Community

So far we have circled twice around that part of the ancient township of Applethwaite, south and west of Orrest Head, where the infant village of Windermere began to rise. During the first tour in the early 1800s we saw a quiet, tranquil and sparsely populated sylvan landscape, almost untouched by tourism, devoid of all but a handful of rural souls.

During the second tour we witnessed a gradual awakening and the opening in 1847 of a railway link from Oxenholme via Kendal to Windermere, a branch line whose primary purpose was not the usual transportation of freight, coal or ore. It was intended solely for the conveyance of passengers – tourists of every class – into the scenic beauty of central Lakeland. In the decade that followed, up to 1860, we also observed the construction of many stylish villas for the first influx of affluent off-comers; and the early arrival of a working class, many with building skills – masons, carpenters, artisans, shop keepers, labourers and domestic servants; and the marking out of the first new streets for terraced houses and shops, the genesis of a permanent village settlement.

The 1850s initially brought wealthy in-comers and their villas to a previously empty landscape. So rapid was their arrival that, perhaps surprisingly, the great rush of villa construction was almost complete by 1860, preceding much of the working village. Of their owners, attracted primarily by the sylvan beauty of the place, its soft climate and unpolluted air ––– some were transient and seasonal part-time residents. Others settled permanently around Revd Addison's little church, ending their days, content in their adopted home. Whilst others, perhaps disillusioned with the parochial isolation of the first community, moved on to more populace watering holes and warmer climes, to be replaced by successive waves of similar in-comers.

We are about to embark on a third tour during which we will circle around many of the grand houses for a third time, finishing on the Ambleside turnpike below the Station.

91. The early success of Windermere Hotel brought pressure for enlargement in 1857, a decade after its opening, to provide additional guest accommodation (on left of the tower). A large stable block for Richard Rigg's new Coach Service was also added, following his take-over of the Royal Mail contract from William Sheldon. The hotel site was perfectly placed overlooking the Kendal-to-Ambleside turnpike and the new Railway Station.

Courtesy of Kendal Local Studies Library

4.1 Hoteliers – Rigg and Bownass Family

We will start our new tour at Windermere Hotel, opposite to the Station. During the previous circuit we met Richard Rigg, proprietor of the newly built hotel, and his wife Sarah Bownass, both of them from Middleton in Lonsdale. They were the first permanent residents of the village after the opening of the railway, the genesis of a Lakeland inn-keeping dynasty. During the following two decades they built a thriving trade in what was variously known as Birthwaite Hotel, Windermere Hotel, and Rigg's Hotel. On their arrival in 1847 the couple already had two young boys, and by 1860 the family had grown steadily to seven children. Sadly, in 1861 Sarah died before her time, at the age of 43, of chronic alcoholism. Her youngest child was barely 18 months old. Five years later Richard Rigg also died a long, lingering and distressing death from kidney and liver failure, probably induced by alcohol.[312] Their children at that time ranged in age from 6 to 20 years, placing a heavy burden on the two eldest sons. As trustees of Richard Rigg's estate they were encouraged by his last will and testament

'--- to renew the lease --- of the premises wherein --- the said business may be conducted, at such rents and --- conditions as they --- may think proper', and if possible '--- to purchase the fee simple --- of the whole or any part of --- the Windermere Hotel and the outbuildings lands and grounds and premises to the same belonging --- .'

Clearly the hotel that bore the family name was not yet in Rigg ownership.

The beneficiaries of the will were all of the Rigg children in equal measure, each on attaining the age of 21 years. The two eldest sons, John (b.1846) and Thomas (b.1847), were exhorted to take over the management of the hotel. In the event, John Rigg succeeded his father as innkeeper at Windermere, and Thomas took a similar position at Grange Hotel in Grange-over-Sands.

John Rigg remained as proprietor of the Windermere establishment for a quarter of a century, during which time the business prospered and he progressively acquired ownership of part of the premises. This is revealed in evidence presented in 1887 to the Committee considering the Ambleside Railway Bill, during its unsuccessful progress through Parliament:

'Mr Rigg is the owner of a portion of the Windermere Hotel, and lessee from the London and North Western Railway Company of the remaining portion, and the occupier of the whole.'

The business of the Committee was to consider petitions for and against the proposed railway and, in particular, the objections of land and property owners along the proposed route of the railway from Windermere to Ambleside.

'The proposed railway will pass through the front garden of the hotel in a covered way, within about 10 yards of the front of the hotel, and underneath one of the coach-houses. The depth of the covered way below the ground is so slight that it is likely to be a cause both of annoyance and danger, and it will make the said garden, instead of a place of quiet retreat, practically useless to him. And the annoyance and discomfort caused by trains passing so close to the buildings will seriously depreciate the value of your said petitioner's property.' [313]

Following the retirement of John Rigg in 1891 after a very successful career at the head of the Windermere business, a third son, also named Richard Rigg (b.1854), took over as innkeeper. He relinquished his profession as alkali manufacturer[314] in St Helens[315] to succeed his elder brother as proprietor of what was now accepted as Rigg's Hotel.

Succeeding generations of the expanding Rigg and Bownass families grew in stature and accomplishment. After retiring from the Windermere Hotel, John Rigg and his cousin John Titterington Bownass, a Bowness solicitor, purchased Belsfield mansion from the estate of Henry Schneider, for conversion as a hotel. They quadrupled the size of the mansion built in 1844 for the Baroness de Sternberg, adding an extra floor to the original villa and a large new dining and bedroom wing.[316] This building has served ever since as a first class hotel in Bowness, the most impressive landmark overlooking the bay.

John Titterington Bownass was raised at the Royal Hotel in Bowness where his parents, William and Jane Bownass, were innkeepers for Thomas Ullock. Like many hotel proprietors, they also ran a farm of 300 acres at Gilpin Bridge, with upwards of 200 head of cattle. Their second son, William Titterington Bownass, briefly took over the Salutation Hotel in Ambleside before his untimely death at the age of 25.

In 1891 John Rigg purchased a block of College land on the west side of College Road, from Benjamin Irving. There he built a large residence called Applegarth, named after his grandparents' farm in Middleton. He was nationally recognised as an expert horseman, and alongside the new house he built an excellent private stable. Well into his later years he rode to hounds, both in Westmorland and in Somerset, and continued to run Rigg's Mail Coach service almost until his death at the age of 81.

During this period John Rigg carried on a very successful business as a horse dealer *'--- admitted on all hands to be the finest judge of horseflesh in the north of England.'* He owned a valuable stud of Shetland ponies, much admired in the fields and lanes around Windermere. When he died in 1927 he had out-lived five of his younger siblings, his longevity being widely attributed to lifelong abstinence from alcohol and tobacco.[317] The funeral cortège to Bowness Cemetery was said to be the longest procession of motorcars ever seen in the Lake District. The probate value of his estate was £63,702.[318]

The inn-keeping profession spread throughout the extensive Rigg family. Mary and Sarah Agnes, the two eldest daughters of the first Richard Rigg and Sarah Bownass, married brothers John Thomas Logan and William Bruce Logan. These lads were raised at the Low Wood Hotel near Ambleside where their father, Robert Bruce Logan from Scotland, was innkeeper for many years. The elder brother took over at Low Wood on his father's retirement in the 1870s; and William acquired fame as innkeeper at the new Ferry Inn from 1881, a popular venue during many Windermere Regatta seasons. Land of the Ferry Inn bordering the Lake, found favour for sporting and wrestling events; and the hotel jetty was employed by yacht owners, who entertained onlookers by swinging down the rigging to board their yachts as their hired crews sailed slowly by. The hotel's lawns and lounges provided comfortable vantage points for ladies to socialise and converse, whilst watching their men-folk race, sheltered from the Lake's fickle weather.

Jane and Lucy Alice, the two youngest daughters of Richard and Sarah Rigg, remained unmarried throughout their lives, occasionally taking overflow guests at Rock Side when Windermere Hotel was full.

92. New Ferry Inn, opened in 1881 for William Bruce Logan and his wife Sarah Rigg.

John Rigg and his wife Annie Sutton from Dalkeith had one son, a third Richard Rigg (1877-1942), a man of considerable importance far beyond Windermere. He read law at Cambridge, and was called to the Bar at the Inner Temple. In 1900, at the age of 23 he was sensationally elected as the youngest-ever Member of Parliament, taking the North Westmorland constituency, which included his grandparents' birthplace in Lonsdale, from the Tories. Perversely, after great initial promise the political career of young Richard Rigg came abruptly and prematurely to an end. Only three years after his election as a Liberal he rashly defected to the Conservative Party. The voters of Appleby and Lonsdale took hard against him, preferring the rival Liberal candidate in the resulting by-election. Rigg was inundated with abusive mail and was physically attacked on his own doorstep in Windermere, so that he and his wife fled to London on police advice.

However in 1909 and still young, Richard Rigg was appointed as High Sheriff of Westmorland, and promoted to Major as a volunteer in the Border Regiment. Thereafter he moved to London where he was elected to Westminster City Council, serving intermittently for almost 20 years. In 1939 he was honoured as Mayor of Westminster.

Such was the considerable heritage bestowed on Windermere and beyond by members of the Rigg, Bownass and Logan families, rooted in rural Lonsdale and Scotland.

93. The first Elleray mansion, built for the young John Wilson in 1808. It was largely designed by himself, conceived in the picturesque manner to blend low and unobtrusively into the landscape. The light and airy conservatory room featured floor-to-ceiling windows, with easy access to and from the garden. It was demolished in 1869 by Manchester banker A.H. Heywood, to be replaced by a much grander and more dominant pile.

© *Ian Jones*

4.2 Elleray Revisited – Arthur Henry Heywood

Moving a few steps down the turnpike road from the Station and Rigg's Hotel, we will revisit Elleray mansion, built by the young John Wilson in 1808.

Thomas De Quincy penned the following description of the view from Elleray terrace for his friend.[319]

> *'Stepping out from the very windows of the drawing-room, you find yourself on a terrace which gives you the feeling of a "specular height," such as you might expect on Ararat, or might appropriately conceive on "Athos seen from Samothrace." The whole course of a noble lake, about eleven miles long, lies subject to your view, with many of its islands, and its two opposite shores so different in character — the one stern, precipitous, and gloomy; the other (and luckily the hither one) by the mere bounty of nature and of accident — by the happy disposition of the ground*

originally, and by the fortunate equilibrium between the sylvan tracks, meandering irregularly through the whole district, and the proportion left to verdant fields and meadows wearing the character of the richest park scenery; except indeed that this character is here and there a little modified by a quiet hedge-row, or the stealing smoke which betrays the embowered cottage of a labourer. But the sublime, peculiar, and not-to-be-forgotten feature of the scene is the great system of mountains which unite about five miles off at the head of the lake to lock in and enclose this noble landscape. The several ranges of mountains which stand at various distances within six or seven miles of the little town of Ambleside, all separately various in their forms, and all eminently picturesque, when seen from Elleray, appear to blend and group as parts of one connected whole; and, when their usual drapery of clouds happens to take a fortunate arrangement, and the sunlights are properly broken and thrown from the most suitable quarter of the heavens, I cannot recollect any spectacle in England or Wales of the many hundreds I have seen, bearing a local, if not a national reputation for magnificence of prospect, which so much dilates the heart with a sense of power and aeriel sublimity as this terrace-view from Elleray.'

Following William Eastted's acquisition of Elleray in 1849 and his abortive attempt in 1855 to sell building plots for villa residences below the mansion, a wealthy lady, Miss Maria Sabine of London, leased the mansion for several years. Renting unoccupied villas in Windermere for periods of months and years was commonplace in Victorian times. She moved to Windermere to be near the northern home of her brother, Rear-Admiral Sir Thomas Sabine Paseley, Commander-in-Chief at Portsmouth Naval Dockyard. It was he who built The Craig, and then Craigfoot, above Bowness.

In March of 1856 the Admiral caused a stir on his arrival at Windermere Station, following service in the Crimean War and the siege of Sebastapol. A great throng of townspeople from Birthwaite and Bowness turned out to greet him, and his carriage was drawn from the Station to Craig Foot, not by horses but *'by 50 stout lads'*, amidst great cheering and adulation. The procession was led by the Windermere Brass Band, formed the previous year, and wearing special naval caps for the occasion. That evening an 18 gallon cask of ale was consumed by revellers in front of the Royal Hotel at Bowness.

In June of 1861 Miss Sabine died at Elleray, having lived there for almost six years, and was interred in the churchyard at nearby St Mary's. Ironically, William Eastted had previously opposed the establishment of a burial ground at the Church, believing that it would *'--- interfere with the amenity of the place'*, as seen from his proposed villa sites.

In 1865 Arthur Henry Heywood, a partner in Heywood Brothers' Bank of Manchester, spent part of the summer with his second wife and daughter at the Royal Hotel in Bowness, seeking a retirement property. They wasted no time selecting from the building sites on offer at Elleray; instead they acquired the whole estate including the mansion and Christopher North's Cottage, Professor Wilson's favourite abode. Unfortunately, one of the first actions of Mr Heywood was to order all gates and paths through the Elleray estate to be closed to public access. This proved extremely unpopular with local people and visitors alike, as it closed the customary route to Orrest Head. However in later years, when an alternative path behind Windermere Hotel was also closed, he purchased 10 acres on the summit of Orrest Head and reinstated public access through Elleray Wood to the scenic beauty spot.[320]

Confusingly, there were two Heywood banking companies, founded at different times in two great northern towns by different generations of the Heywood family. The Manchester-based bank was founded in 1788 by Benjamin Heywood, independently of the bank in Liverpool which had been founded almost 30 years earlier under the name Arthur Heywood, Sons & Co. Much of the initial wealth of the family derived from their merchant ventures in Liverpool and the three-sided slave trade. How they reconciled this bestial business with their Unitarian beliefs is difficult to discern. So successful was the original Liverpool bank that two brothers moved to Manchester a generation later. There they opened Benjamin Heywood, Sons & Co. in 1788, with assets of £10,000. The Manchester bank devolved through three generations, flourishing in the early 1800s under Sir Benjamin Heywood, MP. Possibly influenced by Wilberforce with whom he was certainly acquainted in Parliament, the attitude of the Heywood family to slavery was reversed. Sir Benjamin declared

> '--- I am especially opposed to colonial slavery, because I think it a disgrace and a curse to any nation that permits it, and I shall rejoice to give my support to any measure by which the West Indian slaves may be, with safety to themselves, emancipated.'

Sir Benjamin Heywood had a direct and indirect influence on many important institutions in Manchester, including the founding of the Mechanics Institution in 1824, and served as its President for 17 years. The Mechanics Institute building became the birthplace of the Trades Union Congress (TUC), the Co-Operative Insurance Society (CIS), and later the University of Manchester Institute of Science and Technology (UMIST).[321]

As they attained the age of 21 years four of Sir Benjamin's sons were progressively taken into the Manchester bank as partners, and following their father's retirement in 1860 the bank was re-named Heywood Brothers & Co. It was one of these wealthy partners, Arthur Henry Heywood, who purchased Elleray estate in 1865 and subsequently retired to Windermere. A decade later, in 1874 the brothers sold their Manchester banking business, with all its assets and goodwill, to the Manchester and Salford Bank for £240,000.[322]

Arthur Heywood and his new wife, Margaret Helen Foster, spent three years planning a replacement for Professor Wilson's idiosyncratic and rambling mansion, which bore so much of his character but lacked the image they desired. In 1869 Wilson's mansion was demolished and construction of a larger and more imposing residence began on the site, taking almost two years to complete. The new house was constructed of dressed local greystone at considerable cost, reportedly £13,000.[323] Set high on the hillside overlooking the Church, it presented a sombre and ponderous appearance, dominated by a heavy water tower like those at nearby Hazelthwaite, The Grange and St Mary's Abbey, all of which it overlooked. The house embodied a curious mix of styles, neither gothic nor Italianate, but undeniably impressive.

94. Arthur Henry Heywood, daughter Alice Sophia and his second wife Margaret Helen Foster, in front of John Wilson's original Elleray mansion ca.1866.

Courtesy of Elleray School

A.H. Heywood was certainly one of the wealthiest gentlemen living in the village of Windermere by 1870, equalled only by Robert Miller Somervell, his neighbour at Hazelthwaite. Positions of civic importance were quickly pressed upon him, and progressively Mr Heywood became Chairman of the Windermere Institute,[324] a member of the Vestry Committee at St Mary's Church, County Magistrate for Westmorland, governor of the Windermere Endowed Schools, member of the Burial Board, and member of the Windermere Local Board.

He was a lifelong teetotaller and a rather pious man. To foster his religious convictions he built a small assembly room at his own expense on the edge of Elleray estate, adjacent to Rigg's stables. Its use was restricted solely to meetings of a religious nature.

Arthur Heywood married twice, first to Alice Langton, daughter of the Head Clerk and Managing Director of the Manchester bank. They had one daughter in 1855 named Alice Sophia, but sadly Mrs Heywood died ten days later. In 1861 he married Margaret Helen Foster of Alderley Edge.

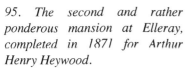

95. The second and rather ponderous mansion at Elleray, completed in 1871 for Arthur Henry Heywood.
Courtesy of Miss Joan Whitworth.

Towards the end of his life Arthur Heywood suffered from progressively debilitating health, becoming reclusive and withdrawing from all public life. He took exercise in the grounds of Elleray each day but seldom ventured beyond its gates, like his neighbour William Pollard at St Mary's Abbey. He died in 1901, two months after Queen Victoria. In his memory Mrs Heywood and Alice Sophia, now Mrs Gladstone, gifted the summit of Orrest Head to the use of the public for ever, placing it in the custody of Windermere Urban District Council

> '--- to the use of the Council, their successors and assigns for ever, --- for the purpose of public walks or pleasure grounds and as a viewpoint of Lake Windermere and the surrounding district'. [325]

Following the death of Mrs Gladstone, eleven acres of Elleray Wood were also gifted to the Urban District Council in 1943 for the same purpose, securing unimpeded public access to the summit forever. In each case the gift was covenanted with the injunction that

> '--- no person shall use any indecent or obscene language, or behave in a riotous, indecent, offensive or disorderly manner.'

Old Elleray – Christopher North's Cottage

If we leave the grounds of Elleray mansion by the back gate beside the stables, an ancient track leads north towards Cleeve How and Elleray Bank. Almost immediately on the upper side of the track stands Old Elleray Cottage, popularly known today as Christopher North's Cottage.

When A.H. Heywood arrived in Windermere part of the cottage was occupied by James Newby. For over half a century he had served as gardener, general servant, caretaker, and occasional coachman to Professor Wilson at Elleray, and then to Mr Eastted. Fittingly, and probably due to his advanced age, he was retained by the Heywoods. Before his death in 1869 and burial at nearby St Mary's churchyard, he was described by a Kendal newspaper reporter as

'—— turned 80, —— still a hale, hearty, lusty man, straight as a poplar, and broad-shouldered as an oak, with a strong, cheery voice, more like a man of 60 than 80.'

96. Alice Sophia Heywood and James Newby, gardener, servant, caretaker and coachman, outside his home, part of Christopher North's Cottage at Elleray, ca.1866.

© Ian Jones

4.3 Elleray Bank – Revisited

Continuing north along the track, a large house towers above, perched on the western slope of Orrest Head. This is Elleray Bank *(3.15)*, designed for George Godfrey Cunningham in 1855 by a young architect, Alfred Waterhouse, who later acquired great fame for his work on Manchester Town Hall and the Natural History Museum in London.

When G.G. Cunningham died in 1860 his widow, Isabella Crawford Laurie, continued to occupy the house for a further decade. Their son, George Godfrey Cunningham junior (1845-1904), read law at Oxford, and in the Scottish parlance became a *'Writer to the Signet'*,[326] being called to the bar in Edinburgh in 1871. In the same year he married Mary Louisa, daughter of Major General George Cumberland Hughes le Fleming of the Indian Army, owner of Rydal Hall. Initially they took up residence at Manor Place in Edinburgh, a fashionable district to the west of Princes Street, and adjacent to the new Cathedral Church of St Mary. They later moved to Liberton House, Dalkeith, just beyond the south-east city limits. In later life he adopted the surname spelling of *Cunninghame*.

During the 1880s and into the 1890s Elleray Bank was let to Miss Elizabeth Earle, daughter of Sir Hardman Earle, one of the merchant princes of Liverpool. Their roots stretched back several generations to the West Indies trade, when they owned plantations and slaves in Barbados, even as late as 1834, the year after the Slavery Liberation Act.

In 1897 Elleray Bank was re-occupied by the Cunninghams and became their second home, until the death at Liberton of Isabella in 1903, shortly followed a year later by her son. It was the younger G.G. Cunningham who, in 1900, published the first contemporaneous history St Mary's Church and the village of Windemere.

97. Attractive gateway to Elleray Bank, originally on the carriage drive to the summit of Orrest Head (now private). If it had been approved, the Ambleside Railway would have sliced through this gate and driveway.

4.4 Cleeve How – Sladen Brothers

Leaving Elleray Bank and descending the winding carriage drive, we pass the Bingle and Oakland again. After the departure of Robert Braithwaite and his wife from Windermere in 1859 *(3.13)*, the Bingle passed through four owners in fairly rapid succession before the arrival of the youthful Sladen brothers in 1887.

The first of these short term owners was **Thomas Toulmin**, an attorney and partner in a well known Liverpool legal practice, Toulmin & Carruthers, specialising in land and property sales. On acquiring The Bingle he purchased a parcel of adjacent land from The Wood estate to the north, which carried the covenant '--- *on which no house costing less than £600 is to be erected'*.

However the Bingle was never Mr Toulmin's principle home and the additional land was not built upon, but was taken in as garden. The Toulmins must have liked the Bingle for they adopted the name for their home in West Derby. Unfortunately Thomas Toulmin, a magistrate and Alderman of Liverpool Town Council, was indicted in 1855 along with two of his neighbours for

> '--- *suffering sewerage water to run from their respective properties over the highway at Mill Lane, so as to be a nuisance to the inhabitants.'*

The same problem was repeated three years later at Mr Toulmin's next residence in Liverpool. On a separate occasion, Alderman Toulmin was summonsed by the Liverpool Town Clerk, since

> '--- *he had neglected to pay his rates, and had gone in a thundering passion to blow them all up.'*

An unseemly and public spat ensued in the columns of the Liverpool press, during which an accusation of lying was made, and strenuously refuted by the Clerk.

For 60 years at Windermere an open drain flowed downhill from The Bingle, past Oakland, Hazelthwaite and The Grange, the home of Dr Bradley *(3.19)*. Ironically, as we already learned, this gentleman was a vociferous campaigner for deep drainage in Liverpool and in Windermere.

In November 1858 Thomas Toulmin retired from the Liverpool Council along with eleven other Aldermen. The Liverpool Mercury reported

> '--- *there has not been such an opportunity for years of clearing out in one ship and entering in one manifest such a lot of thoroughgoing partisans as these.'*

It was in the following year that Mr Toulmin acquired The Bingle in Windermere and for six years it served his retirement. But on Toulmin's death in 1866 his widow sold the property for £4,000,[327] a rather modest price for such a residence.

Another Liverpool merchant, **William Thornley**, was the next to acquire The Bingle and remained its owner until 1877 when he departed for Hampstead. His stay in Windermere was unremarkable, making very little impact on the community.

In that year **Revd John Blurton Webb** became the fourth owner of The Bingle and it was he who changed the name to Cleeve How,[328] probably after his rectory at Old Cleeve in Somerset. Webb was unmarried and lived at Cleeve How with his sister, Elizabeth Webb, until his own death in 1883. He left the property to three nephews and nieces, jointly.[329] During the hearing of the Ambleside Railway Bill in 1887 they protested that the proposed line would pass between Cleeve How and Ellery Bank, within yards of both properties, destroying them as residences. This was undoubtedly true and probably the main reason why the younger Webbs never occupied the place.

98. Cleeve How in snow ca.1892 before a billiard room was added between the tower room and the stable block on the far right.

Courtesy of Kendal Local Studies Library

Sladen Brothers

The demise of the Ambleside Railway Bill in 1887 was followed by the start of a prolonged period of settled residence and ownership at Cleeve How. The house was initially leased in that year from the executors of Revd Webb's estate by Alfred Sladen, then aged 21 and the elder of two brothers. It was subsequently sold outright to young Sladen in April 1891 and remained his home for the next half century.

Alfred Reyner Sladen and his younger brother John Mortimer Sladen had roots in three wealthy cotton families of Ashton-under-Lyne and Stalybridge – Reyner, Cheetham and Sladen. Their maternal grandfather, Alfred Reyner, died tragically in 1871 after being bitten and seriously wounded by a builder's horse. As a result, over time the brothers inherited a very considerable fortune.[330]

The boys were educated at Harrow and then at Trinity Hall, Cambridge, where Mortimer became a rowing blue in 1890. Shortly after taking up residence in Windermere they joined the Royal Windermere Yacht Club, serving the club with great distinction for most of their adult years. They achieved great success at the helm of Windermere Class yachts, which were at the peak of their performance and fame at this time. Alfred became a talented amateur yacht designer, producing around twenty of the magnificent 20-foot and 22-foot yachts. For two decades he was one of the top helmsmen in the club, winning 38 Challenge Cups and serving as Commodore in 1896 and 1907. The brothers were wealthy enough to commission a new yacht almost every year, with Mortimer usually acquiring his brother's cast-off boats of previous years – sometimes achieving greater success. He also held the post of Commodore in the turn-of-the-century year of 1900.[331]

It is said that the brothers were both engaged to the same lady at different times, and that the lady may have been Miss Catherine Tomkyns-Grafton of Fellborough on the west shore of the Lake. Like the Sladens, she was an enthusiastic sailor, and the first lady permitted by the Club to compete in amateur races. Perhaps surprisingly and unexplained, none of the three were ever married.

In 1892, following their purchase of Cleeve How the Sladens built a large extension to the house. It featured a billiard room of unconventional design, topped at second-floor level with a large lantern-like glass-sided cupola, probably to provide good overhead light for the billiard table – and possibly also for Alfred's drawing board.

99. This large lantern-like cupola at Cleeve How provided overhead light in the billiard room.

100. Completed in 1854, the impressive south front of Oakland mansion in snow, set amongst young conifers and a monkey puzzle tree. Native to South America, araucaria araucana was a popular planting in Victorian gardens from the 1850s onwards.

Courtesy of Kendal Local Studies Library

4.5 Oakland – W.F. Palmer

Stepping further down the carriage drive, close below Cleeve Howe stands the magnificent mansion of Oakland, built as the retirement residence of John Gandy, a Kendal banker and mill owner *(3.14)*. Following his death in 1859 his widow, Magdalene Agnes Gandy, remained at Oakland for several years with her niece and namesake as companion. However the house was much too large for the two of them and Mrs Gandy moved to live with her son, Revd James Hunter Gandy, in Northamptonshire until her own death a decade later.

The 1870s saw a succession of short term tenants at Oakland until the arrival of William Frederic Palmer, the next owner. Palmer sprang from a Staffordshire family engaged in building and architecture. But in 1842 he broke from the family business, taking a junior post with Platt Brothers & Co. of Oldham, a firm of iron manufacturers, machine makers and colliery owners. He began as cashier and through time rose to the position of director and finally Vice-Chairman of the company. Under him, the commercial side of the business grew rapidly until they became the largest manufacturer of textile machinery in the world. At its peak in the 1890s Platt Brothers employed 15,000 people in Oldham.

101. William Frederic Palmer with his four daughters (right rear) and four grandchildren, at Oakland in the early 1880s. The lady with hat, seated on the left, is probably his second wife, Alice McMullin, born in India —– and younger than three of her step-daughters.

Courtesy of Kendal Local Studies Library

William Palmer and his first wife, Frances Brownson of Salford, had four daughters. Following her death he remarried in 1881 to a much younger lady, Alice McMullin, who was born in Bengal, daughter of General J.R. McMullin of the Indian Army. They continued to live at Higher Broughton, Oldham, using Oakland as a weekend retreat. W.F. Palmer died in 1894 after more than 50 years' service with Platt Brothers, leaving a considerable fortune of £90,000.[332] His young widow moved initially to Croydon, but returned to Windermere in the early 1900s, living at nearby Inglegarth on the opposite side of the Ambleside Road, for the next thirty years.

102. *The pretty villa, Ingle Garth, built for the Misses Cheetham.*

Kendal Local Studies Library

4.6 Inglegarth

Leaving the carriage drive of Oakland where it joins the Ambleside turnpike, a few steps north there stands a rather pretty house built in a half-timbered Cheshire style for the Misses Cheetham in the 1890s. This is Inglegarth.

Mabel, Katherine and Clara Cheetham were cousins of the Sladen brothers of nearby Cleeve How. And like the Sladens, they inherited a large fortune from their grandfather, Alfred Reyner. After 1900 they gravitated from Inglegarth to St Mary's Abbey, having inherited a further part of his fortune via their mother, Jane (Reyner) Cheetham.

4.7 The Wood – G.B. Crewdson

Continuing north on the Ambleside turnpike, The Wood can be seen set back on the right above the road, followed by Winlass Beck, immediately before Cook's Corner, the intersection of the turnpike with the Low Bowness and Troutbeck Road.

When we last visited The Wood *(3.21)*, Miss Jane Yates, the benefactor of St Mary's Church and school, had died and in 1863 Mrs Pennington, at that time living in Sedbergh, advertised the property to let. A very suitable tenant emerged, a Kendal banker named George Braithwaite Crewdson, who was already renting one of the gothic houses at The Terrace above the Station.

103. George Braithwaite Crewdson was a pillar of the Kendal business community. As a partner in the Wakefield Crewdson Bank, he was one of the first eight stake holders in that bank; a director of the Kendal & Windermere Railway; and Mayor of Kendal in 1849.
With kind permission of Kendal Town Council

George Braithwaite Crewdson, JP

For several generations the Crewdson family had been deeply immersed in the trade and commerce of Kendal, and had intermarried with other Quaker families in the town, notably Braithwaite and Wilson. Although G.B. Crewdson (1800 –1876) was born into this non-conformist tradition, and married Eleanor Fox of Perran near Falmouth, he was one of many younger members who left the Society of Friends around 1840 and crossed to the Church of England.

At Birthwaite his family frequently used one of the houses in The Terrace as a weekend retreat from Kendal, following their completion in 1854 for the Railway Company, of which he was a director. He may have been the first businessman to commute regularly by rail, to and from Kendal and his office in Highgate. Like Miss Jane Yates, he supported the public acquisition of St Mary's Church and Birthwaite School from their founder, and like her he made a substantial donation to the appeal fund. Following consecration of the church and churchyard in 1856, Mr Crewdson took charge of the parish finances. He also served three times as churchwarden. His younger sons, George and Henry, were pupils at St Mary's College, which was by then in the ownership of George Hale Puckle and Benjamin Atkinson Irving.

Following the death of Miss Yates in 1862 G.B. Crewdson moved his family to The Wood, with its more commodious accommodation, continuing to lease the house for almost 30 years. Mr Crewdson died in 1876, survived by his widow Ellen until her own death in 1890. Both were interred in nearby St Mary's churchyard. Fittingly, three years later their middle son, George Crewdson, returned to the village of Windermere as incumbent of St Mary's Church, a fitting compliment to Revd Addison's social engineering plan.

The Wood remained in unbroken ownership of successive generations of Penningtons until 1925, eighty years after its initial acquisition by James Pennington.

4.8 Winlass Beck, revisited

Peter Kennedy left Winlass Beck[333] in 1863, shortly before his wife's untimely death in Heidelberg *(3.22)*. Over four days in March, the complete contents of Winlass Beck were sold by public auction at the house. Comparing a selection of items from this sale with the historic inventory of James Robinson's possessions at Cook's House in 1719 *(2.4)*, the new-found wealth of Windermere in-comers 150 years later is huge[334]

- *collection of oil paintings, some by Brueghel and Canaletti;*
- *foreign painted glass transparencies;*
- *busts of Michael Angelo and Raphael;*
- *grand piano forte, by Collard & Collard;*
- *furniture by Messrs Gillow of Lancaster; and Jackson & Graham of London;*
- *noble and lofty mahogany four-pillared bedsteads, upholstered in French chintz;*
- *family pleasure boat;*
- *double-seated Brougham carriage, by Holmes of Derby & London; painted brown, black and orange fine-lined; complete with silver mounted lamps; trimmed with embossed blue French silk; and crimson French silk curtains;*
- *Dublin jaunting car, painted royal blue, black, and white fine-lined;*
- *smelting furnace and gas apparatus; double-barrelled fowling piece.*

The new owner of Winlass Beck was Mrs Catherine Jeffray, widow of a Glasgow-born minister, the Reverend Lockhart William Jeffray, who had been rector of Aldford in Cheshire. She was a daughter of Thomas Miller of Preston, senior partner and founder of the vast cotton empire of Horrockses, Miller & Company. With her ecclesiastical connection and personal wealth, Mrs Jeffray possessed all the right credentials sought by Revd Addison for residents of his village community.

In 1867 her only daughter, Katherine, married a young Scottish-born doctor named Archibald Hamilton, newly arrived in Windermere. He set up practice at Oakthorpe in the centre of the village *(6.5)*, where he served as the highly esteemed village doctor for almost 40 years.

Around 1880 Mrs Jeffray moved to The Haigh, a large house opposite Oakthorpe, to be closer to her daughter and the doctor. Winlass Beck changed hands again when Maria Taylor, widow of Samuel Taylor JP DL, of Ibbotsholme at Troutbeck Bridge, acquired the villa. It was Samuel Taylor's father who had so strongly supported the rescue of St Mary's Church in 1855, and its purchase by public subscription. Winlass Beck remained in Mrs Taylor's hands for the next 40 years.

104. The Priory is an exuberant architectural flourish, a statement of considerable wealth. Built for William Carver in 1860 as a summer residence for his wife, it overlooks the Lake from a magnificent elevated site between Highfield and Cook's Corner. The mansion presents a dramatic fairytale appearance on one of the finest sites in Windermere.

© Ian Jones

4.9 The Priory – Carver Family

Leaving Winlass Beck and turning left at Cook's Corner towards Bowness, almost immediately on the right stands a dramatic new mansion, grandly named The Priory.[335] It was built in a flamboyantly gothic style in 1860 for William Carver as a summer residence for his wife. It enjoys a spectacular panorama of the northern reach of the Lake, the western fells and the Langdale Pikes. Like several large residences built in the early years of the village, it features a tower probably for water storage. This was supplied from a small private reservoir located beside the road to Troutbeck, on a parcel of land bought from Mrs Pennington of The Wood.[336]

William Carver was born in 1800 at Hipperholme near Halifax, into a family that for generations past had worked as packhorse carriers. As a boy, William often accompanied his father on horseback, taking a great interest in their packhorse and carrier business from an early age. With the introduction of canals in the north of England the Carvers expanded their business, and at the age of 18, William took over management of their Manchester stable and warehouse. In 1822 they merged with another carrier to form a partnership of Carver, Scott & Company, expanding into wagon and canal boat transport between all the major towns in the north of England. The advent of the railways brought further expansion, and warehousing was opened at every major station in industrial Yorkshire and Lancashire. Altogether they had stabling for 2,000 horses and Carver was now the largest carrier business in the north.

105. William Carver
Courtesy of Kendal Local Studies Library

In 1822 William Carver married Elizabeth Airey from Ravenstonedale, a lady raised in the non-conformist Congregational tradition, which governed much of their future lives.

They lived initially at Mount Clifton in Old Trafford, where they had five children. The office in Portland Street was ideally located close to the intersection of all major land and water arteries of trade, the canal network linking Leeds and Liverpool with Manchester, and the Liverpool & Manchester Railway. It could not have been better placed.

By 1860 the Carvers owned two weekend and holiday retreats, in which to escape the soot and grime of Manchester, one appropriately named Winterholme at Southport, and the other The Priory at Windermere. As the carrier and cartage business prospered the

Carvers became frequent visitors to the Windermere area where they usually attended the little Independent Chapel at Troutbeck Bridge, opened in 1858, and largely funded by their distant neighbour Robert Miller Somervell.[337]

Mrs Carver died in 1867 at Southport and William survived a further seven years. On his death at Winterholme the estate was valued at nearly £250,000.[338] With the rapidly growing population of Windermere, William Carver had recognised the need for a larger independent church to serve the growing needs of the village. He had made initial plans, but died before construction could begin. In tribute to both their parents the family engaged a young Kendal architect, fellow-Congregationalist Robert Walker, to design and build a new church in Windermere. The result was the Carver Memorial Church, situated on old Lake Road near Oldfield Farm, and completed in 1879 entirely at their own expense.

in his will William Carver bequeathed the *'business of common carrier'* to his eldest son, also named William, who was already in partnership with his father. The Priory mansion was left in trust as a residence for his youngest daughter, Mary Isabella, *'--- my daughter's settled premises'*. She also received £5,000 in cash, a considerable sum in those days. His twin sons John and Thomas Carver had previously received £15,000 to found a cotton spinning business near Stockport, at Hollins Mill in Marple. This became a successful diversification from the carrier business, the largest employer and benefactor in that part of Cheshire, where the brothers built another church.

Mary Isabella Carver continued to live both at The Priory in Windermere and at Winterholme in Southport for the rest of her life. When she died in 1906 at Southport her estate was valued at £58,919.[339]

4.10 Highfield, revisited

A few steps along the Low Bowness Road sits Highfield. When William Sheldon departed from Windermere in 1859 *(3.21)*, Highfield was purchased by **Hatton Hamer Stansfield** JP, a woollen merchant from Leeds. Stansfield was Mayor of Leeds in 1843 and extremely wealthy. In 1844 he visited a health spa in Silesia and was so impressed with its therapy that, on returning to England, with four friends he formed a company to build a similar establishment near Ilkley. It was known as the Ben Rhydding Hydropathic, and was equipped with private bathrooms for guests, a great innovation at that time. The establishment was run on strict religious lines, with scripture readings in the dining room after breakfast each morning.

But Mr Stansfield's presence at Windermere was short-lived, he died at Highfield in 1865. The house was sold by his widow to **Edward Banner**, JP, a prominent solicitor in Liverpool and President of the Liverpool Law Society. Mr Banner joined the recently founded Windermere Sailing Club,[340] probably as a social member since his name never featured in the racing results. Highfield served for 20 years as a holiday retreat for the Banners, until in 1885 the house was sold to their neighbour at The Priory, Mary Isabella Carver.

106. Edward Banner JP, a Liverpool solicitor, the owner of Highfield from 1865 to 1885.

When Miss Carver and her brothers completed construction of the Carver Memorial Church in 1880, they installed a prominent minister of the Evangelical Union from Kendal as its first incumbent. Grandly titled the **Reverend Professor William Taylor,** he was a Scot by birth who had served the non-conformist community in Kendal for over 30 years.

During that time he had often preached at the little independent chapel frequented by the Carvers, at Troutbeck Bridge, and was considered well qualified to be the first minister of the new and larger church that bore the Carver name. Mr Taylor was also known to them through his mother-in-law Mrs Sarah Cleasby, since she and Mrs Carver had been childhood friends in Ravenstonedale. Family acquaintances endured.

Following Revd Taylor's appointment to the new Windermere church in 1880 he and his family took up residence on Church Street at Orrest House, for five years. However, this address was not a prestigious residence for the incumbent of what was now the second largest church in Windermere, particularly compared with the more commodious and impressive St Mary's Vicarage. It seems that Miss Carver had high and generous purpose when she purchased Highfield, for it became the residence of the Taylor family for the next six years. In 1891 the patronage of the Carver family extended further, to the building of a fine manse alongside their Church on Lake Road, where the Taylors now took up residence.

Highfield was no longer required by Miss Carver and was sold to Kendal banker William Dillworth Crewdson.[341] He purchased the house for the use of his sister, **Frances Mary Broadrick,** who had been widowed at an early age. Her husband, Lt George Broadrick of High Wray Bank, perished in Windermere Lake when he fell through the ice in 1879, whilst crossing on foot from Wray to Low Wood.[342] She and her three sons occupied Highfield in succession for over half a century.

Tragedy continued to hang over Mrs Broadrick's family. Her second son, Richard Wilfred Broadrick, who had been a master at the prestigious Fettes College in Edinburgh, fell to his death in 1903 whilst climbing on Pinnacle Rock at Scafell. Her eldest son George Fletcher Broadrick rose to the rank of Lieutenant Colonel in the Army, but like so many men of Westmorland he fell at Gallipoli in 1915. Her third son Harry Crewdson Broadrick graduated from Trinity College, Cambridge, and became Headmaster at Orley Farm School near Harrow. He was the only Broadrick to reach his natural span, and retained Highfield as a northern home until his death in 1956. He was a dedicated church-goer, donating two panels of stained glass in the west window of St Mary's Church, and wrote a centenary history of the Church in 1948.[343]

Leaving Highfield, descend the steep hill southwards towards Bowness. At Miller Bridge turn left and climb the old packhorse trail through Rayrigg Wood back to St Mary's Church. Here, there are considerable changes to the Church and the cluster of nearby houses to see.

4.11 Evolution of St Mary's Church

When we left the Church during the previous tour, Revd Addison had departed under a financial cloud, never to return to Windermere *(3.14)*. The purchase of his Church and school by public subscription was finally complete and monies paid in January of 1856. The negotiations were managed by a committee of ratepayers and property owners on behalf of the township, headed by John Gandy of Oakland, John Lingard of Holehird, and G.H. Gardner of Ellerthwaite. The school was immediately placed under the control of a management committee, together with the restored endowment fund of £1,000 originally left in the will of John Braithwaite of Orrest Head House. The Church was conveyed to the Diocese of Carlisle, following the re-drawing of Diocesan boundaries.

An ecclesiastical district named St Mary's Applethwaite was annexed from the ancient Parish of Windermere, leaving St Martin's at Bowness as the mother church. St Mary's Church was consecrated on 8 August 1856 by Bishop Villiers of Carlisle with all due ceremony and considerable celebration – unfortunately marred by a violent thunderstorm that broke just as the service commenced. For the first time a church in Birthwaite was licensed for the conduct of baptisms, marriages and burials. Following the consecration ceremony 150 guests and ladies sat down to a cold collation served in the hall of Windermere College, with the willing consent of its new Principals, Messrs Puckle and Irving.

The burial ground was formally consecrated in better weather on the following day, after the storm had abated. Several baptisms of local children had been held back for some time so that they could take place in St Mary's, at a beautiful christening font donated by John Lingard of Holehird. Amongst these children was Mary Charlotte, the daughter of William and Charlotte Harrison, who was baptised at the age of six months.

The first incumbent of St Mary's was Revd Charles Clayton Lowndes, lecturer at St Cuthbert's in Carlisle. Like Revd Addison, he was born in Liverpool and a graduate of Brazenose College, Oxford. In 1862 the Lowndes family were the first to occupy the new Vicarage, the house previously known as Annesdale which had finally been purchased for the purpose. He served the village well for almost 18 years, but died tragically and suddenly in his study, when his head struck the fire grate following an *'apoplectic fit'*.[344] Under Mr Lowndes' quiet leadership and guidance the Church was now well established at the parochial heart of the emerging village, which Revd Addison would certainly have applauded.

Before 1880 the fabric of the building underwent four rather unsatisfactory additions and alterations, but was repeatedly found to be too small to meet the ir-repressible growth of the township population:

- John Gandy of Oakland, who had been so instrumental in managing the purchase of the Church, donated £1,000 for a new north aisle, in memory of his two sons who

- had died in the service of the Crown. The work was carried out by Abraham Pattinson before the consecration in 1856, under the direction of Joseph Crowther, architect of several neighbouring grand houses including Gandy's own Oakland mansion;

- In 1861 Crowther was again called upon to extend the nave westwards, but leaving the aisles unaltered. The visual effect was universally disliked, but funding to lengthen the aisles was not available at that time;

- In 1871 William Inman, new owner of St Mary's Abbey, donated a north transept and a more commodious vestry;

- In 1874 alterations to the west end of the nave and its window were gifted by Mr Gandy's son-in-law, Benjamin Irving, and a porch was added to the north aisle in his memory. The result was a much more satisfactory entrance from the turnpike road.

Revd Lowndes was succeeded as incumbent by the Revd Henry Ainslie, vicar of Easingwold in Yorkshire. Born in Bengal, he came from a family of considerable academic attainment, with roots at Monk Coniston, a graduate of Trinity College, Cambridge, and a man of great ability and persuasion.

In 1880 Revd Ainslie began a drive to extend the length of the aisles to equal that of the nave, and for a proper bell tower to be constructed to complete the Church. Paley & Austin of Lancaster were commissioned as architects, with Robert Atkinson of Windermere as builder. William Pollard, the next owner of St Mary's Abbey, unwittingly became the benefactor. Initially, he offered £1,000 towards the cost of alterations, on condition that a similar sum would be subscribed by parishioners. However, his contribution grew incrementally when he was persuaded to meet additional costs, to be agreed between himself and the building committee headed by the vicar. Building work began in 1881 under control of the committee, which included Dr Hamilton and the churchwardens (John Garnett, the postmaster, and George Hale Puckle, headmaster of the College). Predictably, the project grew almost out of control, with additions to the original plan of a massive central bell tower, complete with a peal of eight bells, a clock with faces on two sides of the tower, extension of the aisles to equal the length of the nave, and reconstruction of the vestry and chancel. Ultimately, most of the total cost of £6,009 was borne by Mr Pollard.

Following his death in 1892 Revd Ainslie was succeeded by Canon George Crewdson, son of G.B. Crewdson of The Wood. As a boy, he had been one of the first students to attend St Mary's College during Revd Addison's stewardship, and a perfect choice as leader for the reverential society which the founder had sought to create.

107. *St Mary's Church before addition of the bell tower. The chancel and that part of the nave under the darker coloured belong to Revd Addison's original chapel. The lighter slates on the right cover the 1861 westward extension of the nave, but the Gandy aisle nearest to the camera has not yet been lengthened. Together with the absence of the north porch and north transept, the photograph can be dated within the period 1862-1870. Revd Addison's little bell turret sits neatly atop the nave. A second gate, on the left, provides entry to Birthwaite School, just visible through the trees. Behind the Church, wisps of smoke rise from Low Birthwaite cottages.*

© Ian Jones

108. *St Mary's Church after alterations and addition of the bell tower in 1882 by Lancaster architects Paley & Austin.*

109. Annesdale, which became St Mary's Vicarage after enlargement in 1860. The south facing range, just visible on the right, and a further extension behind the original cottage, doubled the size of the living accommodation.

© *Ian Jones*

4.12 St Mary's Vicarage

When we left the Vicarage on the previous tour, the house known as Annesdale had just been purchased in 1859, with the help of a generous donation from Miss Jane Yates of The Wood *(3.9)*. The need for a vicarage close to the Church was urgent, and Annesdale was most appropriately sited, overlooking the chancel and the east window. But considerable building work was required to enlarge the house sufficiently to accommodate Revd Lowndes and his family. Mrs Lowndes had recently given birth to their seventh child, and the accommodation had to be nearly doubled in size.

Purchase of the house was being handled jointly by John Rowson Lingard of Holehird and John Gandy of Oakland when Mr Gandy suddenly died, leaving Mr Lingard as *'sole tenant'* and holder of the title to the property. Legal complications together with the necessary building work, delayed the final conveyance of the house to the Ecclesiastical Commissioners until December of 1861.

4.13 St Mary's Abbey, revisited

Miss Anne Marriott (1796 – 1879)

Return a few steps now to the bend in the turnpike road and the gate to St Mary's Abbey. This was the first mansion built in Birthwaite after the opening of the railway in 1847 *(3.1)*. Over the next half century the house was greatly extended by successive owners.

Before the ignominious departure from Windermere of Revd Addison and his family, the Abbey was leased to Miss Anne Marriott, a cotton heiress from Liverpool and generous benefactor of the Church and school. In July of 1854, while she was still a tenant, the mansion and approximately 10 acres of land were sold at auction. Reporting the auction held in Windermere Hotel, the *Kendal Mercury* revealed how anxious (and unsuccessful) Revd Addison had been to dispose of his assets for cash.[345]

> *'The only sales effected were of Lots 1 & 2 which were put up together. These consisted of St Mary's Abbey and a parcel of building ground containing altogether 9 acres, 2 roods and 27 perches. The price at which the sale took place was £4,030, exclusive of about £120 for wood and fixtures. The purchaser was understood to be R. Kershaw Lumb, Esq,[346] at present residing at Cheltenham. Miss Marriott, the present tenant, who we believe was also a bidder, has an unexpired term of three years in a lease.*
>
> *The beautiful residence of Annesdale, Lot 4, was offered first, and was bid to £1,250, but though it was subsequently declared at that sum, no sale was made. The grounds, garden and outhouses attached are about an acre.*
>
> *Lot 3, St Mary's Cottage, with about an acre of land in all, was bid to £800, but it was declared a sale at £1,200, and bought in.*
>
> *The 5th Lot was St Mary's Church and Schools. A very keen competition was anticipated for this, as various rumours were afloat of biddings from influential and determined parties; but the event proved they were nothing beyond rumours, for the offers amounted to only £1,100, while the reserve was £2,500.'[347]*

Miss Marriott continued quietly in residence at The Abbey as tenant to Richard Kershaw Lumb of Cheltenham, attended by five servants, and often companioned by her niece of the same name. In 1856 she joined her friend good Jane Yates of The Wood on the committee of six ladies assisting with management of the girls' and infants' schools. However in 1864, following the death of her friend, Miss Marriott moved to the spa town of Cheltenham to be closer to relations, where she died in 1879.

William Inman (1825-1881)

In 1864 St Mary's Abbey was acquired by William Inman, a wealthy shipping tycoon from Liverpool. He was born in Leicester, the son of Charles Inman, a successful cotton broker, Director of the Bank of Liverpool and partner in Pickford & Co. Described as a human dynamo, the young William Inman began his dynamic career as a clerk in the Liverpool office of Richardson Brothers, and by 1849 he was a partner in the business!

Inman was one of the first passenger carrying lines to serve the Atlantic run with an iron-hulled steamship driven by screw propellers (*'Inman screws'*), the *'City of Glasgow'*. Prior to 1850 ships on the Atlantic crossing were bulky timber-constructed paddle steamers, assisted by sail, all of which restricted internal carrying space. Because of their lighter and stronger iron construction, the new ships contained considerably more usable internal space. In 1852 the Inman Line pioneered the introduction of a cheap steerage class to accommodate the many migrants travelling to America, particularly the Irish escaping from famine. Inman and his wife are said to have travelled incognito on their own ships to identify potential improvements for passengers. One of their innovations was the introduction of cooked meals for all passengers. On earlier ships, passengers were required to bring their own food for the whole voyage, which often resulted in death from starvation when adverse weather extended journey times.

110. William Inman, ship owner

In 1855, at the age of 30, William Inman assumed full control of the company when his Quaker partners opposed the chartering of their ships by the French Government to carry troops to the Crimean War. This proved to be a profitable enterprise for the young owner. In 1859 he won a contract for carriage of the US Mail, and by 1865 he was operating a fleet of ships built by Tod & MacGregor of Glasgow, with speeds in excess of 13 knots from Liverpool to New York and Philadelphia. Although it continued to be popularly known as the Inman Line, the official name became the Liverpool, Philadelphia and New York Steam Ship Company. The ships were named after cities such as *'City of Glasgow'* and *'City of Manchester'*. By 1870 the Inman Line had reached its peak, with 18 ships carrying 44,000 passengers a year, mainly to New York.

111. The first mansion built in Windermere after the opening of the railway in 1847 was St Mary's Abbey. Seen here in its gothic-revival splendour ca.1865, it has been greatly extended for William Inman. Three of his twelve children are charmingly juxtaposed with the gardeners on the lawn.

While young Ernest Inman poses at golf, the gardener's apprentice learns his trade by towing the newfangled lawnmower, a task often performed by ponies in Victorian times. Sadly, Cecil Alma, right, died in 1870, and young William seated on the grass, died in 1888.

© Ian Jones

On his arrival in Windermere in 1863, with a family of twelve children and a domestic household to match, William Inman set about a substantial enlargement of St Mary's Abbey to accommodate them all, doubling the size of the mansion. However it was always their weekend home, their main residence remaining Upton Manor at Birkenhead.

From the beginning, Mr Inman participated actively in Windermere village life. He was quickly persuaded to act as President of the Institute committee; and in 1871 he funded a new north transept and vestry for St Mary's Church.

In that year he also served as Commodore of the Windermere Sailing Club, sailing an imported yacht named *American Eagle,* a yacht which never fulfilled its promise against the locally built Windermere Class of 20-foot yachts. He experimented briefly with a steel hulled yacht, constructed for him in Glasgow, a venture that brought considerable ridicule from Windermere competitors. William Inman responded by commissioning in successive years, three new yachts from the local boat-builder James Barrow of Bowness, but with little racing success.

Perhaps surprisingly, William Inman was a rather timid sailor, always accompanied by his 45-foot steam yacht *Wave Crest,* acting as rescue vessel in case of capsize. He also owned a rather novel manually propelled paddleboat, described as a *velocipede,* capable of taking up to four pedallers.

Unfortunately, sailing brought him to court when he was accused of recklessly ploughing through the *'lath'* [348] of a local fisherman on the Lake near Ambleside. Mr Inman had been at the helm and was warned of the danger by the man, but failed to steer away. In the remonstration that followed he accused the poor man of poaching, which clearly was not the case, and would not apologise. Although Inman had previously been involved in a similar incident with another fisherman, the court dismissed the case as an accident. But William Inman's standing in the community was irrevocably tarnished by the publicity.

William Pollard (1828-1893)

By 1874 the Inman family had departed from Windermere and The Abbey was now in the ownership of William Pollard from Preston. He had started from small beginnings as a clerk in the commercial department of Horrockses, Miller & Co., and rose rapidly to the position of partner[349] in the giant cotton firm, employing more than 3,500 workers.

The cotton industry in England suffered badly from recession during the American civil war. The cotton famine of the 1860s hit manufacturing throughout industrial England, with many workers being laid off in Preston, as elsewhere. Partly due to the efforts of Mr Pollard, Horrockses succeeded better than most firms in keeping some production going by means of part time working – two or three days per week was typical. However, in 1869 the meagre wages of those Preston workers who were still employed were further cut by 5%, causing great hardship. It was little consolation that employees at rival firms, locked out by their *'masters'*, became destitute and were left in a pitiful state. Wealthy residents throughout the north of England, with some compassion, held charitable events to raise funds for poor relief.

112. William Pollard in a typical Victorian studio pose, principal benefactor of St Mary's Church in 1883.
Courtesy of Geoffrey Dunlop

Against this background, at the age of 46 William Pollard was a wealthy man indeed. He began to reduce his involvement in the cotton firm following the departure of his co-partner and friend, Edward Hermon, who entered Parliament for Preston. Mr Pollard commuted briefly from Windermere to Preston by train, but by 1880 had retired completely.

His first wife had died in 1864 after giving birth to their third daughter, at a time when they were living at Avenham Tower, near the wealthy Winckley Square district of Preston. He married again in 1871 his housekeeper, Miss Ellen Hooper, the ceremony being conducted in Lancaster by her brother, Revd Richard Hooper.

William Pollard made little impression on the life of Windermere village until 1881, when St Mary's Church was extensively rebuilt, including the addition of a central bell tower and new chancel *(4.11)*. Inevitably, the initial plans grew to include a peal of eight bells, a clock, lengthening of the two side aisles, rebuilding of the vestry, relocation of the organ, and a new heating chamber. The final cost of £6,009 *(equivalent to half a million pounds today)*, was more than double the original estimate of £2,746. Yet despite this, William Pollard honoured his pledge and met the additional costs. His final contribution rose five-fold, to £4,700.

For the rest of his life he lived quietly at St Mary's Abbey, taking little part in village affairs. Following the death in 1886 of his second wife Ellen, he suffered from depression and became increasingly reclusive, seldom venturing beyond The Abbey garden. Perhaps surprisingly, both he and Ellen were interred at Jesus Church in Troutbeck instead of at St Mary's churchyard. This may be explained by the proximity of Jesus Church to The Howe, home of his second daughter, Emily. In 1886 she married Arthur Brook Dunlop, who was raised at nearby Holehird mansion.

William Pollard's eldest daughter, Elizabeth, married Francis Pierpoint Barnard, headmaster of Reading School. On her father's death in 1893 they inherited The Abbey, which had been further enlarged for Mr Pollard following his purchase in 1875.

113. The very pretty Miss Emily Pollard, daughter of William Pollard. She moved to The Howe in the Troutbeck Valley on her marriage to Arthur Dunlop in 1886.

Courtesy of Geoffrey Dunlop

114. The ornate and architecturally diverse west side of St Mary's Abbey in 1893.[350] The gothic ranges on the left were previously added for William Inman by architect Joseph Crowther. The range on the right of the picture was raised in height for William Pollard, probably in 1875. The original octagonal 'watch tower' of 1848 has observation windows at every level, and a second, higher tower, just visible behind the first, was added in 1875. The central part of the house was built on solid bedrock to support the huge weight of both towers.

Courtesy of Cumbria Archive Service, Kendal

(St Mary's Abbey was demolished in 1962 to make way for a modern housing estate)

4.14 Windermere College

Now we should take the footpath along the west side of the Church, and pass Low Birthwaite cottages to reach Windermere College.[351] By 1860 the College was well established under new ownership as a school for young gentlemen aged 10-18 years *(3.11)*.

The principal, George Hale Puckle, was a Suffolk man born into an ecclesiastical household. He purchased the College in 1855, during the winding-up of Revd Addison's affairs in the village. Mr Puckle was a graduate of St John's College, Cambridge, initially becoming a master at the Royal Institution School in Liverpool. When his father died in France in 1853 he probably inherited some wealth, enabling the purchase of St Mary's College. On his mother's side he was descended from General John Hale, who fought with Woolfe in Canada and subsequently became a Canadian politician.

The Vice-Principal in 1855, and eventual co-owner of the College, was Benjamin Atkinson Irving. Like Mr Puckle, his father was a minister of the Church of England in a rural Yorkshire parish. He graduated from Emmanuel College, Cambridge, and also taught at the Royal Institution School in Liverpool from 1851.

The two friends moved to Windermere during the spring term of 1855, taking over St Mary's College and most of the boys enrolled at that time by Revd Addison. Addison's rather exclusive aim for the College had been to attract

> '--– *the sons of clergymen chiefly, though not exclusively, –--' and to provide*
> '--– *a cheap and thorough education on sound church principles –--'*
>
> to prepare them for the cloth.

By contrast, throughout the summer of 1855 advertisements in the press announced that the newly named Windermere College under Mr Puckle and Mr Irving

> '--– *will for the future be conducted upon moderate Church of England principles, and the courses of instruction will embrace all that is essential for the Learned Professions and for Business.'*

The College was now firmly cast in a role close to that of Revd Addison's proposed Middle School, aimed at the sons of farmers and traders, a college that never properly got started.

Within weeks of the take-over an unfortunate incident occurred when some of the boys rebelled at the strict discipline imposed by Mr Puckle in order to establish his authority. A train of events began when a boy poured water over the bed of a fellow boarder, a common but silly prank. He was made to suffer for his folly when the Principal

'--- administered severe corporal punishment to the offender while in bed, which rendered his limbs perfectly stiff next morning'.[352]

So severe was the thrashing, and so unpopular with the other boys in the dormitory, that they foolishly resolved to repay the Principal by setting fire to the water closets. Luckily the wind on the night did not co-operate with the arsonists and structural damage was limited to £100. But the perpetrators were uncovered and summarily dismissed.

From that point on Mr Puckle ruled by fear at the College – and later also as County Magistrate and chair of Windermere Local Board. By contrast his deputy, Mr Irving, was much loved by the boys, who never heard him utter a harsh word.

At this time, apart from the Church the village had no building large enough to seat any kind of meeting of more than a handful of people. In a bid to improve community relations the College premises were loaned for approved events. On Easter Monday in 1856 the children of the neighbouring Birthwaite School enjoyed a feast in the College, generously provided by Mrs Rigg of Windermere Hotel. This was followed by a very popular magic lantern show for the children and their parents, provided by Mr Whitwell, owner of the Kendal Brewery. An expert commentary was provided by Mr Irving, describing scenes of foreign lands and places never before perceived by the audience. This meeting became the genesis of the Windermere Mutual Improvement Society which flourished for the next decade.

The College prize-giving, at the end of the academic summer term in 1856, marked a successful first year for the new owners. Increasing numbers of boarders were living-in, several day boys attended from nearby communities, and others travelled free of charge from Kendal by train due to the generosity of the railway directors. By 1861 Windermere College had over 100 boarders in the charge of six masters, supported by ten domestic staff. Some of these lads came from as far afield as India, America and the Tonga Islands, as well as from many parts of Britain and Ireland.

The summer of 1856 also saw the continuation of regular cricket matches on the College playing field, sport which had commenced under Revd Addison's patronage. The College was large enough to field two elevens, with Mr Irving and Mr Puckle often joining in. There were regular matches against schools from Sedbergh, Kendal, Appleby and Carlisle; and closer to home, the Birthwaite Cricket Club. Those who scored most runs were often the boys and not the masters.

In 1867 an extremely sad incident occurred when a young village lad, Thomas Christopherson, died of an injury to the head as a result of being struck by a marble from a catapult. He was an ordinary boy of five years, playing innocently with his younger brother in the Bowness Road at Ellerthwaite, when they became targets. It was several weeks later that young Thomas died.

The coroner's inquest determined that two boys from the College had fired at children near Ellerthwaite on several occasions, despite one of the boys having previously been reprimanded by the headmaster and his catapult confiscated. Unfortunately the jury could not agree on whether death was accidental or manslaughter, and the magistrates' court subsequently dismissed the case somewhat peremptorily, on the grounds that the evidence was '--- *very weak and contradictory*'.

115. George Hale Puckle

By 1873 Mr Puckle had retired from teaching to devote his time to public duty as local and county magistrate for Westmorland, and Deputy Chairman of the Quarter Sessions (1884-1893). He also served as chairman of the Windermere Local Board from its inception in 1866, and the Urban District Council when it took over in 1895.

For recreation G.H. Puckle sailed a 19-foot yacht named *Mayflower*. He was a founder member of the Windermere Sailing Club in 1860, which eventually gained the title of Royal Windermere Yacht Club. Mr Puckle won the Challenge Cup in two successive years, giving him outright ownership of the handsome trophy.

Benjamin Irving was now elevated to Principal and owner of Windermere College, in sole charge from 1873, with approximately 100 boys. In addition to the Principal, there were a dozen servants including a groom, and the teaching staff were sufficiently numerous to field a cricket team.

Mr Irving was a knowledgeable geographer who published several books specializing in the Indian Empire, and a teaching atlas, '*An Atlas of Modern Geography for the use of Windermere College*'.

In 1861 he married Mary, a daughter of the late John Gandy of nearby Oakland. Like his colleague, Mr Irving served on the Windermere Local Board, and as President of Windermere Young Men's Mutual Improvement Society. Messrs Puckle and Irving clearly had a strong influence beyond the walls of the College on the people of Windermere, bringing their knowledge to bear for the benefit the working population of the village, on its civic and cultural development.

In the early 1870s around 90-100 students were enrolled as boarders at the College, ranging in age from 10 to 16 years. They came from all parts of Britain and Ireland, and several came from overseas. There were seven teaching staff, approximately 12 maids and domestic servants, and a groom.

116. Students at Windermere College, photographed around the time when Benjamin Irving became Principal in 1873. The gentleman seated in the middle is believed to be Mr Irving. Many of the boys are wearing brightly striped blazers and caps, whilst others have a less colourful uniform. The building behind this group is still known today as The Sycamores. In the background a three-storey dormitory wing of the College can be seen.

© Ian Jones

But by 1881 the number of students had diminished to 21, mainly from Ireland. The staff had also been reduced to three masters, in addition to Mr Irving, a matron, nurse and five domestic servants. Shortly after this, Benjamin Irving retired from teaching. He converted part of the buildings into five letting apartments, whilst he and Mrs Irving occupied Birthwaite House. The entrance tower of the College and an adjacent building were let to Arthur Hamilton Raikes, and the Red House[353] was built to accommodate the new headmaster, but it later served as the sanatorium for the isolation of sick pupils. This was a pleasant little villa, built in the same gothic revival style, complimenting the adjacent College buildings. Conveniently, stone for the house was quarried from a large outcrop of rock that had obstructed the College playing field for years.

In 1886 Mr Raikes took over those parts of the College known as the Tower House and End House, where he opened a preparatory school for around 20-30 boys, to prepare them for Eton and Harrow. This was a happy school, with a high reputation for outdoor pursuits as well as for academic attainment. Mrs Raikes, an Australian lady from Sydney, became matron, housekeeper and friend to the boys.

117. Members of staff from Windermere College, probably photographed in the 1880s, a cricket eleven and umpire.

Courtesy of Kendal Local Studies Library

118. The pretty little house known as The Red House. It was built ca.1890 by Mr Irving for Arthur Raikes, the in-coming headmaster of the Old College prep school, but which later served as the sanitorium. Its gothic revival style blended well with the original College buildings.

By the 1890s a cycling club had been formed at the college in which Mr and Mrs Raikes enthusiastically participated. They were equipped with penny-farthing bicycles and tricycles, with high front wheels and solid tyres. Years later Mr Raikes wrote in the school diary, known as the Red Book,

'Nearly every boy had a high machine. Our favourite race was from the Station at Windermere to the Pier in Bowness —–– that was a country road then; and the little traffic there was used to clear for us, and the people used to come out of their houses to cheer the bicycles as they passed. Fancy trying that now ! The Club would be up before me the next Monday morning and fined ten shillings a head.

We played cricket and football, and started a shooting class, a thing till then unheard of in preparatory schools; we climbed Helvellyn in the winter, and lost ourselves; we printed the Red Book; we began to take scholarships; we gave a concert in the gym, and had sports with mile races; we were a jolly lot and enjoyed life hugely. And all the while we worked hard, every minute of our school hours.'

119. Mr and Mrs Raikes (right) and boys of the Bicycle Club, pictured ca.1890 with their high 'spider bikes' and tricycles. They had solid tyres, tensioned radial spokes and front wheel diameters tailored to the inside-leg-length of the rider. The club was listed in the school prospectus, and a challenge cup was awarded annually on Sports Day. [354]

Courtesy of Kendal Local Studies Library

4.15 Church Street

Next, if we leave the College grounds by the main driveway and rejoin the Ambleside turnpike just above St Mary's Vicarage, we will find two new houses on opposite sides of the College gateway, Fountain Cottage and Annesdale.

Fountain Cottage and John Titterington

Fountain Cottage was built around 1860 as a guesthouse for John Titterington and his wife Betsy. He was a slightly eccentric character who worked initially as head waiter at the Windermere Hotel. Before 1870 he took up portrait and landscape painting, emulating a distant cousin of the same name who painted with Branwell Bronte. But with the advent of photography the fashion for portraiture as a lucrative means of making a living had receded since Daniel Gardner and George Romney were at their peak. The business of running the guesthouse was largely undertaken by Mrs Titterington, occasionally taking overflow guests from nearby Windermere Hotel.

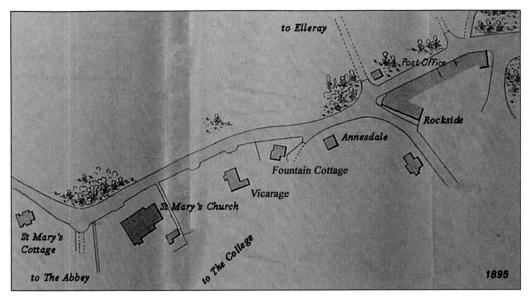

120. Part of an 1895 map by John Banks, showing well separated villas and other buildings ascending Ambleside Road and Church Street from St Mary's Church to the Post Office.[355]

Courtesy of Cumbria Archive Service, Kendal

Annesdale – Miss Preusser

A few steps up the hill towards the Station, the next property on the right is Annesdale. This small villa was built in 1861-62 by Abraham Pattinson for Anne Annette Preusser, a German lady from Leipzig, the cultural and trading capital of Saxony. Along with J.R. Bridson, a wealthy calico bleacher and printer, she introduced the beginnings of musical culture to the infant village of Windermere when they jointly formed a choral and music appreciation society.

Miss Preusser was a granddaughter of John Frederick Wehrtmann, described as *'an opulent merchant'* of Hamburg and St Petersburg, two of the principle cities of the old Hanseatic League. During the French Revolution and the Napoleonic wars many minor nobles and merchants fled to England and London, particularly from Prussia and Germany. Mr Wehrtmann brought his family to London around 1810 where they lived comfortably in fashionable Montague Place, near Hanover Square. Later, Miss Preusser's father became a merchant in Leipzig, and a Director of the Leipzig-to-Dresden Railway Company. Significantly, he was also a member of the management committee of the Leipzig Konservatorium der Musik, founded by Mendelssohn. It was here that Miss Preusser had the rare privilege of meeting and studying music under the master himself.

Anne Annette Preusser brought her passion for music to Windermere where she helped to found the choral group which met variously in Harrison's Assembly Room[356], and also at Annesdale, her home. She shared the house with her uncle, John Michael Frederick Wehrtmann, the first of the family to be born in London following their exile from Europe.

In 1869 Miss Preusser promoted a movement to help poor and destitute orphaned girls by educating them for domestic service. But finding there were no such children in Windermere, she offered to adopt a group of four such girls from Bethnal Green, London. After some initial legal complications the so-called *'boarding out'* scheme gradually gained favour and expanded. For this she received the interest and approval of Her Majesty the Queen. In 1872 she had 13 London girls in her charge, placed out in the Windermere area,[357] and at least one of these young ladies was employed by her at Annesdale a decade later.

Annette Preusser was preceded to the Windermere area by her aunt, Caroline Wehrtmann, who had married George Anthony Aufrère in Hamburg. In 1834 Abraham Pattinson built the villa of Burnside on a commanding site overlooking Bowness Bay for the Aufrères, where they settled for the next 50 years. During this time George Aufrère and J.R. Bridson co-founded the Windermere Sailing Club in 1860.[358] It was largely her aunt's presence that attracted Miss Preusser to take up residence in Windermere where she lived until 1889.

In the next Chapter we shall begin to explore the development of a working township on virgin ground below the Station, a surge of intensive building work lasting four decades up to 1900. Here, we will criss-cross the site of the working village to witness the explosion of urbanisation that produced a vibrant Victorian township, with the infrastructure ––– the essential services, boutiques, bazaars, businesses and social amenities, required to serve the rapidly expanding population, both of visitors and permanent residents.

Chapter 5 – Village Centre and Working People

During previous circuits of the village we witnessed the arrival of a community of wealthy in-comers, largely a self-made and leisured class escaping from the miasmata of the industrial north of England. Their villas, and the ecclesiastical and educational institutions which they created, were scattered in a sylvan landscape to the west of the Bowness Road from Elleray Gate, and on both sides of the Kendal-to-Ambleside turnpike road as far as Cook's Corner. By contrast, construction of the working village trailed several years behind. It rose close to the railway terminus, tightly clasped within a triangle of land, to the east of the Bowness Road, west of Orrest Lane and south of the turnpike road. But the working people who followed, contributed in their own particular way and in considerable measure to the birth and growth of the village of Windermere.

Before 1847 the existing roads in and around Birthwaite were little better than rough dirt tracks, with many rocky and awkward outcrops presenting awkward physical hazards, especially to coaches and wagons. Orrest Lane, which ran almost directly south from Orrest Head Farm to Bowness, was steep and rough. The turnpike road from Kendal to Ambleside,[359] and the Bowness Road from Elleray gate were little better, being notoriously twisty and rough. Several attempts were made over many years since 1820 to improve black-spots on the turnpike by straightening, widening and levelling rocky outcrops. The Bowness Road was renamed firstly New Street; and subsequently in three sections as Elleray Road,[360] Main Road and Ellerthwaite Road. It became the principle artery south to Bowness, joining Orrest Lane at Oldfield Bridge to become Lake Road.[361]

Three builders were responsible for most of the construction up to 1860:

- Abraham Pattinson, a master mason, was already well established in Bowness as the most important builder of his day, working with architects of the calibre of George Webster, Miles Thompson and Joseph Crowther. He built many of the larger civic buildings in the new village – Windermere Hotel, Windermere Station, St Mary's Church, Birthwaite School, St Mary's College – and several of the villas;

- William Harrison, a master joiner originally from Skelsmergh near Kendal, arrived in Birthwaite in 1849 as a vigorous and enterprising young man aged 30, having previously worked in London and Wales. He quickly established himself as a prolific builder of lower cost terraced housing, lodging houses and shops. During the next half century he built over 100 dwellings in the centre of the village;

- Richard Medcalf, a stone-mason from Fellside in Kendal, built bridges for the K&W Railway Company. In the centre of Birthwaite he built a row of working class cottages and a larger terrace on land adjacent to William Harrison's land.

As time went on, at least two other builders emerged:

- Robert Atkinson and his brothers Thomas and Matthew; initially they worked as masons for William Harrison, but branched out on their own account around 1865;

- A new generation of Pattinsons, following the death of Abraham.

5.1 Church Street and the First Shops

It was not until 1850 that the first shops and commercial premises began to appear in the village. They rose first on the south side of Church Street, a steep part of the turnpike road above Annesdale, before any new streets were cut through the empty land below the Station. These first premises were probably built by William Harrison:

- Orrest House at the top of Church Street, an attractive lodging house and china shop for Thomas and Rebecca Davies; [362]

- their grocery and provisions store next door, with living accommodation above; [363]

- the head Post Office and house for John Garnett;

- Rock Side, opposite to Elleray Gate, built in 1853 for John Taylor; it opened as a lodging house, alongside a corn and produce merchant's shop, where he also sold Peruvian guano from the back yard !

Within five years, two of these three young men had died. The third became a stalwart of village life and commerce, starting a proliferation of businesses that continued for the next half century.

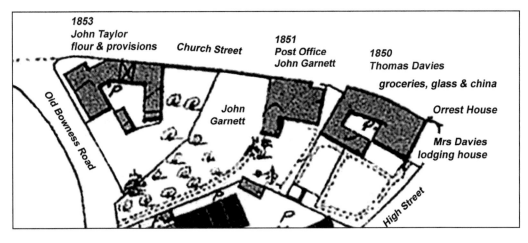

121. Early 1850s, the first shops and Post Office in Windermere were built on Church Street.

122. *Orrest House with its shrub studded garden, on the corner of High Street and Church Street, a prominent site facing the Station. Erected in 1850, it was the first commercial building in Windermere after Rigg's Hotel. The picture shows a building of good quality, made of finely cut dressed stone. For 30 years it served as a comfortable lodging house, containing nine bedrooms and four sitting rooms. Just visible on the right side is the display window of the original glass and china shop. By the date of this photograph in 1890, the whole building had been acquired by the Lancaster Bank to serve as its Windermere branch and manager's house.*[364]

Visible in the centre of the photograph are the chimneys of the four Low Terrace cottages, and the rear of Windermere Cottage, intended originally as a girls' school.

© *Ian Jones*

Orrest House was built in 1850 for Thomas and Rebecca Davies. It was a well made building, constructed from high quality dressed stone on a prominent site at the corner of Church Street and High Street. Intended as a respectable and comfortable lodging house with nine bedrooms and three sitting rooms, it faced travellers emerging from the Station entrance 50 yards away. On the Church Street side it incorporated a shop where Mrs Davies carried on her trade in china and glass. Before their marriage she had been a glass and china dealer in the Carlisle area, and possessed funds to launch their businesses in Birthwaite. They also built an adjoining provisions shop on Church Street where Thomas Davies, from Ireland, sold groceries, grain and other produce. This building had living accommodation above, where the Davies lived, and extensive warehousing behind.

When Thomas Davies dicd in 1853 at the early age of 46, he left Rebecca with three children. She bravely continued running all three businesses in Birthwaite for more than a decade, but was only moderately successful. When her family left home Mrs Davies sold up and followed them to Manchester in 1867.

123. The first shop on Church Street, built for Thomas and Rebecca Davies in 1850, adjacent to Orrest House. They traded in groceries, corn and provisions, living above the shop. (The shop frontage shown here has been considerably altered from the original, see photo 128)

The auction of her premises in 1864 took place at nearby Windermere Hotel, the notice for which reveals their considerable extent: [365]

'Lot 1. —— dwelling house called "Orrest House", containing four sitting rooms, nine bedrooms, bathroom, water closet, two kitchens, and pantry; garden and appurtenances thereunto belonging; large shop fronting the main road leading to Ambleside.

Lot 2. —— dwelling house adjoining Lot 1, containing two sitting rooms, five bedrooms, kitchen, pantry, and scullery, together with the shop fronting the main road leading to Ambleside, two large warehouses and a cottage house, packing shed, and yard.'

Orrest House was acquired by James Atkinson, a coal agent trading from a yard at the Station. His wife, Jane Atkinson, ran the lodging house for many years, a type of accommodation that was much in demand by respectable visitors. In the 1870s the china shop fronting on to Church Street was used as a part-time branch of the Bank of Kendal. This became a fulltime service in the 1880s when the whole building was acquired by the Lancaster Bank to serve as its Windermere branch and manager's house.

At the lower end of Church Street, opposite to Elleray gate, John Taylor's corn and flour business also came abruptly to a stop within a year of opening. Sadly, in 1854 he was found hanging from a tree at Millerground, by two college lads walking by the Lake.

William Sheldon was called to the scene from Highfield, who cut the body down with the help of two other men, but the poor man was already dead. An inquest conducted by the County Coroner, Richard Wilson of nearby Fairhaven, heard that John Taylor was considerably in debt to his brother for a loan, and had been served with notice of bankruptcy, causing great depression. The jury returned a verdict of temporary insanity.

John Taylor's extensive group of buildings on the corner of Church Street, including the dwelling house named Rock Side, were built to enable him to transfer his previous business from Kendal to Birthwaite. Along with additional building land, the premises were advertised for sale at Windermere Hotel in September 1854:

'--- recently erected very extensive and commodious premises at Birthwaite for the carrying on of his business on an extensive scale.
All those two newly-erected, well-finished, and very convenient dwelling houses, with the extensive warehouse, stable, hayloft, coachhouse, garden, plot of building ground, and requisite conveniences thereunto belonging, situate in Birthwaite near the terminus of the Railway, and recently erected by Mr Taylor.

Lot 1. --- A most desirable triangular plot of building ground comprising 280 square yards, with a frontage adjoining the Ambleside Road of the extent of seventeen yards.
Lot 2. --- An equally desirable plot of building ground, comprising 246 sq. yds.
Lot 3. --- the dwelling house occupied by Miss Tyson,[366] and the garden on the west and south sides thereof; also a portion of the yard comprising an area of 193 sq. yds.
Lot 4. --- the dwelling house lately occupied by Mr Taylor, the garden on the west and north sides thereof, and a portion of the yard comprising an area of 218 sq. yds. [367]
Lot 5. --- The warehouse, stable, coachhouse, necessary dunghillstead, and that portion of the yard shown upon the plan. This Lot comprises 195 sq. yds.'[368]

The property was sold, leaving his widow Mary Taylor aged 32, with little means of support. She emerged from the ordeal with a small house named Orrest Cottage, built for her father on Lot 1, between Rock Side and Mr Garnett's new printing works on Church Street. There she lived for over 40 years, taking in occasional lodgers of her own, as well as running Rock Side. Her father, John Fleming, was a retired farmer from Ecclerigg, and moved with his wife and another daughter to the adjoining house on Church Street. They were all interred at nearby St Mary's churchyard.

Rock Side, together with its warehouse, stable and gig-house, was purchased by James Fisher of Bowness, a *'proprietor of rented houses'*. He advertised the property to let, offering the opportunity for a tenant to carry on Mr Taylor's established business. This resulted in the separate parts of Rock Side and its outbuildings continuing as lodging houses, with Mrs Taylor as housekeeper. But around 1880 Rock Side was acquired by the Rigg family of Windermere Hotel, where unmarried sisters Jane and Lucy Rigg took in occasional guests well into the next century.

124. Rock Side, on the corner of Church Street and Elleray Road, as it appears today.

Shortly after the opening of the railway in 1847 a neat little house named Windermere Cottage, was constructed on the Bowness Road below Rock Side. It seems to have been built for an Ulverston solicitor and magistrate named John Cranke. After his death his widow, Margaret Cranke, bravely and quite ambitiously opened in 1855 a small day and boarding school for young ladies, offering French, German, Italian and music lessons. If this school had flourished it would have complimented the nearby Windermere College for boys. But the girls' school was short-lived when Mrs Cranke also died in 1857.

Reverting back to 1850, a swathe of empty land between the newly erected Post Office and Rock Side *(121)* was purchased by John Garnett, a prudent investment towards the future expansion of his multi-various trading activities.

125. Known as Windermere Cottage, the date stone reads 1847. This is probably the first dwelling built after the opening of the railway. To the rear (left) is a row of cottages known as Low Terrace, built by William Harrison in 1851, which fronted on to High Street. On the right is the side of Oakthorpe, a villa built around 1854 by Richard Medcalf for Mrs Marriott, a widow from Kendal.

From 1865 Oakthorpe became the residence of Dr Hamilton, Windermere's first doctor. In succession, three of his assistants later lived and practiced next door at The Cottage.

5.2 John Garnett, Entrepreneur

In 1847 coach proprietor William Sheldon had been appointed as the first Superintendent of Windermere Station, where he took over an unused building as stabling for his mail and coach services. John Garnett, a young printer and stationer from Kendal, succeeded him as Stationmaster in 1849, retaining the position until 1856.[369] In May of 1849 he was also appointed as Postmaster for Windermere,[370] a post which he held for almost 40 years until his death in 1896. For a short time he ran the businesses of Stationmaster, printer, bookseller and Postmaster from a single room at the Station, pending construction of a purpose-built Post Office on nearby Church Street. He claimed that by co-locating the Post and Stationmaster's Offices at the Station, a delay of 50 minutes was eliminated in the departure time of the mail train for Kendal. An energetic and entrepreneurial man, he lodged temporarily at Alice Howe Farm until, in 1850 he married Elizabeth Dawson, daughter of a well known Troutbeck yeoman farmer.

The first cluster of purpose-built shops in the village grew in a haphazard and untidy manner at the top of Church Street, below Windermere Hotel. They included in 1851 the new Head Post Office, serving the whole of the central portion of the Lake District. Four of these shops were dominated in succeeding years by John Garnett's many trading activities. By 1860 his letterhead proclaimed businesses as varied as printer, bookseller, stationer, publisher, estate and house agent, fire and life insurance, Postmaster at the *'head post-office and savings bank'* – and vendor of pianos and sheet music. He printed and published guide books, maps and collections of views of the Lake District, working with Harriet Martineau[371] and novelist James Payn.[372] Around 1860 John Garnett opened a chemist's shop alongside the new Post Office, together with a photographic studio offering personal portraits and prints of Lakeland scenes, many of them stereoscopic views.[373]

John Garnett and his wife initially lived over the new Post Office, but the accommodation rapidly became too small for their growing family of seven children. On the adjacent land previously purchased on Church Street they now built a substantial three storey building, appropriately named Caxton House. It housed his printing machinery on the ground floor, and more commodious living accommodation above for the growing family. Over the next 40 years Mr Garnett served as President of the Tradesmen's Association; as a member of the Windermere Local Board; and its successor, the Urban District Council; on the management committee of the parish schools; and as warden of St Mary's Church.

126. Photograph of a gentleman taken in John Garnett's studio on Church Street, ca.1870.

This may be a self-portrait of John Garnett, the photographer of many of the images in this book.
                                        © Ian Jones

H.C. Broadrick of Highfield wrote in 1900 of the man he knew:

'John Garnett was associated as no other individual could be again with every department of parochial life of Windermere. He combined in his own person the duties of postmaster, chemist and printer, carrying on his businesses in the block of buildings in Church Street above George Dobson's stores. Tall and bearded, with a somewhat grand manner, he could be a very formidable figure, especially when presiding in his official capacity at the post office. In his chemists' shop next door he unbent considerably and could be quite human. He filled the post of churchwarden no less than twenty-one times, and was people's warden from 1865 to 1884.'

127. Four architecturally diverse premises built in the 1850s for John Garnett, Windermere's entrepreneur extraordinaire. The building on the left served for 40 years as the head Post Office for Windermere, Bowness and surrounding areas, and the initial home for his family. The pretty little building in the centre was his book and stationery shop, next to ponderous chemist and druggist premises, with photographic studio above. Just visible on the far right, a three-storey building named Caxton House contained his printing workshop on the ground floor, with commodious living accommodation above.

128. Church Street Shops, ca.1890.

© *Ian Jones*

Beginning in 1850, the first shops and commercial premises in Windermere were a rather untidy hotchpotch of buildings on Church Street. Window (B) marks the second shop in the village, originally a glass and china store. Seen here about 1890, the road had not yet been sealed, and was described by Mr Garnett as being '*— frequently quite foul with equine ordure*', despite being swept four times a week. Magnification of windows and signage has revealed the identity of occupiers at this time, confirmed by Census records:

A = Bank entrance
B = Lancaster Banking Co
C = Braithwaite, general ironmonger
D = Post Office, Telegraph

E = Book shop & stationery store
F = Chemist, druggist, photographic studio
G = Caxton House, Garnett's printing works
H = George Dobson, family grocer.

By 1890 the Lancaster Bank had acquired Orrest House, to take advantage of its prominent and convenient business position at the corner of Church Street and High Street, with around 60 feet of frontage to each road. It was preceded there in the 1870s by a part-time branch of the Kendal Bank of Wakefield, Crewdson & Company. This opened in a single room on the Church Street side of the building, serving the village on three days a week. At this time, most of Orrest House continued to be run as a comfortable lodging house by Jane Atkinson, wife of a Windermere coal agent. But by the 1880s it was clear that the growing population, and associated volume of commerce, required a full time bank. The Lancaster Bank opened its Windermere branch on five days a week, with a resident manager, Milner Riley from Morecambe. The bank entrance at that time was still from the Church Street side, with the door to the manager's house on High Street, facing the garden and Station.[374]

High standards of respectability were demanded from bank staff, '--- *great store was set on the quality of the handwriting of applicants for posts'*, and clerks were required to provide a substantial fidelity bond of up to £500 to ensure their integrity. A manager was typically paid '--- *a salary of £180, coals, gas, and taxes to be paid ---'*, although the top salary could be up to £300 in a large branch.[375]

5.3 The First New Streets

Now we should take a few steps to the virgin land of Birthwaite below the Station. Here, in the period up to 1854 three new streets were marked out – Cross Street came first, followed by High Street and Victoria Street *(131)*. Due partly to the sloping and rocky terrain, they lacked the rectilinear regularity normally associated with new town planning, with the exception of Cross Street which lay below and parallel to the railway. The new street arrangement was more an accident of the lie of the land, combined with piecemeal release of building plots by the Railway Company. Limitations imposed on builders concerned minimum width criteria for roads and footpaths; prohibition of any *'inn, public house or beer house'*; nor *'any noisome or offensive trade'*. Happily, the resulting irregular plan and diverse topography of the street scene contributes to the charm of Windermere village today.

Initially, William Harrison installed a joiner's workshop in a surplus engine shed next to William Sheldon's stables at the Station, and quickly assembled a workforce of a dozen masons, carpenters and cabinetmakers. He also employed the finishing trades of plasterers, painters, glaziers, and plumbers from time to time, as and when they were needed to complete the work in hand. He built terraces of solid cottage houses on both sides of Cross Street, interspersed with workshops at the rear – a smithy, stables and even a coachbuilder's premises. The houses were quickly occupied by the first of the working people, and supporting trades – butchers, grocers, domestic servants, and shoemakers. Collectively, they provided the beginnings of service and amenity, in support of a gradually increasing population of residents and seasonal visitors.

During half a century following his arrival in Birthwaite, William Harrison was a tireless supporter of civic matters in the village which he largely created. He loaned a workshop as an Assembly Room for public meetings; was one of the first members of Windermere Local Board and of the subsequent Urban District Council; an original director of the Windermere Gas & Water Company; and of the Windermere Hydropathic Company. And for many years he served as chairman of the Lake District Association. He was a staunch supporter of St. Mary's Church, its first churchwarden after consecration in 1856, serving in the role five times; and a member of the choir as well. Following his death in 1899, and that of Charlotte his wife five years later, their family installed a fine stained glass window in the south aisle of the church in their memory.

Beginning in 1849, Cross Street was the first all-new street of terraced houses constructed in the village, housing upwards of 100 people. It was originally intended that this street would follow a level contour to link with Orrest Lane, but the intervening land was not released for building, and the street remains a cul-de-sac today.[376]

129. Neat stone-built cottages by William Harrison in Cross Street, below the Station.

William Harrison bought land on the north side of High Street in 1851, below the rear of the Post Office. Before building could commence he was required to provide one half of *'a good and proper roadway'* – the new High Street *(131)*. On the north side of the street he built a row of shops with living accommodation above. The first was Richard Middleton's fish shop; and the second served as Middleton and Willan's Refreshment Rooms, run by two widowed sisters, the families being related by marriage. Simpson Willan was a master tailor from Kendal who bought his shop from William Harrison to serve as a drapery and tailoring business. However Mr Willan died the following year and his widow opened the refreshment room and a small lodging house. Their eldest son became the parcels clerk at the Station, and another son was taken on by John Garnett to learn the business of photography, eventually taking over their Morecambe studio.[377] The last shop was occupied by Mrs Harrison for the sale of *fancy goods*, and served as their family home for over 40 years.

Behind this he built four small cottages named Low Terrace, between the rear of Windermere Cottage and back garden of Oakthorpe. These four cottages were densely populated, typically housing more than 30 people, and may have been intended for girls at Mrs Cranke's school. Three years later William Harrison bought most of the land between High Street and Victoria Street, but building work did not commence until 1859. In the fashion of the day this street was named after the much loved Queen Victoria.

130. Queen Victoria.

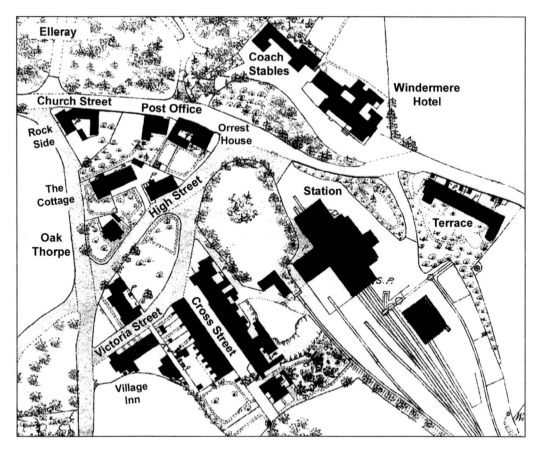

131. Three new streets laid out in the decade from 1849 to 1858 – Cross Street, High Street and Victoria Street. Church Street and the Bowness Road from Elleray gate already existed. Bowness Road was later renamed New Street; then Elleray Road at its upper end, and Main Road lower down.

Oakthorpe

In the meantime Richard Medcalf bought the remaining land on both sides of the junction of High Street and Bowness Road. There, around 1855, he built a pleasant villa of good quality, named Oakthorpe, for Mrs Margaret Marriott. She was the widow of Wilson Marriott, a prosperous Kendal apothecary. Oakthorpe was later to become the home and medical surgery for Windermere's long-serving and highly respected doctor, Archibald Hamilton.[378] Between Oakthorpe and Victoria Street, Richard Medcalf also built a terrace of houses with garden frontage, overlooking Queen's Square.

132. Oakthorpe, built ca.1855 by Richard Medcalf, displays his characteristic mosaic stonework.

The Medcalfs came from an extensive Kendal family, some of whom were stone-masons like himself, and others were linsey manufacturers. It was he who built several of the stone bridges for the K&W Railway in 1846, and the engine shed at Longpool in Kendal. As a house builder, he employed a distinctive building style in Windermere, in the form of stonework which ressembled a mosaic of vertical crazy paving. It can still be seen on on Oakthorpe, on the row of cottages on the south side of Victoria Street, and on the short row of larger dwellings overlooking Queens Square.

At the south end of Victoria Street he built the Village Inn (renamed Queen's Hotel in 1867, the year of the Queen's 30-year anniversary). The hotel was licenced to sell ale in 1851, and was the first public house in the village after Rigg's Windermere Hotel. Although there was a large brewery in Kendal, in many country inns beer was still brewed on the premises. In 1855 the Village Inn comprised cellars, a brew house, malting loft, stable and coach house. Richard Medcalf and his wife lived on the premises for sometime, and Lanty Steele, who lived next door as a lad, remembered them as innkeepers, '--- *a real hearty couple'*, often spoken of as *'--- old Dick and Jinny'*. They advertised the Inn to let in August 1855 before returning to Kendal:

> *'To be let, may be entered upon immediately, The Village Inn, situate at Birthwaite within one hundred yards of the Windermere Railway Station. The Inn comprises bar, tap room, two parlours, and large kitchen with an excellent pump, on the ground floor; on the first floor, four good bed or sitting rooms, and a large club or dining room, also a water closet; and on the second floor six most excellent bedrooms. There are also three large cellars for ale, spirits & co.; likewise brewhouse, tunning room,[379] malt loft, and a good four-stalled stable, coach house &co.'*

Clearly, the initial ban on public houses had been relaxed, and ale could be brewed openly on the premises. A new-fangled water closet was available for the convenience of customers, particularly welcome to ladies; and well-water was obtained from a hand pump in the kitchen.

133. Before returning to work in Kendal, Richard Medcalf built a short terrace of cottages in Victoria Street, just above the Village Inn, which were first occupied around 1856.

By 1859 William Harrison commenced building on the land he had previously acquired between High Street and Victoria Street. At the apex of these streets two houses were built with gothic features, echoing the style of many villas along the Ambleside Road.[380] On Victoria Street he built a terrace of small cottages, juxtaposed with those of Richard Medcalf on the opposite side. In contrast with Medcalf's random stonework, Harrison's masons employed slender rows of horizontally laid dressed stone. On the remaining south side of High Street he also built a row of substantial lodging houses.

134. Albert House, built at the top of Victoria Street in 1859 for John Airey, draper and grocer. The entrance to the shop was on the left side. The wide display window shown here seems to have been a later addition to the front of Mr Airey's original dwelling.

All the Harrison and Medcalf houses were soundly constructed of local greystone, with Lakeland slate roofs, contrasting limestone or sandstone lintels and interlocking quoins. The result produced functional homes of genuine quality, in high demand by the working population which was now occupying houses as fast as they could be built. At the rear of each terraced house there was a privy, usually with access from a back lane for the dung cart. This called inconspicuously at night, a convenience undertaken for several years by two stalwart ladies. Well water was available from 36 public pumps in the village, mostly located at the rear of houses, often uncomfortably close to the middens. Coal agent James Atkinson supplied vital fuel from a coal depot at the Station, brought in by rail for households that could afford it.

Cross Street, followed by High Street and Victoria Street, bustled with labourers, artisans and traders. They were housed in order, according to the need for building trades – masons, plasterers, joiners, labourers, carriers and railway workers came first, followed by provision merchants, grocers, butchers, bakers, shoemakers, tailors, drapers, dressmakers and laundresses – and even confectioners.

Staff for Windermere Hotel were initially accomodated within the hotel, but as business expanded they lodged increasingly with, and were recruited from, households in the village. The practice of taking in lodgers was commonplace, providing a useful supplement to the meagre income of working families. Villa Lodge at the far end of Cross Street was amongst the first of several purpose-built lodging houses.

A few ladies, widows and teenage girls took in laundry, stitching work and dressmaking. Tailors and drapers set up business, notably John Airey at Albert House, offering bespoke garments and furnishings to those who could afford them. And the first shoemaker was quickly joined by six more, a consequence of the high wear on boots and shoes resulting from a harsh combination of un-surfaced streets and Lakeland weather.

135. A row of substantial guesthouses built by William Harrison in High Street ca.1860.

Other early arrivals were blacksmiths, providing repair and farrier services for hard-worked builders' horses and their carts. Along with a wheelwright, they formed the nucleus of a cart and carriage repair business. Edward Deason, a young coach builder and harness maker from Ulverston, eventually manufactured everything from barrows and handcarts to carriages, often bespoke custom-built to order, and a unique design of horse-drawn omnibus for hotel and Station taxi services.

Close to the large Georgian mansion named Fairhaven a few scattered cottages rose along the Bowness Road, which became known as New Street around this time. A pair of quality shops, the Windermere Bazaar, sprang up in the early 1860s; and the village soon boasted the landmark luxury of a coffee shop, a portent of future tourist amenities. A new residential boulevard on St Mary's Road, College Road of today, curved westward opposite the foot of High Street, re-joining New Street below Fairhaven. A short row of three good quality houses named St Mary's Terrace was built at the south end of the road. One of these was occupied by the new incumbent of St Mary's Church, Revd Charles Lowndes, before Annesdale became the Vicarage in 1861.

136. St Mary's Terrace, built in 1855, provided a temporary residence for the incumbent of St Mary's Church, until Annesdale was enlarged to provide a Vicarage in 1861.

137. Stylish Windermere Bazaar, with substantial living accommodation above, and access through the central archway to the yard at the rear for carts and carriages.

By 1860 the original name Birthwaite had been dropped in favour of Windermere, and as we have seen, a busy village was taking shape on virgin land below the Station, with 30-40 dwellings, a dozen purpose-built shops, commercial premises, and the Village Inn. The working-age population trebled from 100 in 1851 to more than 300 within a decade, mostly aged under 50 years; and children doubled the permanent population *(Appendix 7)*. Unsurprisingly, Revd Addison's little church was full to overflowing on Sundays, and his two-roomed school with space for 90 scholars, was bursting with children requiring basic education.

It was not until 1864, more than a decade after the first three streets were first marked out, that a proper street plan for the rest of the village emerged, showing Crescent Road for the first time and an extensive grid of new streets to the east and south. During the next 40 years to the end of the century the streets of Windermere were never clear of builders' tackle.

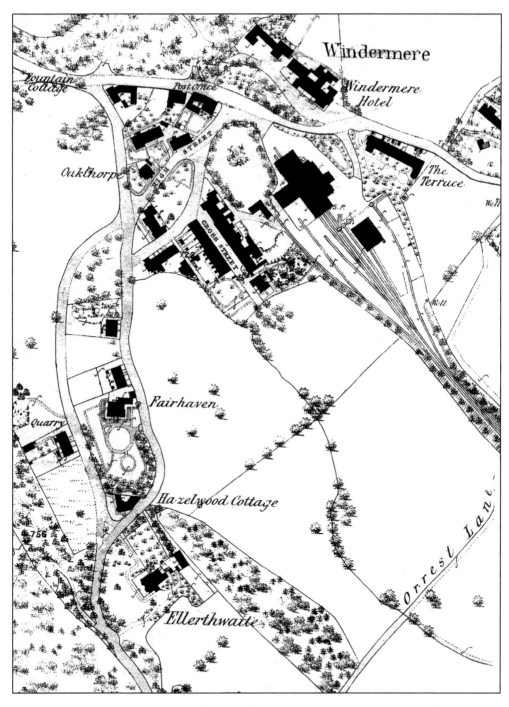

138. The initial phase of village building work, as it was completed by 1858

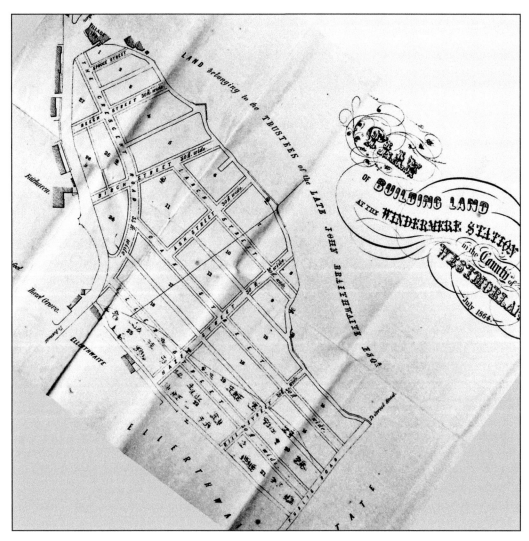

139. *The first street layout for development of the centre of Windermere village, dated 1864* [381].
Courtesy of Cumbria Archive Service, Kendal

Starting from the Village Inn (top), the street names shown running west to east are:
  Spruce Street; back lane; Beech Street; back lane; Birch Street;
  Street; Hazel Street; Gill Street; and Orrest Lane (at bottom right).
Starting at the top and running south-east are:
  an unnamed boundary lane; Larch Street; back lane; Oak Street;
  back lane; Eller Street; back lane adjacent to Ellerthwaite estate.

On the left is New Street (previously Bowness Road), and the broad curve of the new Crescent Road.

5.4 Expansion of the Working Township

Immediately after the opening of the railway, construction concentrated on the grand houses and the larger public institutions adjacent to the turnpike road. But inevitably, pressure grew for provision of domestic services, and the infrastructure of a township. As we have now seen, the first semblance of a working village began to appear around 1850 with the opening of a handful of shops and the main Post Office on Church Street. They were followed by three new streets to house the first working population, mainly on land below the Station, originally part of the Birthwaite estate.

Next we will criss-cross developments at the centre of the village, which began more than a decade later, from 1865. Much of it rose on a large 'inclosure' named Sossgills, released for building purposes by the Reverend Fletcher Fleming from his Rayrigg estate. He was incumbent firstly at Rydal from 1825 and then at Grasmere from 1857, but retired from parochial activities in 1862 due to failing eyesight, when he took up residence at Rayrigg Hall, with more time to devote to civic matters in Windermere and Bowness.

A skeletal plan dated 1864 shows a grid of streets for the centre of the village, and is probably the work of Revd Fleming's surveyor. It is the only evidence of a definitive town plan prior to the advent of Windermere Local Board in 1866. Almost 20 years elapsed before the Local Board took full responsibility for oversight of planning matters. In the interim, arbitrary restrictions imposed by landowners and their agents held sway.

Bowness Road on the west side *(not named)* became known as New Street at this time and anchors the plan in the landscape. At top-left of the map Crescent Road, Spruce, Beech, Birch, Larch, Ash and Oak Streets, fill the area south of Victoria Street as far as Ellerthwaite estate. Confusingly, several streets marked on the 1864 grid were never built, while others acquired different names from those originally shown. An unnamed lane along the eastern boundary borders the estate of the late John Braithwaite, and links the Village Inn with Orrest Lane *(bottom right)*. To the west of New Street most of the land belonged to the owners of Windermere College, Messrs Puckle and Irving.

Spruce Street and the westward extension of Birch Street were not built; Ash Street became Havelock Street; and streets shown south-west of Oak Street were replaced by a single wide boulevard adjacent to Ellerthwaite, appropriately named Broad Street. James Thompson, owner of the Ellerthwaite estate from 1859 to 1881, acquired all nine blocks.

Builders were required to adhere to the grid, particularly with regard to the width of roads and footpaths, which they had to mark out before building was permitted. There appears to have been no other formal restriction, for example to the size or style of buildings that could be erected. So it is to the great credit of builders like Harrison, Medcalf, Atkinson, and the Pattinson family, that they created attractive stone-built houses, shops and business premises, which evolved towards a recognisable Windermere style.

The most prolific early builder of lower cost housing in the village was undoubtedly William Harrison. He is said to have built more than 100 houses up to his death in 1896. While Abraham Pattinson specialised in larger villas and public buildings such as St Mary's Church, Windermere Hotel and Birthwaite College, Mr Harrison concentrated on terraced cottages for working people, lodging houses for growing numbers of tourists and temporary workers, and shops for residents and visitors. Unsurprisingly, he was described by one local resident as '--- *a pushful, energetic worker'*.

In the first phase of construction he built much of Cross Street, High Street and the north-west side of Victoria Street, on land below the rear of Church Street shops acquired from the Railway Company *(3.26)*. Charlotte Kipling, Harrison's great-granddaughter, described how

> '*He was to be responsible for providing one half of a good and sufficient roadway, 24 feet wide, the future High Street. He was forbidden to erect any Inn, Public House or Beer House on the land. He built houses in High Street, and he and his wife lived in no. 10 for the rest of their lives.*' [382]

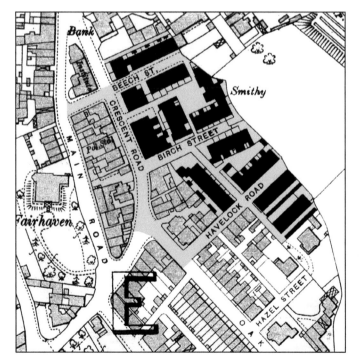

140. *In 1867 and 1871 more virgin land was purchased by William Harrison on which to build much of the new village. Buildings constructed by him are shown here in black. To finance his own building operations, plots on the island on the west side of Crescent Road were apparently sold on to the Atkinson brothers.*

141. Another neat terrace of cottages, built to a high standard in Beech Street by William Harrison around 1868. He used slender horizontal layers of dressed stone, sliding sash windows, limestone lintels and contrasting brick chimney quoins. This was a common theme for many of Harrison's early houses.

From the outset there was no shortage of purchasers for William Harrison's houses. A jeweller from Kendal invested in five cottages in Victoria Street as letting properties. In 1873 Harrison sold a shop with living accommodation above in High Street, to a tailor and draper named Simpson Willan from Kendal. Five years earlier Willan had moved from Kendal to Windermere[383] where his business prospered, attracting patronage from the *'gentry and other residents'*. Unfortunately the poor man died after only a year on High Street, leaving his widow running a guesthouse and refreshment room.

By the mid-1860s William Harrison had completed work at the top of the village and was hungry for more land on which to spread southwards. In 1867 and again in 1871 he purchased a large area of new building land from the *inclosure* known as Sossgill Field, from Revd Fleming. It covered an area extending eastwards from New Street, and included the intended streets of Crescent Road, Spruce Street, Beech Street, Birch Street, Ash Street and the north side of Oak Street.[384]

All new streets were again required to conform to prescribed width limits, and approval for design and construction of Harrison's works on this land was subject to the scrutiny of Revd Fleming's surveyor before construction could begin. Side streets were to be 30 feet wide with *parapets* 6 feet wide.[385] Main Street and the new Crescent Road were intended to be 35 feet wide with footpaths 7 feet wide on both sides, broad and stylish boulevards for shops and business premises.

'Wine, ale, beer, spirits or other intoxicating liquor' were not to be sold without the permission of Revd Fleming. This ruling possibly led to the opening of a temperance hotel on the south-west corner of Beech Street and Crescent Road. Nor was any '--- *noisome or offensive trade'* to be permitted.

It is not clear whether relaxation of the rules preceded the death of the reverend gentleman in 1876, but they did not prevent a smithy being opened in the small Derby Square between Birch Street and Ash Street. Such a smokey and noisome facility was a necessary amenity to care for the horses, carts and carriages of residents, and as temporary stabling for visitors going about their business in the village. A clogmaker in Beech Street provided clattering, but hard wearing footwear for residents.

William Harrison himself was a master joiner, but employed a number of stone-masons, including Robert Atkinson. They built to a high standard, establishing a quality for low-cost housing not previously seen. Their houses were constructed of neat horizontally laid dressed stone, flatter than that of other builders. Quoins, window reveals and chimneys usually featured sandstone or limestone, complimenting the grand houses and villas along the turnpike road.

A large number of buildings on the island created between Crescent Road and New Street, was probably the work of Robert Atkinson and his younger brothers Thomas and Matthew. They came to Windermere amongst the first wave of workers, from Satterthwaite where their father had also been a builder. Around 1865 Robert Atkinson established his own business, employing his brothers. By 1870 he was successful enough to build a fine residence for himself on College Road, with workshops behind.

Robert Atkinson won the contract in 1881 to work with prestigious Lancaster architects Paley and Austin on major alterations and additions to St Mary's Church. Sadly, he died at the comparatively early age of 53, shortly after completing this work. His was one of the last graves to be allocated before the churchyard was closed to new burials.

Following the death of their elder brother, Thomas and Matthew Atkinson continued the building business from an address in Crescent Road. Miraculously, Thomas survived three falls from churches during his career. His obituary in 1909 records that the brothers were responsible for several public buildings in Windermere

'--- amongst these being the later additions to St Mary's Church, the Carver Memorial Church and schools, and St Mary's boys' school; also Holehird [386] and many other large residences in the neighbourhood.'

Most of the shops and commercial buildings at the south end of Crescent Road, and the houses on Oak Street and Broad Street, were constructed by a younger generation of the Pattinson family, who in 1880 were embarking on their prodigious career. They were sons of builder Thomas Pattinson, a brother of Abraham who had constructed so many of the larger buildings at the inception of the village. Abraham died in 1871, also at the comparatively early age of 54, leaving no family.

His brother Thomas Pattinson took over as head of the building firm, working from their Elim Grove and Beresford Road premises in Bowness. He and four generations of Pattinsons dominated the building industry in Windermere, Bowness and Kendal for more than a century, each one specialising in his own trade.

Brothers Joseph and George Henry Pattinson were the powerhouse of building enterprise in Windermere and Bowness. Joseph Pattinson was a talented and prolific architect who studied in Carlisle before joining the family firm. From his drawing board there evolved a succession of styling features which enhanced Windermere and Bowness buildings for the next half century. In Windermere village he designed houses and shops for construction by G.H. Pattinson. Together they built most of the housing south of Oak Street, as far as Bowness, in addition to many villa residences by the Lake shore at Storrs Park after 1900. In 1894 George Henry Pattinson was elected as the first Chairman of the newly formed Windermere Urban District Council.[387]

Thomas's first son, John Allinson Pattinson, set up a plumbing and gas fitting business around 1890 with premises in Broad Street. This was an important enterprise in Windermere at a time when mains water and gas for cooking and lighting, were being installed for the first time in almost every new property. They required lead plumbing, and the fitting of baths, sinks and toilet porcelain, all of which became a significant business.

Another son, with the family name of Abraham Pattinson, set up a successful timber and builders' supply business near Kendal Station, which continued for more than a century.

5.5 More New Streets

Laying out the elegant curve of Crescent Road in 1864 opened the way for a rectilinear grid of side streets of much-needed houses for the growing population of working people. Beech Street, Birch Street (including Beaconsfield Terrace), Ash Street (Havelock Road and Rock Terrace), and the small workshop courtyard of Derby Square, were built by William Harrison on land he purchased in 1867, and completed over the next 15 years or so. He also built several larger lodging-houses and shops on the east side of Crescent Road, which was intended to be a fashionable high street for the village. These included three lodging houses – Crescent Villa, St Michael's Villa, and Central Building, part of which was quickly occupied by Thomas Henry Walton, a grocer and provision merchant. He successfully applied for a licence to sell alcohol despite the previous embargo of Revd Fleming, exposing a more relaxed attitude of the Local Board in such matters.

In 1871 William Harrison purchased all of the land south of the Institute, an island enclosed between Crescent Road and New Street. He progressively resold some of this land in plots to other builders, probably to finance his own building operations.

142. *This unusual and stylish shop at the north end of the Institute, where Crescent Road and New Street converge, was a striking design in its day and very different from the previous gothic revival theme of the grand houses. The date of 1877 on the central panel is framed by scale pans, suggesting its likely use as a chemist's shop at sometime. Adjacent panels contain the words ACME House, a device sometimes used to place a business alphabetically at the head of an address list in a trade directory. In 1880 it was occupied by the Windermere Marquee Company who offered tents of many sizes for hire; and in 1897 it served as an ironmonger's shop.*

143. *Crescent Villa, at the top of Crescent Road, was the first of three large lodging houses on the road, built around 1870. It was later acquired by the Bank of Liverpool, and replaced in 1909 by a purpose-built bank designed by architect Robert Walker.*[388]
Courtesy of Courtesy of Barclays Bank

As construction advanced southwards on Crescent Road a dispute arose regarding the finished width of the street. The roadway was found to be 20 inches narrower than required by the new model bye-laws formally adopted by the Windermere Local Board in 1878.[389] Since the street had already been laid out before the bye-laws were adopted, with a road width of 17½ feet and footpaths 7 feet wide on each side, the Board felt it could not compel a widening. It was deemed to be a matter for negotiation between Robert Atkinson, the builder on the west side of Crescent Road, and James Thompson of Ellerthwaite, the land owner on the east side in the vicinity of Oak Street. It was two years before Windermere Local Board finally agreed that the affected part of Crescent Road and the new street called Oak Street '--— *had been formed and completed in such a manner as was satisfactory to the Board'.*

No further objections were raised, and adoption of Oak Street and Crescent Road could henceforth be '--- *commenced --- as highways repairable at the expense of the public'.*

In 1879, when Church Street and Ambleside Road were *'dis-turnpiked'*, responsibility for their upkeep transferred to the Local Board. Streets in the village at that time had been surfaced with fine grit and pea-gravel, and were mostly in a very poor state of repair due to heavy rutting, pot-holes and accumulated horse droppings. Silt run-off was notorious for blocking rainwater drains, causing large puddles of backed-up and filthy water to form on the surface, to such extent that pedestrians declined to walk on some paths. The public footway from Low Birthwaite, and the footpath in front of St Mary's Church, were notoriously bad on Sundays following rain. It was thought proper that the section in front of the Church, between The Abbey gateway and the churchyard, should be properly kerbed and flagged, and that a limestone rainwater channel should be formed along the opposite side of the turnpike road. A considerable quantity of broken stone was ordered by the Local Board for dressing and rolling into the worst roads of the village, and several more footpaths were flagged belatedly. Theoretically, owners of new properties were responsible for flagging footpaths along their frontage, but many had neglected the responsibility in order to avoid the cost, and no action had so far been taken against them.

One of the first residents in Oak Street, Miss Seeley, founded Mylne Garth Boarding School at No. 33, a school for about 20 young gentlemen aged from eight to twelve years. In 1879 there were still only a couple of houses in the street, and she complained that it had never properly been levelled nor put in order by the Board, yet she was required to pay full rates. The Local Board responded peremptorily that the street was not yet their responsibility. They proceeded to issue a notice requiring owners to sewer, flag and light the street at their own expense, before its adoption would be considered by the Board.[390]

Planning applications recorded by Windermere Local Board and the Urban District Council, together with Census records, reveal that building of new shops, houses, and conversion of some existing premises, continued in the centre and south of the village for 30-40 years, until 1900 *(Appendix 8).*

144. Westbourne Terrace in Oak Street, built in 1883 by Thomas Pattinson

145. A working drawing by Joseph Pattinson, of terraced houses in Oak Street, built in 1884 by his father Thomas Pattinson.[391]

Cumbria Archive Service, Kendal

235

146. *Three stylish shops with elaborate timbered fronts, designed and built on Crescent Road in the 1890s by Pattinsons. The middle shop was a butcher, with a milliner on the right.*

147. *This terrace of shops at the south end of Crescent Road was completed in 1888, with spacious living accommodation above. It illustrates the high standard of commercial architecture and construction delivered in Windermere, helping to establish the village as a stylish Victorian township for residents and visitors alike.*

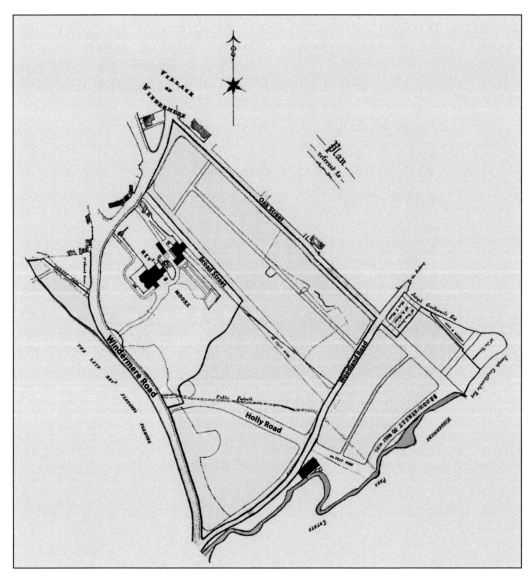

148. An 1882 plan showing 9.6 acres of building land at Ellerthwaite, south of Oak Street (top), including Broad Street (middle), Holly Road (lower-middle), and bounded by Windermere Road (left, Ellerthwaite Road today) and Woodland Road (centre-right).

Courtesy of Cumbria Archive Service, Kendal

All of this land was mortgaged by builder Robert Atkinson and others to raise £2,500.[392] However he died in December 1883. Broad Street and Holly Road are shown as boulevards 36 feet wide, intended for better quality housing. Brook Street (far right, along the beck) was not built. In 1881 Ellerthwaite House and its remaining pleasure ground were conveyed to the Reverend Bernard Moore, rector of Bayfield in Norfolk. Born at Crook, he acquired Ellerthwaite for his retirement, but died in 1884 before taking up residence.

149. *Typical of the first cottages built in Broad Street, these two are from the drawing board of Joseph Pattinson and were built by his brother George Henry Pattinson in 1887. They feature a pleasing style with six-light casement windows, splayed bays and a linking porch canopy sheltering the front doors.*

150. *As work progressed up Broad Street there was a noticeable increase in the quality of design and construction. These houses feature neat glass-sided dormer windows, under-gutter decoration, exposed rafter ends, and interesting window styles. The house on the right was the retirement home for draper John Airey. For some years Broad Street terminated here at a rock outcrop which probably provided building stone for nearby houses.*

151. *Woodland Terrace, overlooking Woodland Road and Ellerthwaite estate. Dating from 1887, this is the last group of houses built in Windermere by William Harrison before his final retirement. One of these became the retirement home of Lancelot Steele, who rose during his long career from ostler in the stables of Windermere Hotel, to manager of Rigg's Coach Service.*

152. Two attractive guesthouses on Holly Road, south-east of Ellerthwaite, built around 1895. They typify the high quality of design established before the turn of the century by Pattinsons and other builders. The detailing of windows, doorways, quoins and rooflines transformed Windermere houses from plain utilitarian boxes into 'poetry in stone'.

Main Road was extended southwards from Ellerthwaite around 1896, the extension being named logically as New Road, linking Ellerthwaite Square directly along the boundary of Rayrigg Wood to Lake Road, and ultimately to Bowness. Ordnance Survey maps reveal that construction on Ellerthwaite Road was almost complete by 1897. One of the few vacant sites was occupied by a small quarry at the junction with New Road. A planning application was lodged in October of that year for a substantial residence, named Crossways, to be built on this corner for Dr John Mason. He gradually succeeded Archibald Hamilton in the 1880s as the village doctor.

Thanks to a generous gift from William Grimble Groves of Holehird, in 1920 Crossways was acquired to become the Edith Cavell Home of Rest for Nurses.[393] In this role it provided much needed recuperation for up to 20 over-worked nurses at a time, typically for four weeks.

153. Originally known as Crossways, a large and unusual residence, built for Dr Mason in 1898. The grand observation room on the first floor has outstanding views of the Lakeland fells. In 1920 the building was acquired as the Edith Cavell Home of Rest for Nurses, the gift of William Groves of Holehird.

5.6 Township Folk

The Cross Street premises of **Edward Deason** were initially used by harness makers, wheelwrights and blacksmiths for repair and sale of second-hand and traded carriages. The business began in 1858 as a branch of the Ulverston establishment of J&E Deason. Two brothers with the same names as their fathers, James and Edward Deason, took charge of the business in Windermere until the younger James was forced to return to Ulverston around 1866 following the unexpected death of his wife.

At the age of 30, and styling himself as a master coach-builder, the remaining brother Edward Deason then took sole charge of the Windermere enterprise, employing eight men and three apprentices.

154. Edward Deason's original harness and carriage repair workshop in Cross Street, with smithy at the rear, established in 1858.

155. On Ellerthwaite Square, the attractive Rayrigg Villa was completed in 1871 for Edward Deason, alongside his carriage works (right).

Carriage manufacturing was transferred from Cross Street to new and larger premises at the south end of College Road where it emerges into Ellerthwaite Square. Bodies were fabricated in the joiners' shop on the first floor of the new workshop by craftsmen such as Thomas Christopherson and John Smeddles, who were employed in the business for over 30 years. Carriage bodies were united with their wheeled chassis and lowered laboriously down an unbelievably steep ramp at the side of the building. Painting, upholstering, trimming and fitting-out were then completed at ground level. Wheels and chassis may have been bought-in from the Deason coach works in Ulverston,[394] or from Kendal. Some completed coaches were even transported from makers in London, probably by train.

By 1871 the coach business had prospered sufficiently to enable Edward Deason, still a young man of 35, to build an impressive home named Rayrigg Villa, adjacent to the carriage works.

The Windermere business prospered from the start, and several auction sales were held in the village when upwards of 40 carriages, phaetons, gigs, carts, saddles and harnesses were offered. The streets of the village thronged with horse-drawn traffic displaying their paces, and prospective bidders milling around the auctioneer.

The following advertisement appeared in the press in June 1877:

'Windermere Carriage and Harness Manufactory, Edward Deason, Coach Builder, begs to inform the nobility and gentry of the neighbourhood that he is prepared to build landaus, broughams, and every other description of first-class carriages, in the most perfect manner and on the most reasonable terms.
Repairs quickly and neatly executed.
A quantity of new and second-hand carriages and harness on sale.
Omnibuses a speciality.'

156. An open carriage of a type that was popular with wealthy private owners and cab drivers.

Another attractive carriage fabricated by Deason in Windermere, possibly unique in its design, was a small two-horse omnibus. It was much favoured by hotels in Windermere and Bowness, to provide taxi services for visitors going to and from the Station. The cab featured a curved glass front, providing the inside passengers with a panoramic view of the scenery – which included the driver's feet and the rump of the horses. For the more adventurous travellers, a bench seat on the roof was accessed by a steep stairway from the rear footplate.

157. Popular omnibus cabs, built in Windermere by Edward Deason, pictured at the Station around 1900. In the foreground is the first streetlight in Windermere, installed in 1863. It was mounted on top of a drinking fountain in front of Rigg's Hotel, and lit by gas.[395]

Courtesy of Colin Tyson

On the whole, Windermere did not attract a wealthy merchant class of incomer. As already described, tradesmen and shopkeepers came looking for opportunities in the new village. Some of them quickly moved on or died, others prospered. One such was **Edward Speight**, born in Kendal in 1851, the son of a butcher. By 1871 he was living in Cross Street, working as assistant to butcher James West. In the following year Mr West retired, allowing the young man to take over the business in Victoria Street, supplying meat to Windermere. In the same year Edward Speight married Grace Clapham of Stybarrow Cottage, where her father had been gardener to Miss Yates of The Wood. They had nine children before Edward Speight's untimely death in 1891.

Like many butchers of the time, Mr Speight became tenant of the 40-acre Oldfield Farm where he raised sheep and cattle for slaughter at the farm, supplying fresh meat to the shop. Unfortunately, his primitive hygiene standards caused great controversy, resulting from the practice of boiling animal waste, prior to its disposal in an uncovered cesspool. Understandably, the procedure was banned by Windermere Local Board in 1880 until improvements were made. They were finally persuaded to grant him a licence to slaughter, after which the sale of meat in Windermere grew steadily, employing two assistant butchers. Edward Speight also sold collie sheepdogs, bred from prize-winning pedigree stock, and he successfully exhibited his animals at local agricultural shows.

By the 1880s the family had prospered, enabling them to move to a larger home at the top of Main Road,[396] where Mrs Speight had two servants in the house. The shop was located in separate premises next door. But once again, her husband quite inexplicably broke the rules by trying to slaughter calves and sheep in a yard behind the shop. In the face of concerted local opposition, especially from near-neighbour Dr Hamilton of the Local Board, he was prohibited from slaughtering anywhere in the village.

158. Mrs Edward Speight, the butcher's wife, née Grace Clapham of Stybarrow Cottage, mother of nine children.
Fenty Collection,
Kendal Local Studies Library

In 1890 Edward Speight gained great kudos from Windermere folk with a novel and enterprising procurement. He purchased several cattle, sheep and pigs from the Queen's Royal Farm at Windsor, to supply his Christmas trade. News of the purchase reached Her Majesty, who responded by placing a substantial order for 36 lb of best sirloin steak from one of her own animals, to be delivered to '--- *Her Majesty, Osborne, Isle of Wight'*.

Unfortunately, Mr Speight died prematurely in the following year, at the age of 40. He left a wife and nine children, the youngest of whom was less than one year old. When Mrs Speight also died before her time, the orphaned family were forced to leave Windermere to live in Blackpool, in the care of the eldest girls. At least one son, Henry Wilson Speight, emigrated to Ontario in 1905, where he worked as a plumber. He served in the Canadian Expeditionary Force during the First World War. He survived the war and returned to Canada where he died in 1959.

Chapter 6 – Infrastructure, Institutions and Services

Clearly, the services and institutions of Windermere were as new as the village itself, and this tour of the working village will not be complete without describing them. Inevitably, we will zig-zag to-and-fro in time and space again, to observe them.

The primacy of the Church of England was established by Revd Addison as progenitor of the community, even before the first house was built. Concurrently with his own mansion, his little Chapel of St Mary was the first building erected in Birthwaite after the Station and Windermere Hotel in 1847. But almost from the start its 220 seats could not accommodate the mushrooming population, leading to several structural extensions before a major rebuild in 1882 *(4.11)*.

159. Congregational Church built on Lake Road in 1880 in memory of William Carver and his wife Elizabeth. The building cost was borne by their family.

Pressure for non-conformist places of worship also grew inexorably as the population grew. In 1858 a modest little Congregational Chapel was erected at Troutbeck Bridge, just outside the township *(3.20)*;[397] and a neat little Methodist Chapel was erected in 1867 at the junction of College Road and New Street, opposite to the Queen's Hotel.[398] However, in 1880 the much larger and impressive Carver Memorial Congregational Church was built on Lake Road, joined in 1884 by St Herberts Roman Catholic Church further towards Bowness. The design of both was the work of Robert Walker, a young architect, who moved from Kendal to embark on a prolific practice in Windermere.

Finally, in 1885 St John's Church was opened, built largely at the expense of the Reverend J.M. Moss, partly to accommodate the ever rising number of residents, but also to relieve the excessive pressure on St Mary's and St Martin's during the visitor season. The site eventually agreed was nearly opposite St Herbert's, just within the township of Undermillbeck, and the architect chosen was Joseph Pattinson. The Ecclesiastical Commissioners annexed another parish from within the ancient Parish of Windermere, alongside the parish of St Mary Applethwaite which included the village of Windermere.

6.1 Windermere Mutual Improvement Society

The grandiosely named Windermere Mutual Improvement Society was the forerunner of an institute for the village. It was founded in March 1861 and met in Harrison's Assembly Room during the winter months. The high-minded aim of the Society's founders was to improve *'the moral, social and intellectual'* well-being of the people of the village and its neighbourhood, an aim that would certainly have found favour with Revd Addison. From the outset the Society was patronised by considerable numbers of people, drawn both from the gentry and from the working people, *'the aristocratic and mechanical portions of the community'*. Upwards of 60 members were enrolled within the first few months, from a resident population of under 1000 people at that time. Robert Miller Somervell of Hazelthwaite, founder of the K Shoe manufactory in Kendal, was elected as its first president, followed later by Liverpool ship-owner William Inman. The Kendal press observed pompously that *'--- the management committee was composed principally of tradesmen and respectable artisans'*.

160. Harrison's Assembly Room – served for several years as a public meeting place in the village. It was built in Victoria Street by William Harrison as a joiner's workshop, occupying the first floor above Airey's shop, but was loaned to village organisations for meetings of many kinds. The Assembly Room, with seating for 60-80 people, first opened in September 1859 with a performance by the Kendal Philharmonic Society.[399]

For almost ten years William Harrison generously allowed meetings to be held in the Assembly Room, a building which was probably intended as a workshop following extensive damage to his joiner's shop in the disastrous fire at the Station *(3.29)*. On the ground floor the new building housed John Airey's grocery shop, behind which there was a small reading room, stocked with newspapers and books donated by the more wealthy residents for enlightenment of the working people.

Through the winter months regular meetings took the form of

- penny readings[400] of poetry and prose, with selections from poets Robert Burns and Charles Mackay, often humorous and delivered in the Scottish dialect;
- musical recitals and soirées by the Windermere Choral Society and others;
- talks on physical fitness, sports, together with demonstrations of gymnastics;
- prayer meetings and bible readings;
- photographic displays, illustrated with the aid of the new-fangled magic lantern projector, an instrument which *'is adapted for the exhibition of dissolving views, and is fitted with the oxyhydrogen light,'* to show images of far off places beyond the ken of most local people; [401]
- lectures from visiting speakers and knowledgeable residents, notably Mr Irving of the College who frequently described far off lands and their peoples, including the war between the dis-united states of America;
- the most popular form of entertainment for children and adults alike, consisted of dramatic demonstrations of electrical phenomena involving high voltage discharge machines, and galvanic experiments producing electricity by chemical reaction.

In December of 1861 a celebration was held in Harrison's Assembly Room to mark the first anniversary of the founding of the Windermere Mutual Improvement Society.[402]

> *'About 200 people sat down to tea, which was provided in a sumptuous manner by the ladies of the neighbourhood, who also presided at the tables.'* [403]

Although there was a considerable element of patronage on the part of the gentry, the meetings of the Society proved so popular with ordinary folk that they frequently overflowed the assembly room, late-comers being forced to stand in the reading room below, straining to hear the occasional word.

By 1865 the pressure of numbers had grown intolerably, and William Harrison needed his premises for building operations which were about to enter a new phase. A fund for erection of a larger community hall had been started, but was still under-subscribed. In 1867 an architectural competition was held for the design of a new building capable of accommodating 500 to 600 people, as a result of which the committee initially favoured erection of a large shed, *'--- the approved plans for which are the produce of local talent'*. [404] Land opposite to the Village Inn, at the junction of Victoria Street and New Street, was offered for a nominal sum by Revd Fleming of Rayrigg. [405]

However the winning plan received lukewarm support from local people, it being held by many residents that the village deserved more attractive permanent premises. Unfortunately the harmony that characterised the early years of the Society evaporated, and views on all sides became acrimonious, preventing commencement of building work.

6.2 Windermere Institute

By 1868 meetings had been transferred briefly to St Mary's Schoolroom, a venue that was wholly unsuitable, '--- *at present there is no place whatsoever for intellectual improvement or innocent recreation.*' It was not until 1871 that the '*poke-noses*' who repeatedly thwarted development, were finally overcome, and

> '--- *plans passed into the hands of a few energetic gentlemen who resolved to float the Windermere Rooms Company (Limited)*'. [406]

Among them was the dominant and assertive secretary of the company, George Hale Puckle, previously headmaster of Windermere College, now a county magistrate and Chairman of the embryonic Windermere Local Board. The site acquired for a nominal price from Revd Fleming lay neatly sandwiched between the recently marked out Crescent Road and New Street, geographically at the heart of the new village. Erection of a large permanent structure in solid Lakeland greystone commenced, and finally on 20 December 1872

> '*the new rooms were opened --- by a grand dress concert given by the members of the Bowness Musical Association, assisted by instrumentalists from Mr Chas. Hallé's orchestra, and professional soloists, the whole being under the able conductorship of J.R. Bridson, Esq, of Belle Isle.*' [407]

Such a prestigious and well equipped institute building, with its library and reading room, was intended to further the education and civic pride of the whole community. But despite high patronage, support of the working people faded and the building eventually reverted to a casual gathering place.

161. The Windermere Institute, opened in 1872 with a grand dress concert that included part of the Hallé orchestra.

6.3 Local Government, Gas, Water and Sewerage Services

In June of 1861 a joint stock company, the Windermere District Gas & Water Works was floated to provide gas and safe drinking water to the village. The public floatation offered 1000 shares for sale at £10 each, seeking to raise capital of £10,000. The directors included property owners and men of standing from industry and commerce:

James Cropper, paper mill owner;   John Crossley, carpet manufacturer;
Thomas Ullock, hotel owner;   George Braithwaite Crewdson, banker;
Robert Pickthall, coal agent;   George Hale Puckle, headmaster;
Abraham Pattinson, builder;   James Wrigley, paper manufacturer.

Production of gas began in May of 1863 at a site on Brantfell Road in Bowness, supplying both townships. The opening of the gas works was marked by installation of the first street lighting

> '--- *two brilliant stars of gas, one in front of the Royal Hotel, Bowness, and the other in front of Rigg's Hotel, Birthwaite*.'[408]

But provision of clean piped drinking water and deep drainage for waste disposal was long delayed; nor was the want of such services unique to Windermere. The Local Government Act of 1858 was intended to encourage communities in all parts of the country to create Local Boards of Health, and empowered them to take control of sanitation matters for the benefit of local communities. They were required to regulate

> '--- *sewerage, drains*,[409] *street-cleansing, nuisances*,[410] *slaughter-houses, lodging-houses, cellar dwellings, and the supply of fresh water*'.[411]

At this time the supply of drinking water in Windermere was obtained from public hand-pumps and springs, usually shared by several households

At The Terrace	5 large houses share	2 pumps
The Railway Station		1 pump
		1 well
Windermere Hotel and stable	private water tower	1 tank
Behind the shops on Church Street	3 large premises share	2 pumps
On the north side of High Street	9 dwellings share	2 pumps
Between High Street and Victoria Street	3 large premises share	1 pump
On the north side of Cross Street	12 dwellings share	2 pumps
On the south side of Cross Street	10 cottages share	1 pump
On the south side of Victoria Street	5 cottages share	0 pumps.[412]

The 1858 Act also empowered Local Boards to exercise control of building works by requiring plans for new buildings, and alterations to existing premises, to be submitted for inspection and approval prior to commencement of work; and to oversee those works to ensure high standards of compliance during execution.

After protracted deliberation, resistance regarding the boundary of the area to be served by the Windermere Local Board (WLB), and wrangling over who would bear the cost of its administration, were finally settled in December of 1865 covering an area below the Station. [413] Nine worthy businessmen and gentlemen were elected to serve for the first twelve months:

R.M. Somervell,	James Cropper,	G.H. Puckle,
B.A. Irving,	Col Renny,	William Harrison,
John Hartley,	John Garnett,	John Titterington.

'It is to be hoped that in addition to the thorough drainage, –––– the board will add a few gas lamps, as one of the great wants of the place.'

At this time, sewage ran in an open stream from the village, through the extensive Rayrigg Wood estate of Revd Fleming, entering the Lake near his residence at Rayrigg Hall, where it polluted the water and created a *'nuisance'* to his property.

Tenders were sought for the laying of four main sewers in the village, totalling about 1,200 yards of 12-inch pipe, to serve the streets then in existence – Church Street (i.e. the upper part of the turnpike road from St Mary's Church to the Station), High Street, Victoria Street and part of New Street.[414] Plans were also drawn for a main drain of 12 inch pipe, 700 yards in length, to be laid at a depth of 4 feet, and costing £350. It was to feed an open cesspool at Beemire costing £100,[415] where solid waste would be extracted. But liquid effluent and storm water spillage still flowed in an open stream to the Lake, its odour being a source of great embarrassment to the area for very many years.[416] Where it crossed the Bowness Low Road at Rayrigg was a particular running sore. With the wind in the wrong direction, the waft from the filter beds at Beemire was plainly discernable on the west side of the village, especially at St Mary's Abbey, The College and at Ellerthwaite. On one occasion it was claimed that a strong smell was emanating from a drain which crossed the College grounds and vented near the stables. The source was strongly refuted by Mr Irving, headmaster of the College, a member of WLB.

Dr Archibald Hamilton *(6.5)* gave several eloquent lectures regarding the proper design of drainage for housing, water closets, the evils of sewer gases, and their containment by properly engineered traps.[417] He illustrated his talks with large-scale technical drawings, the clarity of which received considerable acclaim. His own house of Oakthorpe was badly affected by malevolent odours, to the extent that he and his wife were forced to vacate the premises while the floors were taken up. It was found that an old branch sewer near the wall of their coal cellar had never been properly joined to the main sewer. '*It could not have been better arranged —— for conveying the stench into the house*'.

By 1869 plans made by the Windermere Gas & Water Company were slowly taking shape to provide a proper supply of clean drinking water to the village. Dubbs Beck near High Borrans was judged to have sufficient flow for its water to be shared between the domestic needs of the new village and the mills which already drew on its water along the Gowan towards Staveley and Kendal. Initially, two reservoirs were required to be built – a compensation reservoir to maintain flow to the mills at all times, and a small service reservoir near Alice Howe to provide an adequate head of water for domestic use in the village. The Windermere Waterworks Bill was signed and sealed that year.

Perhaps surprisingly, the Kendal Medical Officer of Health reported favourably on the health of the Windermere area, despite a complaint in 1872 from the Inspector of Nuisances of a piggery at the rear of the Queen's Hotel !

Due to a misunderstanding by members of the Local Board regarding its ownership of Cross Street, installation of a sewer in that street had been neglected for nearly 30 years. It was not until the autumn of 1877 that tenders were sought for 85 yards of 6-inch drain to be trenched and laid.[418] Since its inception, Cross Street residents had suffered from the inconvenience and indignity of privies located in their back yards, with all their malodorous airs. The proximity of such facilities to the public water supply, shared hand-pumps and wells, raised concern over contamination of drinking water, and hence the risk of cholera and typhoid fever. John Garnett inflamed the controversy by taking issue with fellow members of WLB when he wrote to the Local Government Board with an apocryphal claim. He claimed to be aware of a doctor in the Windermere area (deliberately including Bowness in his sweep) who had 40 cases of scarlet fever to care for. The Medical Officer of Health replied indignantly: [419]

> '*The general sanitary condition of the village and district is satisfactory, and there is not, I believe, any reasonable ground for apprehension respecting the existence of serious sanitary defects whereby the dangers resulting from the infection of scarlet fever or other fever may be fostered or enhanced. —— I am not aware of any endemic or seasonal prevalence of fever in this district, and save in the instance of an outbreak of scarlet fever in a large household beyond the village, but within the local district, in the winter of 1875, in which my assistance was requested, and where the infection was clearly traceable to introduction from a distant town, I consider that Windermere has enjoyed a happy immunity from zymotic disorders ——*'.[420]

Supporting the Medical Officer, WLB held that Mr Garnett's letter was without the least foundation. However, in 1877 they appointing a Sanitary Inspector, although the Medical Officer of Health had reported that

> '*the sanitary state of the district in the past year was exceedingly favourable*'.

Mr Garnett, a doggedly persistent man, and a match for Mr Puckle in that regard, was not put off. Writing again to the Local Government Board, he disputed each of the statements in the Medical Officer's report in turn, and called for a special enquiry to be set up to investigate urgently the sanitary condition of the district, especially the sewage continuously running in the open stream through Rayrigg Wood.

6.4 The Volunteer Movement

162. A fine body of men – Westmorland Rifle Volunteers on parade at Calgarth Park, possibly in 1861, shortly after formation of the Westmorland Battalion. Several of the men on the left are holding musical instruments, but the only weapons in view are ceremonial swords carried by officers. The bandsmen are wearing hats with decorative tassels, or cockades, which probably identifies them as Kendal Volunteers.

© *Ian Jones*

In the 1850s a widespread suspicion grew in the land that France was preparing to take revenge for its defeats at Trafalgar and Waterloo. England was unable to afford the cost of a large standing army, and so volunteer militias were formed throughout the country as a means of supporting the regular army, by providing a local defence force or home guard. In 1860 six companies of part-time militia were formed in Westmorland, consisting of

1st Westmorland, or Kirkby Lonsdale Volunteers;
2nd and 3rd Westmorland Volunteers, or Kendal Rifles;
4th Westmorland, or Windermere Rifles;
5th Westmorland, or Ambleside Rifles;
6th Westmorland, drawn from Grasmere and Langdale.

They were collectively known as the Westmorland Rifle Volunteers, or more simply as The Volunteers. They had no trouble recruiting local men to the ranks; and the gentry and property owners enjoyed the prestige of commissioned officer titles. Initially the force did not have uniforms or weapons, but all manner of special events were organised to raise funds for the cause.

Monthly drill parades took place, instruction in weapons, and a summer camp each year to consolidate training and firearms skill. The movement was extremely popular from the start, distracting the populace from the hardship of unemployment arising from the cotton famine and American civil war. In August 1861 the first review of 350 officers and men of the Westmorland Battalion took place on a large field at Calgarth.

'The different shades of the uniforms made the various corps easily distinguishable, the Kendal force being further notable by cockades of the "Kendal Green". There were three military bands on the ground, those of Kendal, Windermere, and Grasmere. Among the officers who took part in the proceedings of the day were: Lieut.-Colonel Murray, the adjutant;

> *Lieut.-Colonel Gandy, of the Westmorland Battalion;*
> *Captains Wilson and Whitwell of the Kendal corps;*
> *Captain Ridehalgh, Bowness Rifles;*
> *Captain Pedder, Ambleside Rifles;*
> *Captain Selwyn, of the Grasmere Volunteers'.* [421]

The K&W Railway Company ran a special train of 20 full carriages to bring men and spectators from Kendal to Windermere:

'In addition to these a considerable number of visitors took the road in carriages of various kinds. The road from the terminus to the review ground presented an unusually gay and lively appearance, the more especially as a large assemblage of the better as well as more ornamental sex had been tempted by the novelty and interest of the spectacle, combined with the fineness of the weather. The music of the Kendal Volunteer Band, as the rifles marched from the station to the field, gave additional spirit to the procession.'

In later years, the availability of field guns enabled pyrotechnic manoeuvres to be practiced in a 30-acre field near the Lake at Calgarth. Spectators from miles around flocked excitedly to watch, drawn by the huge percussions that accompanied these events.

6.5 Medical Services – Dr Archibald Hamilton, of Oakthorpe

Until 1864 Windermere people in need of medical services were forced to consult doctors in Bowness or further afield, but in that year an energetic and personable young Scottish gentleman arrived in the village. Archibald Hamilton studied medicine at Edinburgh University, and in 1862 he was recruited as house surgeon at the Cumberland Infirmary in Carlisle. He held that position for two years until, at the age of 25, he resigned from the Infirmary and moved to Windermere in May 1864. He was the first doctor to take up general practice and permanent residence in the village, his friendly demeanour and genial Scottish accent making him immediately popular with residents. When Oakthorpe at the bottom of High Street was offered for rental by Benjamin Irving in 1865,[422] the building was ideally located at the very centre of the village to launch his practice.

Two years later Archibald Hamilton married Miss Catherine Jeffray, whose mother was living at Winlass Beck following the death of her husband, the vicar of Aldford in Cheshire. As the daughter of Thomas Miller, a partner in the powerhouse of Preston cotton manufacturing Horrockses & Miller, Mrs Jeffray was a wealthy lady. In the 1870s she moved to a large villa named The Haigh, directly opposite Oakthorpe, to be close to her only daughter.

The doctor was very active in the community, participating fully in civic and recreational affairs, in addition to his medical practice. As mentioned elsewhere *(6.3)*, he served as a member of Windermere Local Board where his medical knowledge was invaluable on matters of health, hygiene and drainage. He was also Vice-President of the Institute where he frequently presided at penny readings, and gave lectures on topics as diverse as

- alcohol abuse, the effects of heredity and *'whether alcohol in any shape is necessary to the comfortable existence of a body already in health'*;
- healthy and unhealthy arrangement of house drainage; and
- the environment.

Between 1868 and 1879 he served as Warden of St Mary's Church; in March of 1880 he was appointed as county magistrate for Westmorland; in 1892 he was a founder member of the Golf Club; a tennis player; and surgeon to the Windermere Corps of Volunteers.

In the 1870s the village medical practice grew rapidly, requiring an assistant. Dr Roger St Clair Steuart from Edinburgh came first, a cousin of Mrs Hamilton, but tragically the young man died of pleurisy after only three years in Windermere. He was followed for the next three years by Dr Charles Frederic Newcombe from Newcastle-upon-Tyne, before he emigrated to America. Finally Dr John Mason from Kirkby Stephen joined the practice, taking much of the workload off Dr Hamilton and eventually taking over the practice completely. He knew the village well as a boy at Windermere College, which was followed by medical training at St Bartholomew's Hospital in London. All of these gentlemen lived at The Cottage adjacent to Oakthorpe, convenient to the surgery *(125)*.

6.6 Education

As already described in previous chapters, Windermere College was integral to Revd Addison's concept for the village. It was intended to serve *'the sons of clergymen chiefly'*, by providing *'a cheap and thorough education on sound church principles'*, a boarding school for boys after the style of Eton and Harrow. It survived under his stewardship for less than two years, exhausting his financial resources and unfortunately resulted in the departure of the Addison family from the village in 1855. Under subsequent ownership the strongly ecclesiastical influence was moderated and the College flourished with a high reputation for education. By 1857 three students had gained entry to Cambridge, two with scholarships. Smaller educational establishments also appeared in Windermere, aimed at similar clients, but none survived for long. A few families who could afford the cost, employed live-in governesses to teach their children privately at home.

But ' *for the children of the poorer classes in the community'* there was only St Mary's School, founded at his own expense by Revd Addison in 1850, in the shadow of his Church. The pressing need for such a school ensured its survival in spite of its precarious finances, and income from the Braithwaite endowment helped to sustain a master.

Initially the building contained two classrooms, serving boys and girls between the ages of five and ten years. Like the Church, its classes were full to overflowing from the start. In 1865 the school building was extended by her family in memory of Miss Jane Yates of The Wood. She had been a generous benefactor, and a member of the Ladies Committee which oversaw the infants and girls classes. The school was now able to seat around 100 children; but with a considerably greater population of school-age children, many simply could not be accommodated, especially girls and those unable to afford *'school pence'*. [423] Many children of poor parents typically did work at home such as laundering, or made deliveries for traders, to augment the family income. Bright lads, as young as twelve years, were sometimes apprenticed to craftsmen in the village. Those who could attend the school shared the early morning chore of raking out the ashes of the previous day and re-lighting the fires before class.

For some years, a small number of children from Windermere walked to an unusual building connected with the Nonconformist Church at Troutbeck Bridge. [424] From 1858 this school was housed in a large barn at Knotts Farm on the Patterdale Road to Troutbeck. However, in 1873 it was re-housed in a new building gifted by William Carver, near the Sun Inn at Troutbeck Bridge.

For the first time, an Act of Parliament in 1870 required that schooling should be provided for all children aged five to twelve years; but it was still not free to all ! Windermere responded in 1887 when the pressure on St Mary's School became overwhelming. A plot of empty land was procured from William Harrison, just off Woodland Road near

Ellerthwaite, where a new Church of England Boys' School was built. The old school at St Mary's then became available to the girls and infants classes. But despite this they were never comfortably accommodated.

For those children wishing to progress to higher things, a free Grammar School had existed since 1613 in Bowness, where *'grammar, writing, reading, and other good discipline, meet and convenient for them'* were taught mainly to boys from the townships of Applethwaite and Undermillbeck. [425] In 1836 a completely rebuilt school was funded entirely by John Bolton of Storrs Hall. The dramatically sited building designed by Webster of Kendal *'in the old English order of architecture'*, to seat 100 pupils in each of two rooms. It stood like a sentinel high on a crag above Bowness, enjoying commanding views of village and Lake. Since Mr Bolton was too ill to attend, the foundation stone was laid on his behalf by William Wordsworth, in the foulest of weather, when the only public speech he ever made was only partly delivered. [426]

163. Perched high on a crag, dramatically overlooking the church and village of Bowness, this school served boys and girls of both Undermilbeck and Applethwaite. Built in 1836, the gift of John Bolton of Storrs Hall,[427] it was described as 'a great ornament to the picturesque district'.

It was one of the five local schools to benefit from John Braithwaite's will in 1854, favoured with the largest bequest of £1,200 to support the salaries of an under-master and under-mistress *(3.13)*. The trustees of the School were also charged with £2,000 to establish scholarships to St John's College, Cambridge, the bursaries to be tenable for four years each by boys born in the township of Applethwaite or Undermillbeck.[428]

Like others of the time the school at Bowness provided elementary education, but could not deliver a full grammar school curriculum. By the 1880s the Charity Commission had insisted that income from the Bolton and Braithwaite endowments must provide higher as well as elementary education, and do so for both Applethwaite and Undermillbeck. The outcome of protracted argument with the Commission resulted in the continuation of free elementary education in the existing buildings at Birthwaite and Bowness, sparing the pockets of ratepayers; but it was recognised that the site of Bolton's school could not accommodate the required senior school. A site midway between the villages, near to the Carver Memorial Church, was eventually acquired for a new fee-paying grammar school, to include day scholars and boarders. It was designed by architect Joseph Pattinson and opened in 1885 for 70-100 students, with a broad curriculum of academic subjects including mathematics, science, French and Latin. By 1896 bursaries were introduced to encourage greater up-take by promising students of the Windermere and Bowness boys' schools.

So by 1900 the two villages were served by a comprehensive complement of educational establishments, sending a commendable number of students to Universities.

6.7 Cemetery and Burial Board

At its outset, the village of Windermere did not possess a burial ground. The small number of interments each year were split about equally between the churchyards at Bowness and Troutbeck. But in 1855 Bowness was forced to close its churchyard and open a new burial ground on glebe land, near the parsonage. Since the new village of Birthwaite was beginning to expand, a separate burial ground within Applethwaite was now favoured. During negotiations over the purchase of St Mary's church and school from Revd Addison, the possibility of a consecrated burial ground at St Mary's was raised. Not all the residents were in favour, some claiming that '--- *it would interfere with the amenity of the place*', and would require provision for the burial of dissenters. Further complications arose due to a coincidence of events – the transfer of several Westmorland deaneries from the diocese of Chester to that of Carlisle, closure of St Martin's churchyard, sale of St Mary's to the township, creation of a separate ecclesiastical parish of Applethwaite, and the need for consecration of both church and burial ground. But the need for new graves was so pressing that objections were at last overcome, and St Mary's churchyard was consecrated on 9 August 1856 by the Bishop of Carlisle.

This graveyard served for almost 30 years before its limited capacity was exhausted by the relentless growth of the village. Around 1876 it was found necessary to close St Mary's churchyard to non-parishioners. But despite this, by 1883 burials were approaching 20 per year, from a resident population of just under 2,000.[429] A special Burial Board was formed, charged with locating a site for a larger cemetery capable of serving all sections of community for many years to come. After two false starts and considerable acrimony between Windermere residents and some members of the board, a satisfactory site of two acres was located at Holme Field near Millerground. The total cost, borne by ratepayers and voluntary subscription, rose to £2,762 – which covered purchase of the land, levelling and clearance of rock and undergrowth from the site, installation of ground drainage, building of a caretaker's cottage and erection of a heated mortuary chapel. Capable of seating around 90 people, it was innovatively designed by Windermere architect Robert Walker as a single chapel serving all denominations – *'open to all alike'*. Part of the ground, that reserved for St Mary's interments, was consecrated on 18 October 1887 in a ceremony conducted by the Bishop of Carlisle.[430] The first burial in the cemetery took place on 20 December 1888, that of John Cowperthwaite Airey aged 22, the eldest son of Thomas Airey of nearby Millerground Farm.[431]

Finally, in 1889 burials were terminated at St Mary's churchyard to all but those with pre-existing family plots. The Burial Board oversaw interments at the new cemetery until 1895, when the newly formed Windermere Urban District Council took over responsibility.

6.8 Ambleside Railway – Revisited

It was perhaps inevitable that the original idea of a railway from Windermere to Ambleside would be resurrected as traffic on the line from Kendal increased. Excursion trains brought ever increasing crowds of day trippers and holiday makers to the new village of Windermere in summer months, especially on bank holidays. But the town of Ambleside gained little commercial benefit from the crowds of visitors who flocked to Windermere. Relatively few day trippers made the extra journey by lake steamer, or by carriage along the old coach road.

In 1886 a number of Ambleside gentlemen – hoteliers, traders, land-owners and aspiring entrepreneurs – proposed a 5-mile railway extension from Windermere to Ambleside. Although it was not included at this stage, it clearly had potential to be extended to Grasmere and Keswick, a deep scar through the heart of Lakeland which Wordsworth had railed so hard against in 1844. *(3.1)*

Understandably, Ambleside businessmen and hoteliers viewed with some envy the growing commercial success of Windermere as a tourist resort. The proposal for a new rail link came from five prominent Ambleside men

- Lt Col Godfrey Rhodes JP, who owned land where the proposed line would terminate;
- Joseph Fleming Green, owner of Elterwater Quarry, whose stone was laboriously shipped down the Lake for onward transportation;
- Michael Taylor, proprietor of the busy Salutation Hotel;
- Moses Bowness, a photographer with property on the line; and
- Joseph Mitchell.

They succeeded in launching a private members' bill in Parliament, which reached the Committee stage early in 1887. The enterprise also had the unanimous backing of Kendal Town Council – but certainly not of property owners along the planned route in Windermere, residents whose estates were to be violated and their mansions greatly devalued.

Like the earlier plan, instead of terminating at Windermere, the existing railway was to be extended northwards for almost five miles, starting from a point close to Windermere Station. The engineering scheme proposed a line which crossed in a tunnel under the old turnpike road, continuing under the entrance of Rigg's Hotel, to

> '--- pass through the front garden in a covered way, within about 10 yards of the front of the hotel, and underneath one of the coach-houses. The depth of the covered way below the ground is so slight that it is likely to be a cause both of annoyance and danger, and it will make the said garden, instead of a place of quiet retreat, practically useless ---'. [432]

It would then slice through the pleasure grounds of the Elleray mansion of Mr Heywood; pass within 30 yards of the villas of Cleeve Howe and Elleray Bank; and 90 yards from St Catherine's; slash through the garden at newly built Chapel Ridding, 60 yards from the mansion door; bisect the carriage drive and parkland at Holehird mansion; span the Troutbeck ravine on a lofty viaduct near Low Borrans. It would proceed high on the hillside,

> '--- at a considerably higher level than the old coach road --- never less than half a mile from the Lake',

passing Briery Close and Holbeck Ghyll on a second viaduct 70 feet high, then close to Dove Nest and Wansfell Holme; and finish at a terminus above the Salutation Hotel, near Stock Ghyll Bobbin Mill.

The sponsors had little trouble securing sufficient backing from the people of Ambleside to bring the private bill before Parliament. The capital for construction of the line was estimated to be £165,000,[433] for which the promoters would pay interest at 4% per annum.

A Select Committee of the House of Commons was appointed after the first reading of the Bill. In March of 1887 the Committee heard petitions opposing the Bill, and questioned experts from both sides on the engineering and financial viability of the railway.

> *'The plea of the promoters is that it is necessary for the commercial and industrial development of the little town of Ambleside, which contains only 2,000 inhabitants; that it would enable quarries to be worked and mines to be opened, gunpowder works and other manufactories to be developed, and so give life and prosperity to a sleepy little village; that it would, moreover, bring tourists into the heart of mountains, instead of their being landed at Windermere to go forward by car or steamboat to the head of the lake.'* [434]

> *'Mr Gibson is the owner of a residential estate in the township of Applethwaite, called Chapel Ridding. The said estate was recently laid out, and a handsome residence built thereon at great expense, by your said petitioner, for his own occupation, and the grounds have been very carefully laid out. The property adjoins the Troutbeck Road, and commands a very fine view of Windermere, and the railway will pass through the garden within 60 yards of the house.'*

Opponents of the railway also included the great philosopher and art critic, Professor Ruskin of Oxford and Coniston, whose opinions were quoted in newspapers as far apart as Pall Mall and Aberdeen. [435]

The failure of the 1887 Ambleside Railway Bill was a carbon copy of the fate of the earlier proposal of 1844. Both were casualties of the great cost of constructing a viaduct, and of the influence of wealthy men and women whose properties were to be violated. It was an object lesson in who not to quarrel with. Never was there a scheme more guaranteed to incite the wrath of residents in the village of Windermere and the lower part of Troutbeck Valley, wealthy and successful men whose properties would be desecrated following compulsory acquisition of their land, with no power to resist.

Estimates of the total compensation to be paid to owners whose property would be *'damaged'* by the railway, varied wildly between £24,000 at the lower end and £90,000 at the other extreme. For reasons not revealed, the London and North Western Railway, which the promoters hoped would operate the line, withdrew their support. In closed session from which the public were excluded, the Select Committee deliberated, and decided that the proposed Windermere to Ambleside railway was financially unsound. They were *'--- not satisfied with regard to the money part of the transaction'*, and the Bill was thrown out once and for all. [436]

A mighty threat to the residents of Windermere and Troutbeck had been removed, which had concerned them for a decade or more. Commerce in Windermere village continued to benefit from tourists who arrived at their station in summer months, and the prosperity of Windermere grew inexorably to overtake both Bowness and Ambleside.

6.9 Lake District Defence Society

The Lake District Defence Society (LDDS) came about largely as a counter to the Thirlmere Reservoir, and the proliferation of proposed railways in the Lake District as a whole. The society was effectively founded in May of 1883 when Canon Hardwicke Rawnsley, '*the watchdog of the Lakes*', addressed the annual meeting of the Wordsworth Society. The executive committee of the new society were

- Hardwicke Drummond Rawnsley, Vicar of Crosthwaite near Keswick;
- William Henry Hills, Ambleside bookseller;
- Gordon Somervell, Kendal shoe manufacturer, resident of Windermere;
- Albert Fleming, retired London barrister, of Neaum Crag near Ambleside;
- Herbert Moser, Kendal solicitor.

Rawnsley became the first secretary, and Gordon Somervell was appointed treasurer.

Two of the sons of Robert Miller Somervell of Hazelthwaite had been at the forefront of opposition to railway developments in the Lake District for some time. In 1876 when rumours of a line from Windermere to Ambleside first emerged, his eldest son Robert published '*A Protest Against the Extension of Railways in the Lake District*'. He urged like-minded people to pre-sign a protest petition which would be held on file until needed, for presentation to Parliament whenever a railway project arose.[437]

The formal objects of the LDDS were the subject of much debate and wrangling during the following year. But informally, it aimed to thwart developments that might be injurious to the scenery of the Lake District – railways, quarrying and mineral extraction. With most of its 400 members living outside of the area, the Society suffered accusations of elitism, and failing to represent the ordinary people of the Lakes. However the LDDS, with help from John Ruskin, can rightly claim early success in stopping the Ennerdale Railway, and the Braithwaite & Buttermere Railway, both in 1883. Unlike the passenger-carrying Kendal & Windermere Railway, they were primarily for industrial development, intended for conveying iron ore, coal and other minerals to the west coast. And both failed on dubious economic projections. But although the Society opposed the Ambleside Railway, they could not really claim credit for its demise. They vacillated over the Manchester Water Works at Thirlmere, particularly regarding a new coach road to be made on the west side of the lake; and were accused of taking arbitrary decisions in committee, without consulting the membership.

Although the Defence Society initially confined its activities to the Lake District, from its inception Canon Rawnsley clamoured for a wider national platform. The LDDS was one of several pressure groups whose ethos provided a model for the National Trust in 1894. Rawnsley became its honorary secretary, a towering strength in the national body for the next 25 years, acquiring the accolade of '--- *the most active volcano in Europe*'.

In parallel with the LDDS, a separate group was formed in November 1877, confusingly named the **Lake District Association**. Initially, its aims were simply in support of publicity and marketing,

> '--- *to promote the improvement and further the interests of the Lake Country as a Summer Resort'.*

It drew its membership from the business community, hotel and lodging house proprietors in the principal centres; and Windermere was well represented on the committee. As time went on, the association widened its role to become a civic watchdog over amenities affecting visitors, especially improvements to roads, bridges, public footpaths, and in later years the eyesore of roadside advertisements.

6.10 Recreation Ground

Perhaps the greatest civic event by which Archibald Hamilton deserves to be remembered came in 1897, the Queen's Diamond Jubilee year. At a public meeting in the Institute he brought forward a far-reaching and popular proposal for the village to celebrate the Jubilee by creating a public Recreation Ground, particularly for the children. All of the land in the centre of the village had long ago been taken up. Dr Hamilton advocated the purchase of 11½ acres of open land from the Oldfield Estate on the east side of the village, land which had recently become available but was in danger of being swallowed up by new housing. The idea of open green parkland met with immediate favour, and when a public subscription was opened individual donations flowed in. Contributions ranged from a few pence from children, up to £500 from one unnamed donor. Eventually the total funds pledged and donated rose to £3,692, sufficient to cover the cost of purchasing the land and laying it out. Archibald Hamilton and William Burrill, manager of the Crown Hotel in Bowness, were appointed joint secretaries to manage the project.

On 22 June 1897, along with the rest of the nation, the village of Windermere celebrated the Diamond Jubilee of Queen Victoria with a grand procession to the new recreation ground.[438] The gentry of the area and 400 children were entertained to tea in the Institute, followed by sports, each child receiving a special commemorative medal. George Hale Puckle, as Chairman of the Windermere District Council, declared Victoria Field

> '--- *open for ever as a recreation ground for the use of the public of the parish and district'.*

The occasion was also marked by Mrs Hamilton, who planted an oak tree which, with great foresight, had been

> '--- *sprung from an acorn sown at Oakthorpe on --- the Golden Jubilee in 1887'.*

Mr Puckle generously erected a handsome cricket pavilion entirely at his own expense, for the serving of teas and refreshments.

Within a year of Dr Hamilton's death in 1904 a charity, the Hamilton Memorial Fund, was founded in his honour.[439] It aimed to meet the cost for poor residents of Windermere of medical and surgical assistance, including convalescent care and accommodation. Launch funds for the charity donated by friends of the doctor totalled £793, with four influential and wealthy residents of Windermere becoming the first Trustees:

Revd Frank Taylor	Birthwaite Lodge	retired rector of Kirkandrews-on-Esk
William Grimble Groves	Holehird	retired brewery owner from Salford
John Mortimer Sladen	Cleeve Howe	(of independent means)
Gordon Somervell	Hazelthwaite	shoe manufacturer in Kendal.

164. Official opening of the Cricket Pavilion in Queen's Park Recreation Ground, donated entirely at his own expense by George Hale Puckle.

Courtesy of Roger Bowness

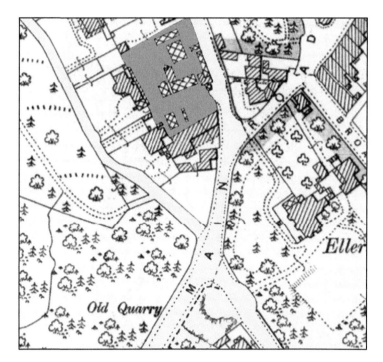

165. *The first nursery, opened in 1897 by the Mawson Brothers, an acre of land and glass on College Road.*

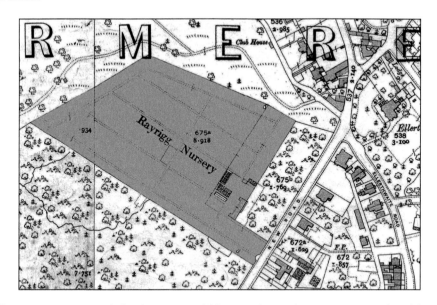

166. *The more extensive Lakeland Nursery of 30 acres, located in Rayrigg Wood and fronting on to New Road ——— 1911.*

6.11 International Garden Designer – Thomas H. Mawson

In the early 1880s three young men arrived in the village of Windermere intent on opening a nursery business. The brothers, Thomas Hayton Mawson, who later attained international acclaim, Robert Radcliffe Mawson and Isaac Mawson were raised near Ingolton. From a staunchly nonconformist family, the boys were largely self-taught after leaving school at the age of 12.

In 1879, when Thomas was 18, their widowed mother moved the family to London where her sons gained valuable horticultural experience, working in several large nurseries. Thomas became interested in garden design and secured a promise of partnership from his employer in 1884. He married a lady from Norfolk, but whilst on honeymoon in the Lake District the employer unfortunately withdrew his offer, a heavy blow. In some disarray, the whole family quickly returned to Windermere in 1885, where there were many large villa gardens requiring maintenance, and with potential for improvement. Thomas and his brothers, Robert and Isaac, bravely opened a nursery and garden design business on an acre of land in Windermere, next to Deason's coach workshop in College Road.

The two younger Mawsons, now aged 20 and 17, took charge of the plant nursery, raising an increasing variety of garden plants and shrubs suited to the Lakeland climate. A successful adjunct to the nursery business became the supply of gardeners to owners of grand houses – *'Mawson Brothers have always on their register a number of thoroughly reliable and trustworthy men'* – providing regular employment for local men. Thomas Mawson was now free to pursue his aspirations in garden design and within four years he had attracted sufficient work to separate the landscape business, leaving Robert and Isaac as proprietors of the nursery.

Thomas Mawson's first commission came in 1886 with a garden design for J.R. Bridson's new house at Sawrey. This was followed in 1889 at Graythwaite Hall for Col Sandys, where he formed a professional acquaintance with the young site architect, Dan Gibson.

A decade later, in 1898 Thomas Mawson had prospered sufficiently to build the attractive villa of Corbels, at Heathwaite, a prestigious private home for his growing family, with a design office for the expanding landscape business. The house was designed by his friend Dan Gibson, by now a talented arts-and-crafts architect, and they briefly formed a partnership – *'Mawson & Gibson, architects, Crescent Road, Windermere'*. After two years they separated on good terms, continuing to collaborate informally from the Crescent Road offices. Together they worked at many important country house gardens in the Lake District, including Holehird, Oakland, Cleeve Howe, Langdale Chase and Cringlemire, with planting stock supplied from the Mawson Windermere nursery. At Brockhole, and Dawstone at Lickbarrow, Mawson aligned the terraces with the Langdale Pikes to exploit the views, a signature element of his style. Both of these arts-and-crafts houses were designed by Gibson.

This success heralded the start of Thomas Mawson's prolific career in landscape design,[440] a subject which became a science and art form when he lectured at Liverpool University. Over the next decade he designed many formal gardens for wealthy clients throughout Britain – the Marquis of Bute, Viscount Leverhulme, and the Rothschilds to name a few; and many of his landscape commissions came from municipal authorities for town parks, cemeteries and garden villages. One such project near to home comprised a civic centre and park for Windermere, below St John's Church – unfortunately never built.

In 1908, with encouragement from no less a person than Andrew Carnegie himself, Thomas Mawson entered – and won – the competition to design the garden of the Peace Palace in The Hague.[441] For over a century Mawson's garden has graced that superb 15-acre site, perfectly uniting the grounds and terraces with the exotic French Renaissance style palace, of global importance to peace and international law.

After 25 years in Windermere, it now became expedient to expand to larger offices in Lancaster and London. Thomas Mawson's family also moved from Windermere to live at Hest Bank, enabling him to be joined in the business by his sons, and a nephew who trained in architecture and town planning. Together they attracted many highly prestigious commissions from across the world – Athens, Salonika, New Zealand, USA and Canada – and many more country house gardens and villages in the UK.[442]

Sadly, both of Thomas Mawson's brothers died before their time; Isaac, the youngest, died of pneumonia in 1901; and Robert died in 1910 after two years of illness. In their hands the nursery business in Windermere had flourished, expanding to a new site of 30 acres in nearby Rayrigg Wood, where it survived for more than a century in the hands of succeeding generations.

Thomas Hayton Mawson died of Parkinson's disease at Applegarth, Hest Bank in 1933. His rise from humble beginnings to world authority on landscape design was truly outstanding. It was his wish that his body should return to Windermere where he had lived for a quarter of a century, the canvas and springboard for his life's work. He was buried in Bowness Cemetery, the gravestone inscribed '*A Lakelander by Adoption*'.

167. Isaac, Robert and Thomas Mawson

6.12 Sporting Activities

An ancient and fast moving **field sport** in the Lake District was the hunting of foxes with harriers, a breed of bloodhound. It was especially popular amongst young men of the area, who followed the chase on foot and on horseback, the baying of dogs on the scent echoing through the hills and valleys for miles around. The Windermere Harriers were a popular pack, kennelled at the Royal Hotel in Bowness. From 1859 they were in the charge of huntsman Thomas Chapman of Patterdale, boots at the hotel. Winter meets sometimes fielded two or more visiting packs, and were set running on fells anywhere from Crook to Langdale, and Winster to Grasmere. The followers, known as *Nimrodians*, frequently retired to the Royal Hotel or the Windermere Hotel, both famous for their hearty food and ale after a strenuous day on the fells.

Over the years there were several attempts to provide a **library** for the working people of Windermere. In many towns libraries were an adjunct to the Mechanics Institute, intended to provide a place for workingmen to spend their leisure time usefully, in alcohol-free premises, particularly when working away from home. In 1860 a small reading room was set aside below Harrison's Assembly Room in Victoria Street. And when the new Institute building was finally erected a decade later, a more commodious and better appointed reading room was provided. But neither of these was manned, and books were provided at the patronage of the more affluent residents.

When Benjamin Irving, the retired headmaster of Windermere College, died in 1905, he left the Urban District Council a legacy of £1,000 towards provision of a public library.[443] Although the Council had insufficient funds to progress the idea at that time, it purchased a plot of land on Broad Street in 1911 where it erected a temporary cabin. But it was not until 1926 when Ellerthwaite mansion and its estate became available for purchase, that a generous gift of £5,000 was offered by William Grimble Groves of Holehird.[444] This gift, together with £1,289 realised from sale of the Broad Street land, enabled the Council at last to make proper provision for a permanent public library and museum in the Ellerthwaite mansion.[445] The building was formally opened in 1927 by the Prince of Wales during his grand tour of the North of England, – but sadly a fortnight after the death of Mr Groves.[446]

Until the opening of the Queen's Park Recreation Ground in 1897 there was no provision for the working population in Windermere village to participate in sport, other than that generously made available by the College. Its playing field was used for the first time for **cricket** in 1854, during Revd Addison's stewardship, when two teams from within the College played each other. In June of the same year a team from Kendal and St Mary's College met at Birthwaite, when Kendal won easily by an innings. A decade later, regular cricket fixtures were played by College lads against teams from Bowness, Windermere village, Burneside, Liverpool, Kirkby Lonsdale, Kendal, Carlisle and others.

Prior to 1886 **Rugby Football** was played during winter months, but the field was notoriously small, rough – and even boggy in places. It was not until Mr Raikes' tenure that the Old College advertised **Association Football** (soccer) in its brochure of school sports, to be played in autumn and spring terms.

In 1863 the marriage of the Prince of Wales was celebrated with town and village sporting activities throughout the nation. A team of 50 Rifle Volunteers organised by Captain Ridehalgh, challenged a team of 50 local lads drawn from the villages of Windermere and Bowness. Unhappily, the match had to be terminated prematurely

> '--- through the breaking in of a few unruly fellows --- it soon became a very unfair match, and the ball was taken up.'

In 1891 the game of **golf** also came to Windermere. A number of enthusiastic players gathered at Ellerthwaite, at that time in the tenure of Revd Moss of St John's Church, to found the Windermere Golf Club. They commissioned the professional from Lytham St Annes to survey a tract of glebe land ' *amidst picturesque but wild scenery'*, located at Cleabarrow between Ferry Nab and Crook. They proposed to create a fell-side course to serve the central part of the Lake District. An article in the press reported that

> '--- the entire area of the allotment consists of clusters of rocks and heather-clad knolls, so that there are hazards innumerable to be encountered whilst driving a ball over the course.' [447]

Mr Lowe from Lytham reported favourably and within a year he had laid out the first nine-holes of the course on 200 acres of glebe land which the founders had leased for £70/year. In the first year of the club its membership grew rapidly to 130 men and ladies, enabling a further nine holes to be added almost immediately.

The first Captain of the club was Stanley Hughes le Fleming, who had created his own private course on parkland at Rydal Hall, north of Ambleside. Many members of the Yacht Club with houses around Windermere, also joined the club, seeking sporting recreation in all seasons of the year for an exclusive group of people. They included the Sladen brothers, Benjamin Irving, Gordon Somervell, George Broadrick, Dr Hamilton, Revd Moss, and Hubert Coutts of Windermere; S.H. le Fleming, Gordon Wordsworth, and Arthur Redmayne of Rydal; Revd Stock of St Martin's, Dr Dobson, and T.D. Lingard of Bowness.

6.13 Yachting

The most illustrious sporting activity for which Windermere Lake was famous throughout the 1800s, and is still known today, was **yacht racing**. Even Revd Addison competed in the 1850s with a small 16-foot yacht, appropriately named *St Mary*. For many years wealthy gentlemen raced against each other during the summer regatta season in craft of many shapes and sizes, the largest usually winning despite a handicapping system. Initially, they hired sailing crews of boat-builders and fishermen, known as *'--- the professionals'*; but later the owners also helmed their own yachts, and were appropriately dubbed *'--- the amateurs'*.

Wealthy residents of the area joined the Windermere Sailing Club when it was founded in 1860.[448] The competitive spirit, and a wish to eliminate hull size and wealth as the winning factors, resulted in agreement of one-size rules that produced the famous 20-foot Class of Windermere racing yachts.[449] By fixing the dimensions of waterline length and sail area, it was intended that the skill of the helmsman and his crew would determine the results, not cheque book and yacht dimensions. But inevitably, the ingenuity of designers and boat-builders found unintended ways of exploiting the rules to increase speed. The sight of a dozen or more of these beautiful craft, heeled hard over until the tips of their booms drew streamers of water, brought crowds of excited spectators from far and wide.

Two wealthy owners were the Sladen brothers of Cleeve How in Windermere *(4.4)*, one of whom became a talented and successful amateur yacht designer, and both of whom served as Commodore.

Others members included

> George Anthony Aufrere, officer at Waterloo, of Burnside *(founder of the Club)*;
> Joseph Ridgway Bridson, cotton bleacher, of Bolton and Belle Isle *(founder)*;
> Col George John Miller Ridehalgh of Fell Foot *(founder)*;
> the Crossley family, carpet manufacturers, of Belsfield and Halifax *(founders)*;
> William Inman, ship-owner, of Liverpool and St Mary's Abbey;
> the MacIver family, partners in Cunard Shipping Line, of Liverpool and Water Head;
> Otto Burchardt, son of the Prussian Consul to Liverpool, *(helmsman extraordinaire)*;
> the Crossley family, gas engine manufacturers, of Cheshire and Pull Wood;
> the Scott family, cotton spinners, insurance owners, of Bolton and The Yews;
> Sir William Bower Forwood, cotton broker and banker, Mayor of Liverpool.

In 1887, the year of her Golden Jubilee celebrations, Sir William Forwood petitioned Her Majesty the Queen, who was graciously pleased for the Club to be styled the

'Royal Windermere Yacht Club'.

Next page:

168. Launch day at Bowness of a classic 20-foot Windermere Class yacht in the 1870s. The proud owners are accompanied by the boat-builder, possibly James Barrow sitting on the stern. These yachts had a huge sail area of 700 square feet, a lance-like bowsprit 6 feet long, and a full length keel containing 1.5 tons of lead, cast in the open on the lake shore. Only the wealthiest of men could afford to commission a new yacht each year to stay competetive, but the professional crews had the sheer enjoyment of sailing them – and were rewarded for the pleasure.

© Ian Jones

169. An immaculately attired lady and gentleman, posing in the cockpit of their new yacht and proudly proclaiming their wealth. He is wearing an unusual and stylish pale coloured bowler hat with flat brim, and a gaberdine jacket. His lady is wearing an expensive silk coat (the sheen is almost tangible), a large lace cravat tied in a bow, and a hair net as protection against the breeze. The hand stitching on her fine kid glove can be seen, and the reflex curve of her elegant parasol is a thing of beauty. This couple is typical of the nouveaux riches who made the Lake District their playground and weekend retreat in Victorian times – a place to relax, be seen, and have fun.

© Ian Jones

They are believed to be William Inman, Liverpool ship-owner, and his wife Anne (Stobart). St Mary's Abbey in Windermere village was their weekend and holiday retreat (4.13). He served as Commodore of Windermere Sailing Club in 1871-1872. If this is indeed Mr and Mrs Inman, the yacht shown on the launching slip would be Magpie or Sea Mew. Both were built for him by James Barrow in 1873 and 1874 respectively, and the hull shape is consistent with these dates.

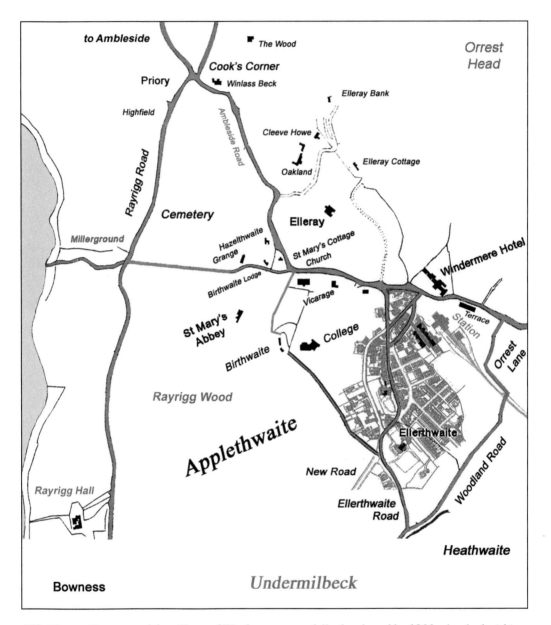

170. The working area of the village of Windermere was fully developed by 1900, clutched within a triangle of land west and south of the station, most of which was previously part of the Birthwaite Estate. It lies adjacent to the many villa residences, widely scattered along both sides of the Kendal-to-Ambleside road, between the station and Cook's Corner.

Chapter 7 – A Vibrant Victorian Township

During successive perambulations around the emerging village of Windermere, we have observed the birth and burgeoning growth of the township during the 1800s. We have covered the 50 years of quietude before the opening of a railway link from Kendal in 1847 – and contrasted this with the second half century of intensive construction, which resulted by 1900 in a vibrant Victorian township. Unlike most other railways, the K&W was intended not for industrial haulage or mineral extraction, but solely for the conveyance of tourists into Lakeland – which it accomplished to considerable effect from its inception. The settlement which rose on the virgin soil of Applethwaite below Orrest Head, where no settlement had existed before, consisted initially of a scattering of widely spaced villas and mansions, mostly completed by 1860. Over the next 40 years they were followed by more densely packed streets of terraced houses, shops, hotels and business premises – the infrastructure and services to support 2,000 permanent residents, wealthy and working class – and the many visitors who arrived by rail in summer months.

For the convenience of our walks the village has been artificially bounded on the north and east by Cook's Corner, Elleray Bank, Windermere Hotel, Orrest Lane, and Woodland Road; to the south and west by Ellerthwaite Road, Rayrigg Wood, Millerground, Highfield and The Priory. For many years after 1900, building work continued to spread beyond this artificial boundary, an aggressive urban expansion southwards into the neighbouring township of Undermillbeck, eventually linking seamlessly with Heathwaite and Bowness. This later expansion lies beyond the geographic limits which are sufficient to define the village of Windermere at the turn of the century, and has been excluded from the present study.

From the start, we have observed both the built environment, and also the social heritage created by the many in-comers drawn to the area – who they were, where they came from, and what they contributed to the growth of the community, their culture, wealth, and attainment – and the artisan skills of the working people.

In 1800 the tiny population scattered between Alice Howe and Cook's Corner consisted of a handful of Westmerians from long established local families, tenant farmers and farm labourers, wresting a hard-won living from difficult terrain in one of the wettest climates in England:

- the Robinson and Dixon families of Cook's House, Wood, and Millerground;
- the Crosthwaites and Ellerays of Birthwaite;
- the Braithwaites, of Orrest Head.
-

By 1840 a tiny handful of in-comers had acquired parcels of land and built the first three villa residences:

- Parker and Hoskins – farming folk with roots in the Lune Valley and west Cumberland, who settled at The Wood and St Catherine's;

- John Wilson – a Scottish-born student at Oxford in 1805 when he purchased Elleray. Known as *'Christopher North'* when he wrote for Blackwood's Edinburgh Magazine, he became Professor of Moral Philosophy at Edinburgh University, for 30 years from 1820; and despite early financial ruin, he retained Elleray as his summer residence;

- James Pennington – a solicitor who acquired The Wood estate as a retreat from the soot and grime of Kendal, providing financial security for his widow and family after his early death;

- three generations of Gardners of Birthwaite, with roots in Kendal and London – portraitist, barrister and solicitor.

The opening of the railway in 1847 brought an initial flurry of building work which lasted for a decade, during which time St Mary's Church, a school for *'the children of the poorer classes'*, a prestigious boarding college for young gentlemen, and most of the grand houses rose on virgin land, close to the turnpike road. Driven by missionary zeal and youthful ambition, the Reverend Addison's grand romantic vision was to shape the township as an ecclesiastical community, with his little chapel at its centre, surrounded by seats of learning and villa residences fashioned in his beloved gothic style. He aimed to attract a populace of genteel and reverential residents of quality – retired clergy, clergy widows, and wealthy gentlefolk – with Revd Addison ministering to their pastoral and parochial needs.

The advent and ease of rail travel attracted off-comers in significant numbers to construct weekend retreats and retirement homes in Windermere – bankers and mill-owners from Kendal, cotton-tots from Manchester, ship-owners and merchant princes from Liverpool. But Revd Addison's grand plan for the village terminated prematurely when his finances were exhausted, and a misdemeanour of trust forced the untimely departure of himself and his family from Windermere in humiliating circumstances – never to return.

The first commercial premises – provision merchants, Post Office, and lodging houses – rose from 1850 on Church Street, the upper part of the turnpike road close to the station. Three new streets of terraced cottages progressively populated open land below the station, the genesis of a village for working people – stonemasons, labourers, blacksmiths, traders, butchers, bakers, shoe makers, to name a few – and their families.

Around 1860 a second, more protracted phase of construction began, which extended for almost four decades to the end of the century, during which time most of the trading and residential heart of the village was built. A rectilinear grid of streets emerged, covering much of Birthwaite farmland and a large parcel of land from the Rayrigg Estate. The layout comprised Main Road, and the curving boulevard of Crescent Road, flanked by a geometric complex of new streets, providing increasing quality of housing for working people. By 1900 a vibrant Victorian township had emerged, together with the services and civic amenities required for a viable and largely self-supporting community.

When his financial resources were exhausted, John Addison was unable to carry through to completion the last and most ambitious institution of his grand plan, a prestigious boarding college for the sons of clergymen, yeoman farmers and tradesmen. Ironically, the unfinished college was purchased by off-comers, who succeeded in achieving the high standard of education for young gentlemen that Revd Addison had sought. His little church and school were acquired by public subscription on behalf of the community; and his mansion and other houses were acquired by the kind of genteel folk he had wished to attract.

Most of the early residents came from Kendal, Liverpool, Manchester, and Yorkshire, escaping from the *miasmata* of the industrial hinterland, to their weekend and holiday retreats in Lakeland. The new-found speed, convenience and comfort of rail travel opened the possibility for gentlemen to commute daily from Windermere to their offices, whilst their families and domestic households enjoyed the pastoral serenity of Lakeland life.

But the tiny initial population and the parochial nature of the first township did not suit everyone; several in-comers moved on to larger Victorian watering holes like Cheltenham. But many of those who stayed contributed enthusiastically and generously to the creation of a thriving social network and to popular civic amenities. In keeping with the time, much social activity centred around the churches; but notably, the more secular Windermere Mutual Improvement Society was a considerable success with the working people from the start. As the forerunner and genesis of a village society, it promoted events such as music, drama, public talks and scientific demonstrations, all of which flourished. With the expansion of population, sporting activities also grew, assisted greatly by the loan of the College buildings and its playing fields for village events.

That many of the original buildings of the village and their architecture survive almost unscathed today, is a tribute to the high quality of construction employed by the Victorian builders – William Harrison, Richard Medcalf, the Atkinson brothers and especially the Pattinson family. Streets retain their individual character, functionality and history, and architectural features imparted by the builder.

Hotels, lodging houses and visitor amenities increasingly attracted people of every social class, from all across the country. The fame and beauty of the Lakes were at last accessible to all. Coaches from the station, linking with steamers from Bowness, conveyed people deeper into Lakeland in search of spiritual and emotional refreshment, engendered by stunning scenery – *'salubrious airs and silvery mists that float around the hills'*.

Windermere village was intended to provide comfortable accommodation and service for visitors –– newly mobile retirees and working folk from the industrial hinterland. In this role the township has survived and prospered, continuing to offer today a holistic collection of affordable amenities, services and recreation, in much the same manner as it has always done.

After more than a century, the advent of a Lake District National Park, and the award of World Heritage Status, have extended the global recognition and attraction of Windermere in the 21st century, ensuring that visitors will continue to arrive from across the world, now and in the future. The establishment of Conservation Areas covering much of the twin townships of Windermere and Bowness protects their heritage and architecture for future generations.

Such developments pay tribute to the drive and vision of the early pioneers, men like the first directors of the Kendal & Windermere Railway who foresaw the commercial potential of tourism, and prosperity for merchants and hoteliers.

I wish to pay special tribute to four gentlemen:

Cornelius Nicholson
whose energy and tenacity brought the Kendal & Windermere Railway

William Harrison
builder of much of the working village

John Garnett
trader extraordinaire, who brought enterprise and service in many guises

The Reverend John Aspinall Addison
'the father of Windermere'
whose missionary zeal conceived the township we know today,

the vibrant village of Windermere.

Courtesy of Heraldry of the World

Appendix 1

Long Holme – Isabella's Island

Isabella Curwen was born at Workington Hall on 2 October 1765. On the death of her father, Henry Curwen, on 23 June 1778 Isabella inherited at the age of less than 13 years a vast coal mining fortune in west Cumbria. The male Curwen line had expired with Henry's death after 650 years, leaving Isabella as his only child and the sole survivor of the Curwen dynasty. During her minority her affairs were handled by the two executors of her father's will, Peter Taylor, a Whitehaven merchant and Robert Merrie.

On 30 May 1780, the Great Island on Windermere was sold at auction in London for £1722 to Henry Addison, acting as agent and attorney for Isabella Curwen. She was greatly taken with the beauty and romanticism of the island retreat in the middle of the Lake, with its half-finished Palladian roundhouse. Historically, the island had been variously known as Long Holme, Lang Holme, The Island, Windermere Island or the Great Island, and was renamed Belle Isle in the 1780s after her purchase. A total of three islands, including Small Holme and Ing Holme, were eventually conveyed to her in July of 1781.

In October 1782 Isabella Curwen and her cousin John Christian of Maryport were married in Edinburgh when she reached 17 years. At that time the law in England specified that marriage of a lady under the age of 21 required the consent of her parents, but no such restrictions on age and consent applied in Scotland. It is likely that Isabella's marriage was a rebellious declaration of independence from her guardians, but the union flourished as a successful, happy and enduring one. Two weeks later, on 18 October all her inherited property was settled on her husband by Peter Taylor, the surviving executor of her father's will. The accounts show that the total transaction cost for the three islands had increased to £2,500. *(approx. £300,000 today.)*

After their marriage John Christian and Isabella set about completing the construction of the Round House as their summer residence, and engaged Thomas White to complete the layout of the gardens and perimeter walk.

In 1786, after successfully appealing against *'mushroom votes'* counted in favour of John Lowther, John Christian was elected as Member of Parliament for Carlisle, a seat which he held intermittently for 30 years. Before standing a second time it appeared expedient for electoral reasons that he should now adopt his wife's name. On 1 March 1790 he took the surname and arms of Curwen *'by the King's sign-manual'*, to be known henceforth as John Christian Curwen.

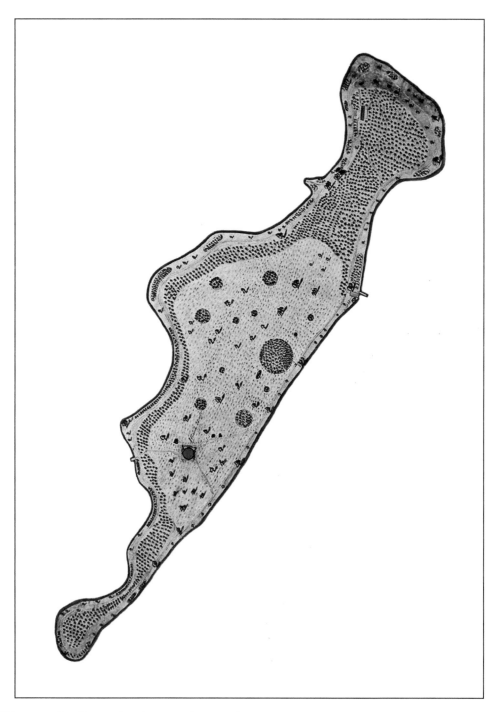

172. Map of Belle Isle by Thomas White, "– for the purpose of landscaping a garden, mainly of trees, and a perimeter walk."

Cumbria Archive Centre (Whitehaven) ref. D Cu/5/232

Appendix 2

Birthwaite Timeline and References

The earliest documents referring to the Birthwaite estate date from the 1600s:

TNA PROB 11/243/140
1654   Will of John Philipson, yeoman, of Birthwaite
       Bequeathed Birthwaite, ploughs and iron gear to second son Christopher Philipson.
       Bequeathed a property named Orrest to first son, John Philipson.

CAC(K) WD/TE VI 316
1670   Christopher Philipson   release of an action from Spooner of
       (of Birthwaite)   Bannerigg.
LRO WRW/K/R466A53/
1708   Will of Christopher Philipson, yeoman of Birthwaite

CAC(K) WD/TE IV 67
1741   Thomas Knipe *(d.1741)*   will proved 1741.

CAC(K) WDX 398 E1-4

1747	Richard Cowperthwaite	deed of assignment & conveyance by Knipe (1712-1757) to Cowperthwaite *(son-in-law)*.
1751	Richard Cowperthwaite	his will dated 26 Aug. 1750, proved 17 Jun. 1751; *held at LRO ref. R 493/122*
1757	Dinah Cowperthwaite, *(née Knipe)*	will of Richd. Cowperthwaite proved, widow inherited on death of husband.
1767	Dinah Cowperthwaite	to James Cowperthwaite *(b.1740)*, release of his mother's widowright, he to pay her annuity.
1770	James Cowperthwaite	release by mother of his obligation to pay annuity
1770	James Cowperthwaite	took a customary mortgage *(from Tobias Atkinson, solicitor, Kendal)*.
1771	James Cowperthwaite	Atkinson to Gawen Braithwaite, .adjustment of Customary Mortgage, a cancelled deed
1771	Leonard Cowperthwaite	his will; *held at LRO ref. R 501/111*

1772	James Cowperthwaite	Cowperthwaite to Atkinson, solr, a bond
1772	James Cowperthwaite ?	Cowperthwaite to Cowperthwaite, indenture
1773	Dinah Cowperthwaite	to Tobias Atkinson, assignment of lease
1773	James Cowperthwaite	to Tobias Atkinson, release of equity of redemption
1774	Atkinson, solr	to Thomas English of Lewisham, customary conveyance, and bond of indemnity
1774	Atkinson, solr	to Dowker (solr ?), adjustment of a term for use of Thos English
1778	Thomas English	to Stephen Lushington, attested copy of office copy of mortgage
1779	(English ?)	(to Gardner ?) sale particulars & contract *(sale of Birthwaite took place at Low Wood 28 July 1779)*
1780		memo of Thos English admittance
1780	English & Lushingto	nconveyance of Birthwaite to Gardner
1782		memo of Lushington's admittance memo of Daniel Gardner's admittance
CAC(K) WDX 398		Gardner family documents.
1774	Thomas English	Birthwaite was conveyed to him with a bond of indemnity; (by Atkinson); also assignment of a term

Thomas English was a tea and coffee merchant in London. He began the construction of the Round House on Long Holme (later named Belle Isle), but ran out of funds in 1778 before completion. Why he bought Birthwaite is uncertain. Both were owned by Christopher Philipson in the 1600s.

Bundle of petitions by "tenants" of Lonsdale, mostly seeking to be admitted to tenements (not dated circa 1721 – 1858)

Petitions of **Thomas English**, first described as Lieutenant in the Westmorland militia, for his customary estates in Applethwaite and Windermere, 1774-1780;

Lancashire RO QSP/4152/15
Bill of costs of prosecution of Thomas English for obtaining money by false pretences c1783

1778		to Stephen Lushington (solr ? provided mortgage of £2000 to English), an attested copy of a mortgage in fee.
1779		Sale Particulars + contract (English + Lushington sell Birthwaite to **Daniel Gardner**)
1779 ?		Applethwaite Inclosure Act
1780		Birthwaite being fenced *(i.e. enclosed ?)*
1780	**Daniel Gardner**	(portrait painter, born Kendal, working London) Birthwaite was conveyed from English by Lushington (solicitor). Conveyance received by Pennington (solicitor, Kendal) *(a rough farmhouse + land)*
1781		improvement work proceeding at Birthwaite for Gardner, Thomas Elleray tenant
Aug 1786 – Jul 1787		admittance of Gardner to Birthwaite, £1-16s. paid to Lord Lonsdale, Lord of the Manor
1805	**George Gardner**	solicitor in London, inherited Birthwaite on death of his father, Daniel Gardner.
1806	George Gardner	mortgage for loan of £2000 from John Machell.

1824	(draft of will)	confirms George Gardner as owner of Birthwaite, copyhold farm and lands with messuage, buildings and woods, watercourses, commons and right of common, and appurts.
1827,	Oct 13 Thomas Elleray	will; held at LRO ref. R 519/92 death and will of Thomas Elleray, tenant of Low Birthwaite allowed George Gardner to take possession of the estate.
	George Gardner	*(did he sell the old Low Birthwaite farmhouse and a parcel of land to Joseph Crosthwaite ?)*
1828	George Gardner	purchased the copyhold of the Birthwaite estate from Lord Lonsdale, built a small villa named Birthwaite Hall.
1828, Feb.2 (codicil 1)		George Gardner *"--- now residing at my house and farm at Birthwaite"*.
1828, Dec.1 (codicil 2)		George Gardner *"--- residing at Birthwaite in my new built messuage"*
1828 Dec.16		Earl of Lonsdale released the freehold of Birthwaite to Geo. Gardner.
1837, May 20 George Gardner		death of George Gardner; interred at St Martin's Church, Bowness.
1837	**George Harrison Gardner**	solicitor in Bowness; inherited Birthwaite on death of his father, George Gardner.
1841	Census	George Harrison Gardner, aged 26, now living at Birthwaite Hall with wife Jane, nee Thompson, aged 19.
		Three dwellings at Low Birthwaite occupied, one by Joseph Crosthwaite. *(Crosthwaite appears to own Low Birthwaite).*
1843	GH Gardner	conveyance to John Wilson (of bank ?) against a mortgage of all Birthwaite for £1600 (reconveyed to Gardner 1845)

1843, Apr.29	CAC(K) WDX 505	small piece of land measuring 11p. sold (?) for £18 to Thomas Crosthwaite, of Low Birthwaite
1845, 16 Aug		Part of Birthwaite estate offered for sale; purchased with Birthwaite Hall, by K&W Railway Co.

"Part of that desirable ESTATE called BIRTHWAITE, situate below Elleray and Orrest Head, about one mile from Bowness, and three quarters of a mile from the shore of Windermere, being part of that "beautiful Romance of Nature" which has been so worthily the theme of the Poet, and the admiration of all Lovers of Natural Scenery.

The Property for sale comprises a genteel residence, with all its Outbuildings, Offices, Gardens, and Shrubberies, together with Twenty-four Acres of Land, undulating in lines of beauty and exact proportions of taste, interspersed with tufts of Larch and other Wood. As to access, and facilities of communication, no property was ever so fortunate, or so well placed. It is bounded by the Ambleside and Kendal road on one hand, and by the Bowness road on the other. The Kendal and Windermere Railway Station will be at the distance of perfection ––– conferring all conveniences, and yet removed from all that may be disagreeable to the eye or ear. The Steam Yacht passes within ten minutes walk *four times a day*; and the London Mail close by the Entrance Gates, twice a day, giving time for reply by return."

1851	Census	Birthwaite house occupied briefly by John Gandy, Chairman of K&W Railway, before his mansion was built (Oakland).
1852		Birthwaite Hall and part of the estate was purchased from the Railway Co. by Revd John Aspinall Addison for his College (£3300)
1853 Sept. John Addison		Birthwaite College opened.
1861	Census	two dwellings at Low Birthwaite unoccupied, one let ?
1871	Census	three dwellings at Low Birthwaite
1881	Census	three dwellings at Low Birthwaite
1891	Census	three dwellings at Low Birthwaite; "Old Birthwaite House" occupied. *(separate entry in census from the College)*

Appendix 3

Kendal & Windermere Railway (K&WR)

Provisional Committee and Directors of the Kendal & Windermere Railway (K&WR) (ref. WG 31 Aug 1844)

Railway from Kendal to Windermere.

Capital: £125,000 in 5000 shares of £25 each.
Consulting Engineers: Joseph Locke, Esq., FRS &c. and J.E. Errington, Esq. (*succeeded by John Harris*)
Solicitors: Messrs Clay and Swift, Liverpool.
Thomas Harrison, Esq., Kendal.

Provisional Committee, Aug. 1844	*Genealogy notes*	
Edward Wilson, Esq., Abbott Hall, Kendal	*banker*	*d.1870*
John Wakefield, Esq., Sedgwick House	*banker*	*d.1866*
G.B. Crewdson, Esq., Kendal	*banker, The Wood*	*d.1876*
John Gandy, Esq., Kendal	*banker, mill owner*	
	Chairman of Directors	
	Oakland, Windermere	*d.1859*
W. Briggs, Esq., MD, Ambleside		
John Braithwaite, Esq., Orrest Head	*yeoman*	*d.1854*
George Burrow, Esq., Lancaster	*West India Merchant*	*d.1861*
Giles Redmayne, Esq., Brathay Hall	*silk merchant*	*d.1898*
John Davy, Esq., MD, FRS, Ambleside	*Lesketh How, Ambleside*	*d.1868*
	Inspector General, Army Hospitals	
Hornby Roughsedge, Esq., Fox Ghyll	*ironmonger, Liverpool*	*d.1859*
James Bryans, Esq., Bellfield	*Bowness*	*d.1863*
J. Hewetson Wilson, Esq., Grange, Sussex	*Ravenstonedale & Hugill*	*b.1784*
William Whitwell, Esq., Kendal	*brewer,*	
	Tolson Hall, Burneside	*d.1886*
Isaac Braithwaite, Esq., Kendal	*drysalter + millowner*	
	Kendal	*d.1861*
Charles L. Braithwaite, Esq., Kendal	*woollen manufacturer*	
	Gill Close House, Kendal	*d.1893*
John Jowitt Wilson, Esq., Kendal	*woollen manufacturer*	
	Underfell House, Kendal	*d.1876*
John Harrison, Esq., Hundhow	*wine merchant*	
	High Hundhow, Bowston	*b.1779*
Cornelius Nicholson, Esq., Cowan Head	*Mayor of Kendal, 1845*	
	later, Deputy Chairman d.1889	
	Secretary of K&WR,	

1845   The K&WR Act received Royal Assent on 30 June 1845
           Linked the Lancaster & Carlisle Railway to Birthwaite

Subscribers named in the Act:

Edward Wilson		*first Director*	*left* £350,000
James Gandy			
John Gandy		*first Director*	*left* £40,000
George Braithwaite Crewdson		*first Director*	*left* £45,000
George Burrow			*left* £6,000
Giles Redmayne			*left* £65,874
Hornby Roughsedge			
James Bryans		*first Director*	*left* £30,000
John Hewetson Wilson		*first Director*	*left* £45,000
William Whitwell		*first Director*	
Charles Lloyd Braithwaite			*left* £23,930
John Jowitt Wilson		*first Director*	*left* £30,000
John Harrison			
Cornelius Nicholson	Esquires	*first Director*	*left* £52,557
John Davy,	Dr		*left* £14,000

Appendix 4

<u>Opening of St Mary's College</u>

This College, of which various notices have appeared in our paper, was formally opened on Sunday last, the occasion being inaugurated by two sermons preached at St Mary's Church by the Revd. T.F. Redhead, of Rock Ferry, the prayers being read by the Revd. Mr Barker, Vicar of Hollins, near Partington, Yorkshire. The disclosures were eloquent and appropriate for the occasion, and were followed by a collection in behalf of the schools connected with the church, amounting to nearly £16.

The opening number of pupils in the institution is 25, and fresh entries are made daily. The College occupies nine acres of ground, including the garden, the pleasure and the play grounds; and when the buildings are all completed, it will form a very imposing structure.

At present the only available building is Birthwaite House, which has been fitted up with much judgement and skill, and, with the accommodation obtained from some adjoining premises which have been converted into excellent school rooms, everything needed at the outset of the undertaking, has been got into most efficient operation. It is intended that Birthwaite House shall form the tower part of the new building. Operations are already commenced for the erection, and when completed it will accommodate 200 youths.

There will be two distinct establishments, viz., a preparatory school, and a College, designed principally for the education of clergymen's sons, though admission will be also open to laymen, and it is this latter institution which is now in operation.

Westmorland Gazette, 10 Sept. 1853

Appendix 5

The Society of Friends and its Relevance to Windermere

Isaac Crewdson (1780-1844) was born into a long established Quaker family of Kendal woollen merchants. His father, Thomas Crewdson, founded the Kendal Bank along with Christopher Wilson and Joseph Maude in 1788, which merged with Wakefields Bank half a century later, to form Wakefield, Crewdson & Co.

When his father died in 1795, Isaac at the age of 15 moved to Ardwick in Manchester where he was apprenticed in the textile industry. He and three brothers entered the calico business in Manchester, eventually enjoying great commercial success.

Throughout the early 1800s Isaac Crewdson maintained strict adherence to the old principles of The Society of Friends, serving as a minister from 1816 to 1836. But as a result of close association with the principles of Quaker theology, he became attracted to a more evangelical view, questioning the supremacy of the *"inner light"* as the only guiding way. In 1834 he published a controversial book *'A Beacon to the Society of Friends'* and *'The Reformer'* newspaper. In these he questioned old Quaker ways, a questioning which found favour more widely than he might have expected, from Kendal, to Manchester, and to Plymouth. His sister-in-law, Sarah Fox, described it as no less than

> *'--- an awakening process as to the great verities of the Christian religion ---'*

which lead to a deep schism within The Society of Friends throughout England – and abroad.

Many Quakers, especially younger members in Manchester and the northern counties of England, split from the Friends, and 50 sympathizers established an assembly of Free Evangelical Friends, loosely associated with the Plymouth Brethren. They renounced *'the wearing of Quaker garb'* and supported the practice of baptism, when Isaac Crewdson was one of the first to go through adult baptism in 1837. Kendal supporters included his brothers William Dilworth Crewdson (II) and George Braithwaite Crewdson; and Robert Braithwaite and Robert Miller Somervell, amongst others. In the late 1830s they migrated with their respective families to the Anglican churches of St George and St Thomas in Kendal, and later to the Congregational Chapel at Troutbeck Bridge.

Appendix 6

<u>Robert Miller Somervell – Founder of K Shoes</u>

Robert Miller Somervell (1821-1899) was born in London, the youngest of three brothers, grandsons of a Scottish Presbyterian minister from Strathaven in Lanark. Robert married Ann Wilson of the Kendal Quaker family in 1849. Mrs Somervell's sister Mary Wilson had already married John Harris, the railway engineer, who sold part of his building land at Birthwaite to Robert. The Wilson ladies shared common great-grand-parents with Robert Braithwaite of The Bingle, and with George Braithwaite Crewdson who for many years lived at The Wood, near Cook's Corner. Clearly family ties and growing Kendal business created strong incentives for the construction of adjacent homes in the growing township. In spite of non-conformist roots, they fulfilled admirably Revd Addison's aspirations for a reverential community around his little church.

William Somervell, the middle of the brother, established himself as a leather merchant in London in 1840, importing fine leathers from abroad, and Robert was quick to learn his trade there. Previously, their eldest sister Margaret had married John Ireland, a woollen manufacturer in Kendal, and their eldest brother John Somervell became a partner in that business in 1838. Sometime after their father died in 1840 their mother moved to join Margaret and John in Kendal, and in 1842 they were followed by Robert. At the age of 21 he started a business which was destined to become synonymous with Kendal for over a century, and eventually its biggest industry. Using borrowed money Robert set out to establish a trade in leather, bringing high quality hide from London and supplying shoe *findings* to the many one-man shoemakers in the north of England.

Shoe making in the early 1800s was a cottage industry and Robert Somervell very rapidly succeeded as the main supplier of uppers and soles of the highest quality leather, and all manner of fine accessories. He transported raw materials from London to small workshops located in every town and village in the north of England; and supplied their hand made shoes and boots to a growing middle class in the larger towns and cities. The trade entailed much travelling, in all weathers, on the worst roads in England, and long hours spent on horseback. In the industrial areas around Manchester and Liverpool he was able to travel more quickly on the growing rail network; but north of Lancaster, coach and horse were the sole means of transport at that time. Robert Miller Somervell was a tall man, over six feet in height, possessed of great energy, determination and entrepreneurship. He was a man of integrity and deeply religious throughout his life, all of which were rooted in his Scottish non-conformist heritage.

He worked initially from a single storeroom at Sand Aire Mill in Kendal, travelling prodigious distances on horseback all over the north of England, even into Scotland, the Isle-of-Man and Ireland, spending up to half his time on the road away from home. So successful was his trading that within two years he repaid completely the capital of £110 borrowed from his mother and brothers. By 1844 the footwear business had expanded to such an extent that larger warehouse premises were leased at Netherfield, in the Kirkland area of Kendal. In 1848 brother John Somervell left his position at Ireland's woollen mill to join Robert as a partner in Somervell Brothers.

In 1847 and 1849, John and then Robert Somervell married Rachael and Anne Wilson, these ladies being first cousins from the well known Quaker family in Kendal. Although the Somervells were baptised in the London Wall Scotch Church and raised as Presbyterians, in Kendal they espoused the Congregational Church; and through their wives the Quaker influence also entered their daily life.

With the investment which John brought to the business, and its growing success, Somervell Brothers acquired the whole of the 2-acre Netherfield site and a sprawl of buildings thereon. This expansion enabled more operations to be performed at base – currying of leather, cutting of uppers and soles. Stitching of uppers to soles and finishing work were still performed by an army of out-workers in small workshops who Robert continued to visit fortnightly. To prevent covert substitution of sub-standard leather soles it became his practice to stamp his products with the letter 'K' before despatch, and this lead eventually to the company name of 'K Shoes'.

The advent of mechanical sewing machines from America transformed the stitching of leather uppers and soles, enabling production line operation to be introduced at Netherfield across the whole site. The business boomed, eventually becoming Kendal's largest employer with 600 employees.

The astonishing growth of their leather merchandising and shoe-making business quickly made the Somervells moderately wealthy men. Within twelve years of starting, Robert was able to build a very fine villa named Hazelthwaite, in Windermere, where he lived for nearly 50 years. Robert and Anne Somervell filled their home with nine children and they became the driving force in the Congregational Chapel at Troutbeck Bridge, where Robert oversaw its initial construction in 1858 and then its enlargement five years later. Throughout his life he often lead the service at Troutbeck Bridge, participating with his brother John in the British and Foreign Bible Society in Kendal, and became chair of the Literary and Scientific Society. Both brothers were ardently opposed to slavery and often spoke on the subject. Robert served for many years as a magistrate and in 1888 was appointed JP for Westmorland.

John Somervell continued to run the business in Kendal, living at Kent Terrace. In 1861 Somervell Brothers participated in the great International Exhibition and won a prestigious award for machine working of leather uppers for shoes. Following the partnership with Robert, John Somervell entered civic affairs, being elected to Kendal Council in 1849. Unusually, he served twice as Mayor – in 1882 and again in 1883.

It became customary at Whitsuntide for the workforce at Netherfield to be treated by their employers to a railway excursion to Windermere, where they were able to enjoy and explore the scenic grandeur of the lake country and to cruise upon the water.

> *'A fiddle somehow or other found its way among them, and its enlivened airs moved heart and foot, to the great delight of the more juvenile.'*

Rather unfortunately, in 1860 religious fervour and an employer's *'powerful influence over the working classes'* led to the dismissal of eight ladies from their employment at Somervell Brothers, *'solely on account of their attendance at a dance at the Shakespeare ballroom'*. It was described in the press as a *'tyrannical act'* and *'zeal without knowledge'*. Sadly, the press does not record whether the young ladies were re-employed following an outpouring of public disquiet against the employers. *(Westmorland Gazette, 27 Oct. 1860.)*

In 1863 Robert Somervell purchased the grand Fairhaven mansion at the bottom end of Windermere village, following the deaths of Richard Wilson and his wife. He paid a bargain price of £1,350 for the property, in a private sale from the trustees of Richard Wilson's estate, the property having been for sale for many months. It came complete with a four-stalled stable and gardener's residence.

Around 1869 there was a downturn in the business of Somervell Brothers and Hazelthwaite was let for three years to A.H. Heywood who was building a new mansion at nearby Elleray, to replace Professor Wilson's house. The Somervell family moved for a while to more modest accommodation in Southport, with Robert living in Kendal during the week to be near the business. An unsuccessful experiment with a cheaper range of shoes was abandoned, and the factory reverted to the traditional high quality products for which they were now famous, especially in overseas markets. Gradually the business recovered and Robert Somervell's family returned to Hazelthwaite in 1872.

Robert Miller Somervell lived quietly in Windermere for over 40 years, only occasionally participating in village life, apart from Sunday service in the little chapel at Troutbeck Bridge which benefited greatly from his benefaction.

In the final days of 1899, eight members of his household contracted influenza and Robert Somervell died on 30 December, two days before the start of the new century *(Yorkshire Post, 1 Jan. 1900)*. The funeral was so extensive that special trains from Kendal brought workers from the Netherfield factory, some of whom provided music at the house. Two processions, one from Hazelthwaite and the other from the little chapel, converged at Cook's Corner and proceeded to the Rayrigg Road Cemetery for the interment. Robert Miller Somervell was buried on 2 January 1900, almost within sight of his mansion, and his wife Anne was laid to rest by his side in 1905. His estate was valued at £21,246 *(equivalent to well over £2 million today)*.

Like their father, the Somervell family were high achievers. Probably at the wish of their mother, several of the children attended Quaker schools in Kendal and then in Southport. Four of the six sons of Robert and Anne Somervell graduated from King's College, Cambridge. Robert (junior) became a master at Harrow School where he taught English language with great effect to a young Winston Churchill. Frederick Somervell also became a schoolmaster, in Oxford, and High Sheriff of Oxfordshire. Clifton Somervell became a Congregational minister and married his cousin Helen, daughter of John Somervell. Arthur, the youngest son, was a renowned composer of choral works, and was appointed professor at the Royal College of Music. In 1929 he was knighted for a lifetime's contribution to music.

Colin and Gordon Somervell became the mainstay of shoe manufacturing in Kendal, after their father's death, and Colin was appointed High Sheriff of Westmorland in 1916.

A truly remarkable family, with long standing roots in Windermere.

Wilson - Braithwaite - Crewdson - Fox - Lloyd - Masterman - Dillworth - Jowitt - Harris - Somervell

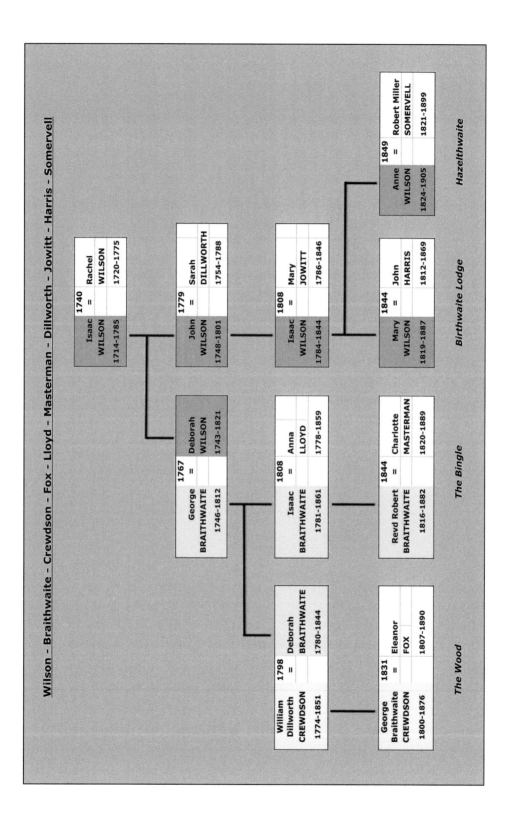

The Wood   *The Bingle*   *Birthwaite Lodge*   *Hazelthwaite*

Appendix 7

<u>Trades and Occupations – Census returns</u>

Occupations of people living on the new streets of Cross Street, High Street and Victoria Street

Occupations	1851	1861
builders, joiners, masons, plasterers, glaziers, painters, etc.	25	32
professionals ––– teachers, post masters, chemist etc.	2	7
transport ––– coach, rail, blacksmiths, wrights, grooms	3	17
food and provisions ––– butchers, bakers, grocers, etc	6	24
clothing ––– dressmakers, milliners, tailors, shoemakers	4	21
servants, laundry, char, garden, coach, carter etc	12	30
unemployed, guests, others		17
Total working population	52	148
Wives, children, dependents		153
Total population (three streets)		301

Timeline of Development Noted in Planning and Census Records

(Cumbria Archive Centre (Kendal) ref. WSUDW W1)

	Dates of Planning applications	First Census record of this street
Cross Street	– 1896	1861
Church Street		1861
High Street		1861
Victoria Street		1861
New Street/New Road	– 1898	1861
St Mary's Terrace		1861
St Mary's Road		1891
College Road/Park Range	1891 – 1900	1861
Crescent Road	1885 – 1901	1871
Beech Street		1871
Derby Terrace		1871
Birch Street		1881
Salisbury Place		1881
Hazel Street	– 1885	1881
Ash Street		1881
Oak Street	1884 – 1893	1881
Upper Oak Street	1895 – 1900	1881
Woodland Grove		1851
Broad Street	1884 – 1900	1891
Holly Road	1884 – 1896	1891
Woodland Road	1892 – 1898	1881
Ellerthwaite Road	1896 – 1904	1901
Main Road	1895 –	1881

Clearly, building work started at the north of the village near the station, and progressed southwards to completion at Ellerthwaite. For nearly half a century some streets were never clear of builders' tackle.

Appendix 9

Relative Value of the Pound, 1750-2010

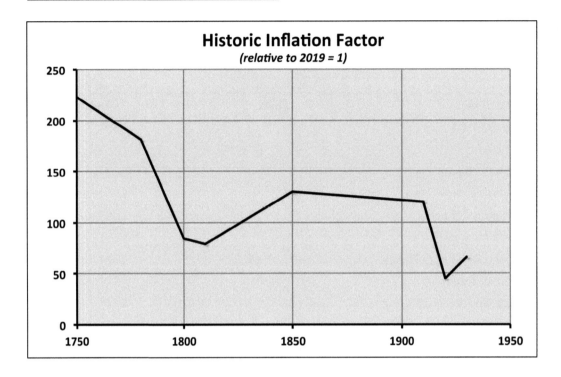

Historic Inflation Factor
(relative to 2019 = 1)

The graph above (*based on Bank of England, and Office for National Statistics data*) illustrates the complexity of converting commodity prices in the 1700s and 1800s to 21st century equivalent values. It provides, at best, approximate factors for converting historic costs to equivalent 2020 values. Pragmatically, for the Victorian period covered by this book, a factor of 100 is an easy and stable rule-of-thumb (although a factor of 125 is more accurate).

The graph contains pronounced dips which coincide with major wars – the Napoleonic Wars, and World War I.

A further complication arises when converting property and land prices. Following World War II the mortgage borrowing limit for property was increased by banks and building societies from typically two-times-salary to four-times-salary (or even more in London). Due to continual shortage of housing, rather than easing the problem of house purchase, the effect has simply been to increase property prices in line with the maximum mortgage that cold be raised.

Therefore, factors for property value can be doubled (or even trebled in London), compared to those given by the graph for commodities, to compensate for increased mortgage lending limits (i.e. a factor of 200-300 above Victorian property prices).

Bibliography

"Guide to the Lakes"   Thomas West (1778)

"A Survey of the Lakes of Cumberland, Westmorland and Lancashire 1789"   James Clarke

"Thomas Gray's Journal of his Visit to the Lake District in October 1769"
                                   ed. William Roberts (Liverpool University Press)

"A Tour from London to the Lakes of Westmorland & Cumberland 1791"   diary of A. Walker

"A Tour in the Lakes 1797"   William Gell (edited by William Rollinson)

"A History, Directory & Gazetteer of Cumberland & Westmorland"   (Parsons & White, 1829)

"Sylvan's Pictorial Handbook to the English Lakes"   Thomas & Edward Gilks (1847)

"History Topography and Directory of Westmorland"   (P.J. Mannex, 1849)

"Guide to Windermere"   Miss Harriet Martineau (published privately, 1854)

"A Complete Guide to the English Lakes"   Miss Harriet Martineau (J. Garnett, 1855)

"Leaves from Lakeland"   James Payn (J. Garnett, ca.1860)

"A Handbook to the English Lakes"   James Payn (J. Garnett, ca.1860)

" Furness Abbey and its Neighbourhood"   James Payn (J. Garnett, ca.1860)

"A Guide to Highways of the Lake District of England"   John Garnett (ca.1860)

"Views of the English Lakes and Mountains"   John Garnett (ca.1860)

"The Lakes in Sunshine"   James Payn (J. Garnett, 1867, 1873)

"Christopher North, a Memoir of John Wilson"   Mrs Gordon (1879)

"The Church & Parish of St Mary, Applethwaite, Commonly Called St Mary's, Windermere"
                                   George Godfrey Cunninghame (published privately 1900)

"Some Records of Troutbeck"   George Henry Joyce (published privately, 1925)

"Windermere – Its Growth and History"   Lancelot Steele (Atkinson & Pollitt, 1928)

"Annals of Troutbeck, Windermere"   C.T. Phillips (published privately, 1933)

"St. Mary's Church Applethwaite Windermere 1848 - 1948"   H.C. Broadrick (1948)

"The Place Names of Westmorland"   A.H. Smith (Cambridge University Press, 1967)

"Wordsworth's Hawkshead"   T.W. Thompson (Oxford University Press, 1970)

"A Visit to Lakeland in 1844"   Revd C.A. Tryon, edited by J.D. Marshall (CWAAS, 1971)

"Old Lakeland, Some Cumbrian Social History"   J.D. Marshall (David & Charles, 1971)

"Road Transport in Cumbria in the 19th Century"   L.A. Williams (George Allen & Unwin 1975)

"Highways and Byways in the Lake District"   A.G. Bradley (Jackson & Sproat 1980)

"Early Railway History in Furness"   Melville & Hobbs (CWAAS, 1951, Tract Series)

"Kendal and Windermere Railway"   Julian Mellentin (Dalesman, 1980)

"The Lake Counties from 1830 to the Mid-Twentieth Century"
                    J.D. Marshall & John K. Walton (Manchester University Press, 1981)

"Traditional Buildings & Life in the Lake District"   Susan Denyer (National Trust, 1991)

"Windermere in the Nineteenth Century"   Westall, Marshall, Walton, Dowthwaite
                    (CNWRS,1991)

"The Place Names of Cumbria"   Joan Lee (Cumbria Heritage Services, 1998)

"Roads and Tracks of the Lake District"   Paul Hindle (Cicerone 1998)

"St Mary's Church in Applethwaite by Windermere, The First 150 Years"   Ian Jones (2001)

"The Estate and Household Accounts of Sir Daniel Fleming Of Rydal Hall 1688-1701"
                    Revd B.G. Fell, Blake Tyson (CWAAS, 2001)

"The House of Hird, the Story of a Windermere Mansion & Its People"   Ian Jones (2002)

"The Fleming Family of Rydal Hall"   Ann Galbraith (Shoes with Rockets, 2006)

"The Baroness of Belsfield by Windermere"   Ian Jones (2007)

"The Royal Windermere Yacht Club Celebrates 150 Years"   Ian Jones (2010)

"The Ferry Inn on Windermere"   Ian L. Muir (2011)

"Village by the Water, A History of Bowness-on-Windermere from the Earliest Times to 1963",
                    John L. Campbell (2015)

Endnotes

1. *'Annals of Troutbeck'*, C.T. Phillips, 1933
2. The terms *in-comer* and *off-comer* are used interchangeably in this book, although the latter is regarded by many people as being a little derogatory.
3. The township known as Applethwaite (an ancient division of land, in this case measuring approximately 4 miles square) extends from the Trout Beck at Troutbeck Bridge on the north, across Moor Howe, the Common and Bannerigg on the east, southwards as far as the Myln Beck, descends westward along that stream to the lake shore near Rayrigg Wyke, and north to the Trout at Calgarth. Near its centre the highest ground is Orrest Head, a rise of 668 feet above the lake. In this book we are concerned with part of this domain, that part which lies south and west of Orrest Head.
4. Birthwaite was the name of a small farm on which part of the centre of the new village of Windermere was built. The village briefly acquired the name of the farm, but was superseded in 1860 following protracted and sometimes vexatious argument between two sets of in-comers, one faction residing in Bowness, the other in Windermere. But from the start the Station was listed in railway timetables as Windermere.
5. A *'statesman'* was the holder of an estate of land, quite small in Cumbria, perhaps 50-100 acres. Alternatively, the term may be derived from *'stead-man'*, someone of standing in the community, referred to by the title Mr, or occasionally Esq., a little above the average farmer.
6. Since this text was written, the following volume has been published: *'Village by the Water, A History of Bowness-on-Windermere'*, John L. Campbell, 2015.
7. The names *Lakeland* and *Lake District* are used interchangeably in this book.
8. Orrest means battle in old Norse. In *'Place Names of Cumbria'* Joan Lee speculates that as two Roman roads crossed near here it may have been the site of a battle.
9. The 1841 Census records 18 people living in the area of the Birthwaite estate.
10. an ancient word for a narrow packhorse trail, sometimes Causeway or Causey or Casie.
11. i.e. surfaced with random local stone, but not yet to the Macadam standard.
12. known as Cook's House today, a name which migrated from an ancient farmhouse nearby.
13. the A591 and A592 of today.
14. A UK hundredweight is one twentieth part of an Imperial ton, or 112 pounds.
15. CAC(C) Ref.: DX 431/2 *'Principal Roads in England and Wales'*, John Ogilby, 1675.
16. *'Roads and Tracks of the Lake District'*, Dr Paul Hindle, 1998. Cunningham gives the completion date of the *'present highway with easier gradients'* as 1768.
17. Paul Hindle states that the southerly route did not exist in 1762 when the turnpike first opened, although a rough track across marshy ground is shown dotted on Jeffreys' map of 1770. The dotted lines denote a track lacking defined boundaries. Roads across marshy terrain were often open-sided before the land was enclosed, and meandered with the seasons according to where the ground was passable.
18. When Celia Fiennes travelled from Kendal to Bowness in 1697 she found that the road through Crook was exceedingly narrow and incapable of taking carriages.
19. William Wordsworth was born in Cockermouth, educated at Hawkshead Grammar School, and scholar of St. John's College, Cambridge.
20. one of the starting points for driving the King's deer to the valley deer-parks.
21. Birthwaite Hall (sometimes Birthwaite House) was built in 1828 for the retirement of George Gardner, barrister.
22. 1½ miles to Bowness Bay.
23. a coarse hard slate-like rock laid down in the Silurian period, more than 400 million years ago.
24. tops and sides for door and window surrounds.

25 'The Church & Parish of St Mary, Applethwaite, Commonly Called St Mary, Windermere', G.G. Cunninghame, 1900

26 his father, also named George Godfrey Cunningham, was a historical writer and publisher in Glasgow and Edinburgh.

27 'The Websters of Kendal', Angus Taylor, 2004

28 G.G. Cunningham married Mary Louisa Hughes le Fleming in 1871. She was a daughter of Major General George Cumberland Hughes of the Indian Army, who assumed the surname le Fleming in 1862 as a condition of inheriting Rydal Hall.

29 he adopted the alternative spelling of Cunninghame in later years, possibly to differentiate from his father of the same name.

30 a stableman employed to look after the horses of guests at an inn.

31 mainly the *Westmorland Gazette* and *Kendal Mercury*.

32 Cumbria Archives Centre, Kendal.

33 *Westmorland Gazette* 24 Apr. 1847.

34 Formed more than 420 million years ago.

35 Clarke's Survey of the Lakes, 1789

36 On the north side of the turnpike a continuation of this lane can be traced to Common Farm, crossing Moor Howe towards Troutbeck Valley, Garburn Pass and ultimately to High Street.

37 Cook's House was for centuries the name of a farmhouse which stood on the site where a Gothic-style villa was built in 1854. The new villa was named Winlass Beck ca.1860 and the name Cook's House migrated to the cottage on the north side of the intersection.

38 e.g. St Mary's Church to Rayrigg; St Mary's Church past Low Birthwaite Cottages to College Gardens; Windermere Hotel, passing Christopher North's Cottage, to St Catherine's.

39 It was John Loudon McAdam who in 1811 developed a durable system of constructing roads for wheeled vehicles, sufficiently robust to withstand the destructive rutting action of heavy wagon wheels and carriages. He enlisted teams of men, women and boys, armed with nothing more than hammers, in order that the top layer of stone was '--- *broken small, resting directly on the sub-soil; every piece of stone put into a road which exceeds an inch in any of its dimensions is mischievous'*. A simple engineering formula which has stood the test of time.

40 In the Rusland Valley, south of Hawkshead.

41 Both spellings, Stile and Style, were used in old documents. It is possible that Droomer is a distortion of Drummer, and Bannerigg is where a flag was hoisted during the ancient battle of Orrest.

42 Causy, Causey, or Causeway, is a name often used to denote a packhorse track, particularly a raised track across marshy ground.

43 CAC(K) WD/Big 1226 Orrest Head Estate

.44 *'Survey of Ancient Monuments of Westmorland'*, p.247; wood carving within the building bears the inscription '*I.D. 1671*'. Unpublished notes by Janet Martin also refer to deeds dated 1596.

45 '*Road Transport in Cumbria in the Nineteenth Century*', L.A. Williams, records that in 1825 John Braithwaite held the offices of clerk, treasurer and surveyor of the Ambleside (turnpike) Trust.

46 '*Records Relating To the Barony of Kendale: Volume 3*'. The office of Surveyor was no sinecure, as he had to keep constant watch that no nuisances were allowed to accumulate, that all grass and saplings were removed and that the adjacent landlords trimmed their hedges so as to allow as much sun and wind as possible to dry them; he had to inspect the bridges and to see that all water courses and dykes were kept scoured.

47 '*Christopher North*', Elsie Swann, 1934; p.31

48 '*Christopher North, a Memoir of John Wilson*', p.88, Mrs Gordon, 1879.

49 Taking guidance from a Scottish portraitist, landscape painter and engineer, Alexander Nasmyth.

50 '*Christopher North, a Memoir of John Wilson*', p.102, Mrs Gordon, 1879.

51 Yachts named Endeavour, Eliza, Palafox, Roscoe, Clyde, Jane, Billy; and the rowing barge Nil Timeo.

52 Windermere Parish Register, Marriages, 1811. It is not clear if the ceremony took place at Jesus Church in Troutbeck, the Revd Fleming's church, or at St Martin's in Bowness, the mother church, where the Parish Register was kept.

53 the Chair of Moral Philosophy and Political Economy was regarded as the most exalted at Edinburgh University. Moral philosophy was described by his daughter as 'the science of mind'.

54 *Westmorland Gazette*, 6 Aug. 1825

55 CAC(K) WDX 398, Gardner papers

56 Surely it would be appropriate for some lasting memorial of this great man to be erected in Windermere.

57 The Wood was conveyed from George Dixon to Miles Dixon in 1756

58 Parsons & White Directory, 1829, records that *'In some parts of Westmorland considerable portions of land are covered with coppices, consisting principally of oak, ash, alder, birch and hazel. These underwoods are usually cut down every 16th year, and wood is chiefly converted into hoops and bobbins, the former being generally sent to Liverpool, and the latter to the cotton, woollen, linen and silk manufacturers.'*

59 Obstructed today by two centuries of tree growth, and by housing.

60 CAC(K) WDB 22/2/1/35, sale particulars dated 1925.

61 Construction of the Palladian style Round House commenced in 1774 for Thomas English, a London coffee and tea merchant, but was sold to Isabella Curwen when his wealth expired before the building was complete.

62 Anne, eldest daughter of Alexander Hoskins of Broughton Hall, near Cockermouth.

63 Old Bellfield today, and not to be confused with Belsfield Hotel.

64 Parsons & White Directory, p.677, lists The Wood as one of the villas of Applethwaite township in 1829, but omits St Catherine's.

65 James Pennington was a cousin of the Penningtons who had fostered George Gardner.

66 Bowel problems.

67 WDB/35 931 map of Cook's House estate (ca.1850)

68 The origin of the name "Cook's House" is lost in the mists of time, but it seems reasonable to suggest that it was named after its owners in the distant past. There is a legend that a dispute over neighbouring land which Myles Philipson of nearby Calgarth wished to acquire, was resolved by foul means. A couple, named Kraster and Dorothy Cook, refused to sell the disputed land. By a nefarious set-up, they were falsely convicted of stealing a silver cup and hanged. It seems likely that Cook's House was their property, from which the disputed land was annexed by Philipson.

69 'Historic Farmhouses in and around Westmorland' J.H. Palmer, and W.T. McIntire, 1949.

70 CAC(K) WD/TE Vol III 47, 1719 (*£41 at that time is equivalent to about £8,000 today.*)

71 Biggs were a hardy form of barley; probably used for animal feed and the brewing of ale.

72 About the value of a worn out old car or tractor today, say £700.

73 Using a factor of 300 for equivalent values in 1700, James Robinson's estate today would be valued around £12,000, before funeral costs of about £900 and debts around £7,200.

74 *Westmorland Gazette*, 29 Sept. 1849

75 In 1860 the new villa built by Peter Kennedy on the site of the old Cook's Farmhouse was renamed Winlass Beck, and the name Cook's House migrated across the road.

76 Low Gate Mill How, High Gate Mill How, and St Catherine's Brow Head seem to have formed the estate known today as St Catherine's.

77 *Liverpool Mercury*, 26 May 1815

78 George Augustus Frederick Henry Bridgeman, 2nd Earl of Bradford, whose estates and seat were mainly in Shropshire and Staffordshire.

79 Tithes were no longer payable in those parts of Applethwaite south and west of Orrest Head where Windermere was built.

80 Miss Anne Agnes Parker is remembered on a wall tablet in Jesus Church in Troutbeck.

81 The Bowness to Ambleside road via Cook's Corner is described in the will of Thomas Ullock (1840) as being a turnpike road. But prior to that date it was notoriously rough and badly maintained, certainly not to turnpike standard.

82 Rayrigg Bank was renamed Adelaide Hill after the dowager Queen Adelaide stood on the hill when she visited the Lake District in August 1839.

83 Clarke's Survey of the Lakes, published in 1789. Attributing Calgarth to Peter Taylor on this map seems to be a cartographic error. Surviving records indicate that Miles Sandys of Graythwaite acquired Calgarth in Feb.1730, following expiry of the Philipson male line, and sold it to Richard Watson, Bishop of Llandaff, in 1788. Revd John Raincock, rector of Bootle, inherited Rayrigg via his mother Agnes Fleming (1749-1809). To secure the inheritance John Raincock adopted the surname Fleming. His grandfather Fletcher Fleming (1715-1770) acquired Rayrigg in 1735 from the survivors of the Philipson line (see 'Wordsworth's Hawkshead', T.W. Thomson, p.305; and 'The Philipson Family' Part I, T.G. Fahy, C&WAAS 1964, p.188) Similarly, Peter Taylor junior was descended from the Fleming line through his mother Isabella Fleming (1750-1826), second daughter of Fletcher Fleming. Isabella married Peter Taylor senior (1740-1789), a merchant from Whitehaven with plantations in America. In 1788 Calgarth was purchased by Richard Watson, Bishop of Llandaff (ref. DNB).

84 Lancelot Steele.

85 C&WAAS Transactions 002_1926_vol26_0003

86 A large rowing boat propelled by one or two men.

87 'There were three customary ferries crossing the Lake, but that from Claife was the principal.'

88 Rhym attributed to Thomas Cowperthwaite (1711-1782), ironmonger in Hawkshead.

89 Apprentices served five years as the underdog in such a place.

90 Arguably, Rayrigg Hall ranks second in architectural importance only to the palladian Round House on Belle Isle. The island is included administratively within the township of Applethwaite but is geographically close to Bowness.

91 George Dixon of Orrest head & Rayrigg is referred to many times in the late 1600s in documents of George Browne of Townend (CAC(K) WD/TE). In the same archive, John Philipson, the last of the male line, is also associated with Rayrigg around 1700.

92 'The Fleming Family of Rydal Hall' Ann Galbraith. (T.W. Thompson in 'Wordsworth's Hawkshead', gives the date of the Fleming purchase of Rayrigg estate as 1735.)

93 A major twentieth century alteration demolished part of the west wing, leaving a more balanced southerly aspect with two curved bays, symmetrically disposed, framing a wide central façade.

94

95 St Mary's, Rydal 1825-1857; St Oswald's, Grasmere 1857-1863.

96 6th baronet, born 1791 at Whitehaven, son of Roger le Fleming. This branch of the Fleming family use the original French form of the name.

97

98 Storrs Hall, ca.1795 for Sir John Legard, slave trader; Croft Lodge at Clappers Gate, ca.1825 for James Brancker, Liverpool sugar king; and Old Bellfield ca.1805 for Isabella Taylor, relict of Peter Taylor, plantation and slave owner in South Carolina.

99 *Kendal Indictment Book, 1811-1817*

100 It is not clear whether the name relates to a mill race channelling water on to a mill wheel. Its proximity to Rayrigg Wood and the sawpit suggests that this was a saw mill. *Stokkr* in old Norse means tree stump. Logs mounted vertically in a frame were often used as stampers to *felt* the fibres of cloth, shrinking and strengthening it. A powerful mill with a good head of water was needed to drive this extremely noisy machinery.

101 From Old Norse *thveit,* a clearing in the birch trees.

102 TNA ref. PROB 11/243/140 Will of John Philipson, Yeoman of Birthwaite.

103 There were several distinct lines of the Philipson family in South Lakeland in the 1600s and earlier, distantly related. They had seats at Calgarth, Rayrigg, Birthwaite, Long Holme, Lindeth, Crook, Hodge Hill, Burblethwaite and more.

104 Confusingly, there are three possible Orrest farms nearby in Applethwaite. Orrest Head Farm is adjacent to Birthwaite, and is the most likely one; Near Orrest Farm is a mile away to the north of Orrest Head; and Far Orrest Farm is still farther north, adjacent to Holehird.

105 The seat of the Knipe (or Knype) family was Burblethwaite Hall, adjacent to the Philipson holding of Hodge Hill in the Winster Valley.

106 If title was copyhold (usual in Cumbria) then ownership could be freely conveyed to members of his immediate family on payment of a 'fine' to the Lord of the Manor.

107 Richard Cowperthwaite bequested Birthwaite to his second son James.

108 1731, Gawen Braithwaite of Brathey married Isabel Hirdson of Dalepark. 1768, Gawen Braithwaite appears on the Electoral Register of Rydal and Loughrigg, apparently a man of substance.

109 'Westmorland Agriculture 1800-1900', Frank Walls Garnett, page 14.

110 The price paid by English in 1772 for the three islands of Long Holme, Small Holme and Ing Holme is not known, but in 1745 the same three islands changed hands locally for £450.

111 CWAAS Transactions 1984, vol.84 0016; 'The Troutbeck Park Slate Quarries, Their Management and Markets, 1753-1760', Blake Tyson

112 'The Barony of Kendale', Volume 3, 'Supplementary Records: Windermere – Undermillbeck and Applethwaite', (1926). John F. Curwen (editor)

113 Philipson owned both Birthwaite and the island of Long Holme, and may have offered them to English together.

114 a total of approximately £1.5 million today

115 At the age of 14 her fortune was in the hands of executors of the will of Henry Curwen, one of whom was Peter Taylor of Whitehaven.

116 Alderman Christopher Redman was three times Mayor of Kendal, in 1749, 1760, 1761.

117 John and William Wordsworth entered Hawkshead School in 1779, and were joined by their younger brother Christopher around 1782. On the evidence of Daniel Gardner's payments to William Pennington, George Gardner entered the same school in 1783.

118 CAC(K) Ref. WDX 398

119 Auctioned at Low Wood Inn, 28 August 1779.

120 more than £1 million today.

121 'Inclosure' is an old or formal spelling of the word. The Inclosure Acts were a series of Acts of Parliament which enclosed previously open pasture and common land. They removed existing rights of local people freely to carry out activities in these areas, such as cultivation, cutting of hay, grazing of animals or using other resources such as small timber, fish, and turf. Inclosure Acts for small areas had been passed sporadically since the 12th century but the majority were passed between 1750 and 1860. Much larger areas were also enclosed during this time and in 1801 the Inclosure (Consolidation) Act was passed to tidy up previous acts. In 1845 another General Inclosure Act allowed for the appointment of Commissioners who had power to enclose land without submitting a request to Parliament. (Ref. Wikipedia)

122 equivalent to about £½ million today.

123 a type of customary land tenure enabling family inheritance.

124 Second codicil to George Gardner's will, dated 1828. The funds for construction of the new villa at Birthwaite came partly from the sale of his chambers at Lincoln's Inn. Unfortunately there is little in surviving records to tell us much about this house.

125 *Westmorland Gazette*, 26 Jul. 1834

126 CAC(K) WDY 552Contains a poor quality photocopy of an Old College Prospectus ca.1910, including the only known image of Birthwaite Hall (demolished in 1957).

127 West India men like John Bolton of Storrs Hall and James Brancker of Croft Lodge.

128 The Bellasis family of Holly Hill, George Aufrère of Burnside, Giles Redmayne of Brathay Hall, and Mark Beaufoy of Bowness to name but a few.

129 G.H. Gardner's father George would have known the Wordsworth brothers at Hawkshead Grammar School, although they were several years older.

130 '--- and as to the said copyhold farm and lands called **Birthwaite** *with the right of common and other the rights and appurtenances thereto belonging to the use of the said* **William Pennington** *of Crosthwaite his heirs and assigns for ever provided nevertheless that if it shall be found that by reason of the customs of the manors of which the said farm called Birthwaite is holden that the aforesaid limitations cannot take effect so far as they relate to the said farm that then I give and devise the said farm and lands with the common and other appurts thereto belonging unto my said son* **George Harrison Gardner**'.

131 CAC(K) WDX/398 13 scrapbook of Jane Gardner

132 N.B. there are four properties close to Windermere with Orrest in their names: Orrest Head Farm, beside Alice Howe; Orrest Head House, on the opposite side of the turnpike road; Near Orrest, beside Causeway; and Far Orrest, above Holehird.

133 Rainfall averages 70 inches per year in the Windermere area, compared with 43 inches for the country as a whole, and 24 inches in London.

134 Cornelius Nicholson's father apparently died quite young leaving his widow, Agnes Coward, to raise at least four of their children. She must have been a remarkable lady for the Census of 1861 records her at the age of 82 years as Post Mistress in Ambleside. Consequently, the family would have been well acquainted with the stamp distributor, William Wordsworth.

135 Cornelius Nicholson (1804 – 1889) served as Mayor of Kendal in 1845.

136 James Cropper came to the area from Liverpool in July 1845, initially leasing Cornelius Nicholson's successful Cowan Head and Burneside mills, and taking full ownership in 1854 *(Oxford Dictionary of National Biography)*.

137 'Railways of the Lake Counties' by David Joy, Dalesman Books, 1973.

138 One proposed route across Morecambe Bay was advocated by George Stephenson himself.

139 It was claimed that the Morecambe Bay barrages would reclaim 20,000 acres (Stephenson) and 46,300 acres (Hague) of valuable new farmland, with potential for a handsome profit.

140 For the next century express trains crossing Shap were hauled by two locomotives in tandem.

141 The work of Joseph Locke.

142 'Kendal and Windermere Railway' by Julian Mellentin, Dalesman Books, 1980. 'The Kendal & Windermere Railway' by Dick Smith, Cumbrian Railways Association, 2002

143 Even with the benefit of cuttings, the gradients on two section of line, one between Bowston and Plantation, and another beyond Staveley, was 1-in-80, quite challenging for locomotives of the 1840s. On the opening day two special trains of 16 and 18 carriages respectively, carrying upwards of 600 passengers, required three locomotives each to climb this gradient.

144 Possibly Low Wood Farm, marked on the first OS map as Low Wood. The farm is higher on the hillside than Low Wood Hotel, so avoiding an impossible gradient from Lake level.

145 'Promises Lost' by Audrey Howard, 1996

146 In December 1844 Wordsworth and a number of influential landowners with property around the Lake drew up a second petition, objecting to the introduction of steam boats on Windermere '--- *to preserve the picturesque, undisturbed beauty which has so long characterised Lake Windermere.*'

147 See ref. – 'Kendal and Windermere Railway, Two letters, Re-Printed from the Morning Post', R. Branthwaite and Son, Kendal

148 'Wordsworthshire' by Eric Robertson.

149 More than £1 million today.

150 CAC(K) ref. WD AG Box 51

151 *Preston Chronicle* 5 December 1846.

152 *Kendal Mercury* 13 February 1847.

153 On 24 April 1847 the Kendal Mercury and the Westmorland Gazette both carried special reports on the opening of the railway, complete with wood-block prints of the scenery and sites in the Lake District (a new technology in Victorian times).

154 Two of the first locomotives on the K&W Railway, *Windermere* and *Langdale,* were built to the 0-4-0 configuration. They were probably similar to the contemporary and better known *Coppernob* locomotive on the Furness Railway.

155 Early locomotives consumed around 600 gallons of water per hour when working hard, requiring frequent replenishment.

156 *Westmorland Gazette,* 24 June 1847: Predictably, two months after the railway was opened an incident occurred '--- *as the six o'clock train was nearing the station. In proceeding down the incline the engine and tender were as usual detached from the rest of the train, and proceeded in advance of the carriages in order to get off to the siding to allow the carriages behind to pass on the regular line. Owing to the slippery state of the rails from the rain, the brakes were rendered comparatively ineffective, and the carriages followed close behind the engine all the way down. The man at the points had no time to turn them in the interval between the tender going off and the carriages coming on. The consequence was that the hind wheels of the tender got off the rails, and being thus at a stand, the carriages behind the tender struck suddenly against it, which dealt to two or three of the passengers a few bruises and scratches. One person who had his head out the window at the time, received a cut on his forehead which caused the blood to flow down his cheek. No blame appears to be attached to any of the brakesmen, but the incident gives additional proof of the necessity for increasing the effect of the brakes on railways.'*

157 Designed by architect Miles Thompson of Kendal, built by local builder Abraham Pattinson, and completed three weeks after the railway was opened.

158 *Kendal Mercury*, and *Westmorland Gazette,* 24 April 1847

159 Due to the great pace of railway building elsewhere, Errington had moved on. He was replaced as chief engineer of the K&WR by John Harris (born in Maryport), who also moved on.

160 It is likely that Cornelius Nicholson abstained from these toasts since he is known to have been a strong supporter of the temperance movement.

161 *'A Well Spent Life',* by Cornelius Nicholson.

162 *Annals of Kendal'* by Cornelius Nicholson, 2nd edition, 1861

163 CAC(K) ref. WQ/R/DP 35.

164 CAC(K) WD/NT Box 81 and WD/MM Boxes 157, 158 £1,725 for 702 perches = £2-48/perch; £5,596 for 2278 perches

165 CAC(K) ref. WDX 505 Item 9

166 Approximately £1 million today.

167 *Westmorland Gazette,* 16 August 1845

168 9 chains measure approximately 200 yards

169 *Westmorland Gazette,* 31 January 1846

170 *Westmorland Gazette,* 29 January 1853, report of the half-yearly meeting of the K&WR Co.

171 Miles Thompson was a pupil, partner and successor to architect George Webster of Kendal.

172 *Westmorland Gazette,* 29 September 1849.

173 *CAC(K) ref. WDX:398*

174 Sometimes known as Windermere Hotel, sometimes as Rigg's Hotel (the name of the first innkeeper), and sometimes as Birthwaite Hotel at Windermere.

175 *Kendal Mercury,* 8 November 1845

176 In August 1848 the report of K&WR Directors stated that the Railway Company '--- *have taken part in the construction of an hotel at Windermere*'.

177 Aged 33 in 1847, he was possibly assisted into the job by the patronage of Edward Wilson of Abbott Hall, a director of the Railway Company, who built Rigmaden mansion at Middleton in Lonsdale and would have known both the Rigg and Bownass families.

178 Richard Rigg was raised on a farm named Applegarth, near Middleton in the Lonsdale valley; and Sarah Bownass came from nearby Close Foot farm.

179 The Riggs were preceded in the coach service by William Sheldon of Highfield, who held the mail contract from 1850 until 1855. *(see also Lancelot Steele)*

180 CAC(K) Ref. WQ/A/H/9 – extract from a map of footpaths through Elleray in 1854.

181 *Westmorland Gazette,* July 1855, K&W Railway Company half-yearly meeting.

182 *Westmorland Gazette,* 18 June 1842.

183 *Westmorland Gazette,* 4 August 1849.

184 William Dilworth Crewdson II (1799-1878)

185 It was his uncle, Isaac Crewdson, who wrote the book 'A Beacon to the Society of Friends' which persuaded many younger Quakers throughout England and abroad to leave the Society (see Appendix 4).

186 '*The Church and Parish of St Mary, Applethwaite, Commonly Called St Mary's, Windermere*', by George Godfrey Cunninghame, 1900.

187 '*A Short Memorial of William Dilworth Crewdson*', by his Wife, after 1878, page 3.

188 '*Christopher North, a Memoir of John Wilson*', by his daughter Mrs Gordon, p.472.

189 **Units of area:** 40 poles = one rood, 4 roods = one acre; 2.47 acres = one hectare.

190 CAC(K) ref. WDB 35/1/178

191 CAC(K) ref.WDB 35 SP179

192 *Westmorland Gazette,* 27 September 1851

193 The Post Office was initially sited within the Station complex, but in the autumn of 1851 it was moved to Mr Garnett's new house on Church Street, opposite to Elleray.

194 *Westmorland Gazette,* 18 August 1855

195 Today, part of the private carriage driveway terminates at Elleray Bank where a linking section is no longer accessible.

196 '*Leck, Cowan Bridge & the Brontës*', by Alan R. Wellburn.

197 For centuries past, Standen Hall had been the family seat of a prominent line of the Aspinall family. '*The Aspinwall and Aspinall Families of Lancashire*', by Henry Oswald Aspinall, 1923

198 A branch line to Sedbergh was built through Middleton in 1859.

199 *Westmorland Gazette,* 16 Aug. 1845

200 Bishop John Bird Sumner of Chester, since the Parish of Windermere lay within the diocese of Chester at that time.

201 *Westmorland Gazette,* 31 July 1847 – Half-yearly meeting of the proprietors of the Kendal & Windermere Railway.

202 '*The Church and Parish of St Mary, Applethwaite, Commonly Called St Mary's, Windermere*', by George Godfrey Cunninghame, 1900.

203 Miles Thompson was commissioned by Mr Addison as architect of St Mary's Church. It is very likely that he was also the architect of Birthwaite Abbey, the two building projects running concurrently. A few months earlier Miles Thompson was also responsible for the Windermere Hotel and Station.

204 Initially referred to as St Mary's Abbey, then as Birthwaite Abbey, Windermere Abbey, but more usually shortened to The Abbey.

205 CAC(K) ref. WPR 104/17/22

206 Anciently called St Marie Holme ('*Sidelights on Mediaeval Windermere*', A.P. Brydson) and frequented by Wilberforce during his summers at Rayrigg.

207 'The Church & Parish of St Mary, Applethwaite', George Godfrey Cunninghame, 1900

208 'History Topography and Directory of Westmorland and Lonsdale North of the Sands, in Lancashire', by P.J. Mannex, 1849

209 *Liverpool Mercury*, 29 March 1849

210 A decade later, in 1860 Annesdale became the St Mary's Vicarage and the name Annesdale migrated to another building nearby.

211 In 2007 the original pointed slates were replaced with conventional rectangular ones.

212 In their half-yearly report to shareholders in July 1849 the Directors of K&WR reported receipt of £1,181 from sale of surplus land. This was acquired by Revd Addison for his college building works, begun in 1852. (*Westmorland Gazette*, 4 August 1849) In all, he acquired about 15 acres over the years.

213 St Mary's Cottage is known as Cedar Manor Hotel today. The magnificent cedar of Lebanon tree guarding the entrance was probably planted by Revd Addison himself because of its biblical connections.

214 *Westmorland Gazette*, 24 November 1855

215 *Kendal Mercury*, 16 January 1858

216 'St Mary's Church in Applethwaite by Windermere', by Ian Jones, 2000.

217 CAC(K) ref. WDB 35/2/605 Birthwaite House Estate, with notes on purchase price.

218 *Westmorland Gazette,*10 September 1853

219 *Westmorland Gazette*, 26 February 1853

220 *Westmorland Gazette*, 18 June 1853

221 One report describes the uniform as being medieval in character with knickerbocker pantaloons and knee-socks.

222 *Westmorland Gazette,* 9 September 1853.

223 Which would equate to a property value of £800,000 today.

224 The bidding stopped at £800 and £1,250 for St Mary's Cottage and Annesdale respectively. For the church itself the bidding failed to reach half the reserve price of £2,500. It was rumoured that the Jesuits were interested in the church, but this was never substantiated.

225 Around 1854 Thomas Crosthwaite of Low Birthwaite became tenant farmer at Alice Howe, one of the farms inherited by his distant cousin Joseph Crosthwaite. The farm remained in the hands of Thomas Crosthwaite's sons well into the next century.

226 Joseph Crosthwaite, who inherited the Braithwaite farms, was the first boy to be awarded a scholarship to St John's College, Cambridge. He obtained a BA degree in 1871.

227 *Westmorland Gazette,* 9 April 1853

228 *Westmorland Gazette*, 25 December 1852

229 'J.S. Crowther in Windermere and Alderley Edge' by Matthew Hyde; Centre for North West Regional Studies, Regional Bulletin, No. 8, 1994.

230 'Villas of Alderley Edge', by Matthew Hyde

231 There is no evidence that A.N.W. Pugin himself ever worked in Windermere. His health and eyesight deteriorated from 1846, curtailing travel beyond his home in Kent. He died of a stroke at an early age in 1852 in Ramsgate.

232 *Westmorland Gazette*, 10 June 1854

233 'Minutes of the Proceedings of the Committee for Purchasing the Church at Birthwaite' CAC(K) ref. WPR 104/109 1854-1858

234 A full account of the protracted events preceding the purchase of the Church and School on behalf of the community is described in 'St Mary's Church in Applethwaite by Windermere, the First 150 Years' pp.26-39.

235 *Sadly, the cross has been snapped off in one of the most vandalised cemeteries in England*

236 Ownership of St Mary's Church was complicated by rearrangement of Chester and Carlisle diocesan boundaries in February 1856, when Windermere Parish was transferred to Carlisle.

237 These boundaries were later modified to some extent by the formation of the consolidated chapelries of Jesus, Troutbeck, and St. John's, Windermere, by Orders in Council, dated 30th November 1882 and 10th August 1888 respectively. To each of the chapelries certain contiguous portions of the parish of Applethwaite were transferred.

238 As a drysalter he dealt in dyes, gums, oils and chemicals concerned with the dying processes for woollen fabric and garments. The achievement of repeatable and permanent colours was more of an art-form than a science in the 1850s, and such skills were highly valued.

239 The Bank of Westmorland was founded by a group of prominent Kendal citizens in 1833 as the town's first joint stock bank. It was absorbed into the Midland Bank in 1893 and a century later into the global HSBC Bank. The original building on Highgate, designed by George Webster, survives today as the imposing Kendal Branch of HSBC.

240 *'Four Centuries of Banking'*, by George Chandler.

241 John Gandy and his wife had ten children.

242 *'Alfred Waterhouse 1830-1905, Biography of a Practice'*, Colin Cunningham & Prudence Waterhouse, 1992; page.21

243 Elleray Bank was built at a time when the pace of building work in Birthwaite and Bowness had exploded and building firms were greatly stretched.

244 1829 *'Foreign Tales and Traditions: Chiefly Selected from the Fugitive Literature of Germany'*; 1832 *'The Parliamentary Gazetteer of England and Wales'* 1837 *'Lives of Eminent and Illustrious Englishmen from Alfred the Great to the Latest Times'* (seven volumes);

1849 *'The Biographical History of England; or A History of England in the Lives of Englishmen'* (eight volumes). *'Bell's System of Geography'* (various editions) 1850 *'The Gazetteer of the World'*

245 G.G. Cunningham's historical works are still in use today by universities, especially in America. Some are available to download free in e-book form. Much of his material seems to have derived from the Latin text of an ancestor, Alexander Cunningham (1654-1737), who, after travelling widely in Europe for many years as a tutor, served as British Ambassador to Venice in 1715-1719. In retirement, Alexander Cunningham wrote extensively about the happenings surrounding the Hanovarian accession; see *'A History of Great Britain from the Revolution in 1688 to the Accession of George the First'*, which was later translated into English.

246 Glasgow citizen said of the new residential district of Lauriston

'--- *a peculiarity of this district is that the streets have all high-sounding names – Portland, Cavendish, Salisbury, Bedford, Oxford, Norfolk, Warwick, Coburg, Surrey, and Cumberland Streets'*. Unfortunately Laurieston lost its attraction as a desirable residential area in the late 1800s when industrial sprawl and pollution from the adjacent Gorbals overtook the south bank of the Clyde.

247 Listed Category A today.

248 The views from Elleray Bank are now partly obscured by trees which have matured in the intervening years, the unintended consequence of professional landscape architecture.

249 Under the new ownership of Puckle and Irving, in 1856 the name changed from St Mary's College to Windermere College.

250 *'Alfred Waterhouse, 1830 – 1905, Biography of a Practice'* p.21; Colin Cunningham & Prudence Waterhouse

251 John Harris, b.1812 in Maryport, railway engineer working out of Darlington; built several railways in the north of England in the 1840s, including the Lancaster to Carlisle. He later became an engine manufacturer.

252 *Westmorland Gazette*, 9 April 1853

253 CWAAS_002_1969_vol69_0018 *'John Harris, Quaker Engineer & Investor'* H.J. Smith

254 Although Joseph Locke was the civil engineer when the route was surveyed for the K&W Railway, J.C. Errington and then John Harris acted as site engineer during the planning and construction work of

1844-1847, submitting the engineer's reports to meetings of the Railway Company up to 1852. Such was the pace of railway development elsewhere that John Harris was redeployed to the engineering company's base at Darlington before Birthwaite Lodge was complete.

255 About £2 million today.

256 CAC(K) WDB 61/13/9/3

257 *Westmorland Gazette*, 25 December 1852; See advertisement for Excavators, Stonemasons and Joiners for works in erecting a house at Birthwaite, architect Mr Crowther. Sealed tenders to be delivered to R.M. Somervell, Esq.

258 *'K Shoes – the First 150 Years, 1842-1992'* by Spencer Crookenden, 1992.

259 leather uppers and soles for shoes and boots

260 Miss Jane Yates' father, Thomas Yates, was a second cousin of the Home Secretary, the Rt Hon. Sir Robert Peel, MP.

261 The first Sir Robert Peel, MP, married Ellen, daughter of his partner William Yates. Peel was ruthless in pursuit of mechanical innovation and cloth of the finest quality. The company exploited Samuel Crompton's spinning mule (probably with little financial compensation to its inventor, since the machine was not patented) and by 1784 they are said to have been '--- *employing 6,800 both directly and indirectly ---*' around Bury and Bolton. They introduced significant innovations in chemical bleaching and pioneered the use of steam power for their spinning mules.

262 variously estimated between £20 million and £40 million at today's value

263 say £9m for each son, and £3m for each daughter, at today's values.

264 Equivalent to £10,000 today.

265 When this little villa became The Vicarage the name Annesdale migrated to another house further up the hill.

266 Equivalent to around £6 million today.

267 Cook's House was renamed Winlass Beck around 1860 by Peter Kennedy. Subsequently the name Cook's House migrated across the Patterdale Road to Stybarrow Cottage.

268 The Kennedy brothers were known to Samuel Crompton of Bolton and later participated in the national movement to compensate him for the widespread, unlicensed use of his invention, the spinning mule. Successive generations of the Kennedy family prospered in Manchester and Leeds as cotton spinners, and in the manufacture of mill machinery.

269 One of the Escher family of Zurich, politicians and railway pioneers, who created the bank known today as Credit Suisse.

270 John Douglass, another expatriate Scot, the 14th Laird of Tilquillie.

271 They had a third son who died in Malta in 1845, aged under a year.

272 With the abundance of water tumbling from the mountains, Austria and Switzerland were home to the earliest cotton mills in Europe. Calico manufacture was already well established in the early 1800s at Geneva and St Gallen. Much of their bleaching machinery was imported from the Ridgways of Bolton.

273 About £10 million today

274 Probate valuation of the estate of John Lawson Kennedy in 1895 was equivalent to around £14 million today.

275 *Westmorland Gazette,* 19 January 1839

276 £250 today

277 *Kendal Mercury,* 5 February 1842

278 *Cumberland Pacquet,* 3 October 1843

279 A unicorn is a team of three horses – a single lead horse and two behind.

280 Huck's Brow is a steep mile-long climb from High Borrow Bridge to Shap Summit, on the old coach road. In 1819 the 'Lord Wellington Coach' overturned while descending this hill, killing two of its passengers and dreadfully injuring two others.

281 Lamplugh was a coach halt on the Sheldon coach route to the west coast.

282 *Kendal Mercury,* 13 March 1847

283 *Westmorland Gazette,* 29 May 1847

284 *Westmorland Gazette,* 31 August 1850

285 around £1½ million today

286 The front elevation of Ellerthwaite was originally dressed stone, not rendered as shown here.

287 named Ellerthwaite Square and Ellerthwaite Road today.

288 The Law Journal 1852, Volume 30, Part 1, page 357

289 Daniel Gardner's legacy of Kendal properties included The Elephant Inn and Elephant Yard, property in Redman's Yard, several houses on Lowther Street, and land on Sedbergh Road.

290 G.H. Gardner died of pulmonary tuberculosis, an infectious bacterial disease of the lungs.

291 on the evidence of maps (see CAC(K) WDX505 and OS2).

292 This extension is not on a map of Jan. 1882 *(CAC(K) ref. WDX 505),* but appears on OS 1897 map. Ellerthwaite was built for George Harrison Gardner (see Note 117 above) who lived there from 1851 until December 1858. The date stone on the extension gives the date as 1850.

293 *Kendal Mercury,* 7 January 1843

294 *Kendal Mercury,* 27 May 1848 and 24 April 1852

295 The Terrace seems to have been the property of the K&WR and successors until after WWII.

296 *Westmorland Gazette,* 27 May 1854.

297 Liverpool did not become a city until 1880.

298 George Holt (1790-1861) founded the Bank of Liverpool and also the Liverpool & Manchester Railway, both in 1831; and first chairman of the Liverpool Fire Insurance Company. His sons were extremely influential in Liverpool commerce: Sir Robert, Alfred, Philip and George Holt.

299 The India Building of 1834 was the first purpose-built office block in Liverpool with large and airy rooms at every level for conducting business. It was replaced a century later on the same site for Alfred Holt & Co., founders of the Blue Funnel Line.

300 trustees of the Ambleside turnpike.

301 *Westmorland Gazette,* 30 December 1854

302 *Westmorland Gazette,* 30 June 1838

303 *Kendal Mercury,* 3 April 1858

304 possibly The Terrace, which is known to have taken longer than normal to complete.

305 In 1853 Windermere did not yet have a fire service.

306 Probably Cross Street, which backed on to the Station.

307 *Westmorland Gazette,* 21 May 1853

308 Large casks holding up to 120 gallons each.

309 Equivalent to £150,000 today.

310 Old Norse for a clearing in the birch trees.

311 'The Lake Scenery of England', by J.B. Pyne, published 1859

312 Richard Rigg's death certificate lists Bright's disease and anasarca as causes of death.

313 CAC(C), ref. DSO 24

314 i.e. production of washing soda and soap.

315 48 chemical companies of Britain and Ireland merged in November 1890 to form United Alkali Company Limited, a parent of Imperial Chemical Industries. It is possible that the wealth of Richard Rigg (1854-1921) derived from sale of his share in one of the alkali companies in St Helens, and that this was the source of funds to purchase the remaining part of the hotel.

316 'The Baroness of Belsfield by Windermere' pp.53-54.

317 John Rigg's abstention from alcohol and tobacco probably resulted from seeing both his parents die before their time of alcohol-related illnesses.

318 equivalent to about £3 million today.
319 *'Christopher North, a Memoir of John Wilson'*Mrs Gordon (1879), pp.85-87
320 later made famous by Alfred Wainwright.
321 A.H. Heywood's cousin Mary Sumner, the wife of Bishop Sumner of Guildford, also founded the Mothers' Union.
322 At today's value the brothers each received around £6 million.
323 approximately £1.2 million today
324 which grew out of the Windermere Mutual Improvement Society shortly before Mr Heywood's arrival in the village in 1865
325 plaque at the footpath gate near the summit of Orrest Head
326 one of a special group of Scottish solicitors and advocates.
327 £700,000 today
328 Cleeve meaning cliff; the approach to the house passes the rock face of a small quarry.
329 Thomas Henry Webb, Frances Lucinda Webb, and Clara Elizabeth Webb
330 their grandfather, Alfred Reyner, left £450,000 (equivalent to more than £40 million today), for the benefit of his two daughters during their lifetime, and subsequently for their children.
331 *'The Royal Windermere Yacht Club Celebrates 150 Years, 1860-2010'*Ian Jones (2010)
332 approximately £8 million today.
333 The spelling of the name appears at various times as Winlass Beck, Windlass Beck, Wynlas Beck.
334 *Westmorland Gazette,* 21 March 1863
335 Listed, Grade II
336 CAC(K) ref. WD/NT/77/8
337 The independent church at Troutbeck Bridge opened in 1858 as a Congregational Chapel. *Kelly's Directory, 1858,* describes it as a Morrisonian chapel, a variant of Presbyterianism which had its origins around the Clyde. But the little church seems to have operated as a Congregational Chapel from the start, having previously met in the large barn at Knotts Farm.
338 £22 million today
339 £0.5 million today
340 the Windermere Sailing Club acquired the title Royal Windermere Yacht Club in 1887
341 William Dilworth Crewdson III (1838-1908)
342 *Westmorland Gazette,* 8 Feb.1879
343 *'St Mary's Church, Applethwaite, Windermere 1848-1948',* by H.W. Broadrick
344 *Westmorland Gazette,* 5 May 1873
345 *Kendal Mercury,* 29 July 1854
346 Richard Kershaw Lumb was a wealthy Yorkshireman who retired to Cheltenham where he founded the Cheltenham Industrial School in 1866.
347 It seems that Miss Anne Marriott did not purchase the Abbey, but continued to lease the mansion from Mr Lumb until 1864.
348 Lath fishing was a method of deploying multiple fly lines, using a small boat to tow a long lath.
349 *Westmorland Gazette,* 14 January 1893 (Obituary).
350 CAC(K) ref. WD/TE Box 28
351 The name of the College changed under the different owners. During Revd Addison's years 1853-55 it was known as St Mary's College; following its acquisition by Messrs Puckle and Irving in 1855 the name changed to Windermere College; in 1886 it became The Old College of Mr Raikes.
352 *Kendal Mercury,* 2 June 1855.
353 The Red House serves today as the Hideaway Hotel
354 courtesy of Kendal Library

355 CAC(K) WDB/133

356 Harrison's Assembly Room opened on 28 September 1859 with a concert given by Kendal Philarmonic Society. It was situated above Airey's shop in Victoria Street.

357 *Staffordshire Advertiser,* 22 March 1873

358 Windermere Sailing Club later became the Royal Windermere Yacht Club in 1887.

359 Ambleside road continued as a profitable turnpike for over three decades after the railway opened. The railway and the turnpike were mutually beneficial since it was the principle route for people and freight arriving at the Windermere terminus, needing to travel further into the central core of Lakeland. Tollhouses at Plumgarths, Staveley, Waterhead and Grasmere were sold in 1875, but it was not until 1883 that the Ambleside Turnpike Trust was finally dissolved by act of Parliament and responsibility for roads and sewerage devolved to Local Boards.

360 This section may also have been known briefly as St Mary's Street or St Mary's Road.

361 New Road linking Ellerthwaite more directly to Baddeley Clock came later, around 1900.

362 Orrest House stood on the site of the NatWest Bank of today.

363 still exists beside the bank, but with revised shop front.

364 In 1898/99 the building was extensively rebuilt in its present form, the NatWest Bank of today. (Plans ref. CAC(K) WSUDW/W1/133)

365 *Westmorland Gazette,* 11 Febrary 1864.

366 Probably Jane Tyson, barmaid, daughter of the innkeeper of the Sun Inn at Troutbeck Bridge.

367 Rock Side

368 *Westmorland Gazette,* 2 Sept. 1854

369 *Kendal Mercury,* 17 May 1856

370 *Westmorland Gazette,* 21 April 1849

371 *Westmorland Gazette,* 19 May 1855, two books jointly published by Whittaker & Co. of London and John Garnett of Windermere were advertized – 'A Complete Guide to the English Lakes', and 'A Guide to Windermere' by Harriet Martineau.

372 'The Lakes in Sunshine' by James Payn; and several other titles.

373 Many of the photographs in this book were the work of the John Garnett studio of Church Street, Windermere, and have survived in remarkable condition for 150 years. They now form the author's collection of glass plate negatives.

374 In the late 1890s the original structure of Orrest House was substantially rebuilt on the same footprint, eventually becoming the present NatWest Bank.

375 'Four Centuries of Banking, Volume I' George Chandler; Batsford 1964

376 A large parcel of land between the Birthwaite estate and Orrest Farm belonged to the Revd Fletcher Fleming of Rayrigg Hall.

377 Willan & Garnett, Victoria Buildings, Market Street, Morecambe.

378 Comparison of OS maps of 1858 and 1897 indicates that the house was extended into the rear garden, possibly to provide a surgery and consulting rooms for Dr Hamilton.

379 A room where beer was fermented in casks

380 John Airey's house at the top of Victoria Street, was appropriately named Albert House.

381 CAC(K) Ref. WDX 505

382 No.10 today is on the north side of High Street, above Oakthorpe Hotel. Confusingly, a photograph exists dating from around 1900, shortly after William Harrison's death, used by the family as a Christmas card with the inscription 'our house'. It shows the last house on the opposite side of the street. Was High Street re-numbered at some stage?

383 *Kendal Mercury,* 11 April 1868.

384 Ash Street is known today as Havelock Road; and Spruce Street was never built.

385 The term parapet seems to have referred to a raised footpath with a defined kerb line. The installation

of kerbstones and paving of footpaths often lagged long behind the buildings they fronted, and the footways were rarely permanently surfaced.

386 Probably 1867-1869 for John Macmillan Dunlop.

387 After a quarter of a century as a member of the WUDC, George Henry Pattinson was appointed High Sheriff of Westmorland in 1921.

388 Courtesy of Barclays Bank

389 To conform with the 1875 Public Health Act. The act brought together a range of Acts covering sewerage and drains, water supply, housing and disease. Each Local Board was required to appoint a Medical Officer in charge of public health, and a Sanitary Inspector to ensure the laws on food, housing, water and hygiene were carried out. Local authorities were ordered to cover sewers, keep them in good condition, supply fresh water to their citizens, collect rubbish and provide street lighting. The Act required all new residential construction to include a running water supply, an internal drainage system and prevent the construction of shoddy housing by building contractors.

390 *Westmorland Gazette,* 15 February 1879

391 CAC(K) Ref. WDB 133, records of Pattinson builders

392 CAC(K) Ref. WDX 505

393 *The Scotsman,* 31 January 1920.

394 Confusingly, Christian names were repeated several times in succeeding generations of the Deason family. James and Edward Deason of Windermere were cousins. In 1853 their respective fathers, also named James and Edward, founded the parent company of J&E Deason at The Gill, Ulverston. Nearby in Ulverston, a third brother Joseph Deason worked as a coach builder on his own account.

395 After a confusing and chequered history of transferred ownership, the Windermere fountain now stands outside the Brewery Arts Theatre in Kendal.

396 Edward Speight rented nos. 14 and 16 Main Road, close to the little Methodist Church, and the stationers W.H. Smith today.

397 This non-conformist congregation previously met in the barn at Knotts Farm on Patterdale Road. They were briefly referred to as Morisonian, a denomination of Presbyterian origin.

398 The Village Inn became Queen's Hotel in 1867.

399 *Kendal Mercury,* 9 September 1859

400 A form of cultural recreation costing a penny for admission, that was popular throughout Victorian England, long before the invention of radio and television.

401 The oxyhydrogen gas burner, directed at a small block of slaked lime, produced a very bright light, sufficient to project a clear image on a large screen or wall. Two early magic lantern machines were loaned by Captain Ridehalgh of Fell Foot (who had a gas producing plant behind his mansion), and by Mr Whitwell, owner of the Kendal brewery.

402 *Westmorland Gazette,* 21 December 1861

403 Teas were also served under cover of the Station.

404 *Westmorland Gazette,* 27 July 1867.

405 The old Bowness Road was known initially as New Street, New Road and then as Main Road.

406 *Westmorland Gazette,* 18 November 1871

407 Joseph Ridgway Bridson and his family owned the largest calico bleaching and printing enterprise in the world at this time, located in Bolton and Horwich. A founder member of Windermere Sailing Club, for several years he leased the Round House on Belle Isle in Bowness Bay as a summer retreat.

408 *Kendal Mercury,* 23 January 1864

409 For the taking away of surface water.

410 'Nuisance' was an oblique term for the stench of gases emanating from drains, sewers, middens and piggeries.

411 *Westmorland Gazette,* 16 October 1858, summary of the Local Government Act 1858

412 Another source gives a total of 30 public hand-pumps.

413 *Westmorland Gazette,* 16 December 1865, Local Government at Windermere

414 In 1866 the Windermere Local Board sought tenders for the laying of 500, 200, 190 and 150 yards each, and then a further 150 yards of drain.

415 Beemire is located between The College and the top of Rayrigg Wood.

416 The Beemire sewage works and its discharge into the Lake continued to be a blot on the Windermere landscape well past 1900.

417 *Westmorland Gazette,* 29 March 1879

418 *Westmorland Gazette,* 22 September 1877

419 *Westmorland Gazette,* 11 January 1879

420 The gentleman concerned was Captain Henry Sandwith of Biscay How near Bowness, who had seven children of his own, together with a large household. He had lived recently at West Derby, part of Liverpool.

421 *Westmorland Gazette,* 3 August 1861.

422 Benjamin Irving moved briefly across the road to The Haigh, a new house built on the edge of the College grounds, and known as *Grey Walls* today.

423 A summer festival for St Mary's School in 1863 is said to have been attended by 150 scholars, but it seems barely credible that two classrooms could have accommodated so many.

424 'The Church & Parish of St Mary, Applethwaite, Commonly Called St Mary, Windermere', G.G. Cunninghame, 1900, p.61

425 'Windermere Grammar School, a History', (anonymous), 1935. The earliest deed suggests a grammar school existed here before 1600. Despite its name, the Free Grammar School was never free.

426 *Westmorland Gazette,* 16 April 1836 William Wordsworth, who had never before delivered a speech in public, agreed to lay the foundation stone on behalf of his close friend John Bolton, who was terminally ill in Liverpool. On the day, 800 good people of church and village, including many ladies, attended the ceremony in torrential rain. To spare them from the ordeal of listening for 20-30 minutes to his prepared speech, the poet hastily delivered a much abbreviated few words, and the company repaired to the nearby White Lion Hotel for refreshments and dinner. Wordsworth's sodden notes were handed to a reporter to be published in full.

427 Liverpool slave trader.

428 i.e. including the villages of Windermere, Bowness and their surrounding areas.

429 *The Lakes Chronicle,* 11 May 1883

430 *Herald and Lakes News,* 21 October 1887

431 *Lakes Herald,* 21 December 1888

432 Ambleside Railway Bill: Verbatim report of proceedings before the select committee on Railway Bills (Group 4) in the House of Commons, 15 March, 1887.

433 equivalent to about £12 million today.

434 *Pall Mall Gazette,* 22 November 1886

435 *Pall Mall Gazette,* 21 April 1884

436 *Manchester Courier and Lancashire General Advertiser,* 22 March 1887

437 After graduating from Cambridge, Robert Somervell became a master at Harrow School where he taught English to Winston Churchill.

438 The Diamond Jubilee year of Queen Victoria also coincided with the 50th anniversary of the opening of the rail link to Windermere and the birth of the village.

439 The Hamilton Memorial Fund (Charity no. 223270) continued for over a century until 2015, when it was absorbed into Lakeland Disability Support (Charity no. 1102609)

440 'The Art and Craft of Garden Making', Thomas Mawson

441 'Thomas Mawson, Life Gardens and Landscape', Janet Waymark

442 *'Life and Works of a Landscape Architect'*, Thomas Mawson

443 *Westmorland Gazette,* 25 March 1905

444 *Westmorland Gazette,* 27 February 1926

445 *Lancashire Daily Post,* 2 June and 25 August 1926.

446 *Westmorland Gazette,* 9 July 1927.

447 *Herald and Lakes News,* 22 April 1892

448 which later became the Royal Windermere Yacht Club.

449 *'The Royal Windermere Yacht Club Celebrates 150 Years, 1860-2010'*, Ian Jones, 2010

Index

X

Z

About the Author

After graduating from Queen's University, Belfast, Ian Jones chose a career in aerospace research. He worked on future projects, pioneering the use of computers and mathematical modelling in aerodynamic research. At the height of the cold war he was seconded to NATO where he led analyses of Central European air defence.

On retiring to the Lake District his interests turned to the Victorian history of Windermere. He was fascinated by the grand houses and their architecture, the off-comers who built them and where they came from, how they acquired their wealth and importance. Along the way, he has published books on the history of St Mary's Church, Holehird mansion, the Baroness of Belsfield, and the Royal Windermere Yacht Club. The present volume on the off-comers and birth of the village of Windermere, is the outcome of this research.

For exclusive discounts on Matador titles,
sign up to our occasional newsletter at
troubador.co.uk/bookshop